ARNE SLOT

ARNE SLOT
THE BIOGRAPHY

Maarten Meijer

EBURY
SPOTLIGHT

EBURY SPOTLIGHT

UK | USA | Canada | Ireland | Australia
India | New Zealand | South Africa

Ebury Spotlight is part of the Penguin Random House group of companies
whose addresses can be found at global.penguinrandomhouse.com

Penguin Random House UK
One Embassy Gardens, 8 Viaduct Gardens, London SW11 7BW

penguin.co.uk
global.penguinrandomhouse.com

First published by Ebury Spotlight in 2025

1

Typeset in 11/18pt Sabon Next LT Pro by Six Red Marbles UK, Thetford, Norfolk
Printed and bound in Great Britain by Clays Ltd, Elcograf S.p.A.

The authorised representative in the EEA is Penguin Random House Ireland,
Morrison Chambers, 32 Nassau Street, Dublin D02 YH68

A CIP catalogue record for this book is available from the British Library

Hardback ISBN 9781529949506
Trade paperback ISBN 9781529970753

Penguin Random House is committed to a sustainable future
for our business, our readers and our planet. This book is made
from Forest Stewardship Council® certified paper.

CONTENTS

1

RED ON TOP

'In terms of outperforming expectations, having young squads and style of football, he ticked all the boxes. I'm surprised it's gone quite so smoothly but [Slot's impact] is not a surprise.'

IAN GRAHAM, *HOW TO WIN THE PREMIER LEAGUE*

The flag of the Netherlands is a horizontal tricolour of red, white and blue. Upside-down Dutch flags along highways became the symbol of the vociferous 2022–23 farmers' protests. Judging the merit of the protests is not the point here, just that the inverted flags did not sit well with many Dutch men and women who are proud of their national standard. In the Middle Ages, special meanings were associated with the three colours, reflecting what people used to see as the natural order of society, with red representing the people, white the church and blue the nobility.

Liverpool defeated Real Madrid, Los Blancos, on 28 November 2024, and three days later beat Manchester City, the Sky Blues, by the same scoreline: 2–0. Under their first Dutch manager, the Reds brushed aside teams that previously had caused so much grief. Red belongs at the top of the rainbow, the Dutch flag and, as every Liverpool fan would contend, the Premier League and Champions League competitions.

In terms of popularity, Arne Slot is at an all-time high. The whole world now knows the coach hailing from a small village in the Dutch countryside. Every day, his bald head features almost life-size on the front of tabloids and, in smaller versions, in the rapt analyses of *The Times*, the *Guardian*, the *Athletic* and *Voetbal International*. He is regularly on television and there is a plethora of videos circulating on the internet. That is the consequence of navigating Liverpool FC to the top of the Premier League and the Champions League. Slot responds to it with calm rationality and characteristic modesty. 'I don't follow how popular I am. The results are good, yes, but that is done by the players. We put a lot of energy into good results, but the credits must go to the players. They keep achieving these results. That's why I've become so popular, I am part of those results . . .' He understands the excitement but is not distracted by it; he just calmly and relentlessly pursues victory, one game at a time.

In the spring of 2024, Arne Slot met with Liverpool sporting director Richard Hughes at his monumental classic mansion in the heart of Zwolle. 'I had a very good relationship from the start with Richard, which is one of the reasons I loved to join the club,' Slot explained when asked about his reasons for choosing Liverpool. Now at the AXA Training Centre, their offices sit side by side on the first floor. Liverpool had meticulously compiled a 60-page scouting report on Slot, which Hughes handed to him during their initial meeting. When Slot mentioned that one of his key strengths was improving players, Hughes immediately pointed him to a section full of stats and personal testimonies backing that claim. Liverpool evaluates managerial candidates using a 20-point system – and Slot didn't just meet expectations, he exceeded them, especially in areas related to player development and availability.

Since arriving from the Netherlands, Slot's impact at Liverpool has been as understated as it has been remarkable. The Dutchman has a relatively mild-mannered presence in the dugout and at the press conference. Meanwhile, everything he touches turns to gold. Few expected Slot to launch a title challenge in his debut season. Common sense suggested there would be a period of transition, with a top-four finish as a credible goal, but the conversation soon changed, even only a handful of games in. Expectations were vastly exceeded. Players who lost their way when Jürgen Klopp's final season unravelled in the spring of 2024 were reinvigorated. Slot beat José Mourinho's 20-year record for the best start by a new Premier League manager, but he is the polar opposite of the Portuguese: humble instead of preening, jokes in press conferences rather than scowls. In 2024, Slot won 23 of his first 27 games in charge, the fastest any manager in charge of a top-flight English club has reached such numbers since William Sudell with Preston in 1888–89 (the inaugural Football League season). For only the third time in their history, Liverpool reached Christmas Day without being beaten away from home (1893–94 and 1987–88 were the other campaigns). Liverpool fans were revelling in the spirit of the holiday season, singing, 'It's beginning to look a Slot like Christmas'.

Slot remained remarkably confident and consistent. 'In general, I think it is difficult to take things from another competition, other players, and bring them to this current situation. The Eredivisie [the Dutch top flight] is a good league, but there are only three title contenders, three teams that can normally take points from each other. The Premier League is completely different from that. We have six, seven, eight teams, maybe nine, that can play top four. I work in the same way as I did with the under-14s in my first year as a manager and when I did the under-21s, at Feyenoord and now. I do the same. I don't change my way of working. Sometimes you change how you handle certain individuals, because people are not always the same, but the idea, our training sessions, the way of playing, hasn't changed a lot in seven, eight, nine or ten years.' He added, 'I never thought that my vision wouldn't work or fit here [at Liverpool]. I was brought in because of that vision, so it would be crazy if I didn't believe in that. But I was very curious when I started: how would these players react to what you say and how you work? But at the same time, top players also need a clear structure and a plan because that's when they can excel individually. What I mean is that they are also quite easy to convince, if the things you say come true in practice.'

Doomsayers cautioned that Liverpool had been ahead at this point in previous years and still lost the title race. At any time, Liverpool's challenge could have crumbled. When three wins at the start of the season were followed by a home defeat to Nottingham Forest, it was instantly suggested the honeymoon was over. That was followed by another sequence of seven straight wins and a draw at Arsenal. Pep Guardiola's team gave them no quarter in 2018–19 and 2021–22, when even 97 and 92 points were not enough to become champions. Unlike previous title challenges that fell short in the Klopp era, Liverpool did not need to think about Manchester City this time. The crisis at the Etihad had Pep Guardiola worried about securing a fourth-place finish. The wide gap halfway through the season alleviated the pressure on the title-race frontrunners. They were the only team performing at the level City had set as benchmark in previous years.

As the season wore on, a familiar storyline began to emerge – the idea that Arne Slot's Liverpool were only on top because Arsenal had been so unfortunate. In north London, some were convinced that the injury of Martin Ødegaard earlier in the season, followed by later setbacks to Bukayo Saka, Gabriel Martinelli and Kai Havertz, had skewed the title race. In their version of events, it should have been Slot chasing Arteta, not the other way around. But that narrative conveniently glossed over what Liverpool had endured. Between October and December, first-choice keeper Alisson missed a significant run of games, and yet barely a ripple was felt because Caoimhin Kelleher stepped up brilliantly. Cody Gakpo, the team's second-highest scorer, was also sidelined for a spell, but that was treated like a footnote. Diogo Jota quietly dealt with his own injury issues, while rising star Conor Bradley overcame multiple setbacks with barely a mention outside Liverpool circles. It's always the losing side that complains about bad luck and refereeing calls. Champions find a way. Runners-up find reasons.

The 'lucky Liverpool' narrative clung on since day one. The thinking was clear: Klopp had to contend with the greatest domestic forces ever, while Slot coasted past mediocre rivals. This is disrespectful not only to Slot but to Pep Guardiola and Mikel Arteta as well. Advocates of this theory ignore the task Slot inherited: stepping out from under the immense shadow of Jürgen Klopp, whose impact reached far beyond the pitch and deep into the fabric of the city itself. This wasn't just a coaching change – it was one of the toughest transitions in modern football, rivalling the daunting hand-overs after Wenger at Arsenal and Ferguson at Manchester United. And history shows just how turbulent those were.

For nine years, Jürgen Klopp's infectious presence defined Anfield. His departure didn't just result in a managerial vacancy, it left a deep void. Klopp wasn't just successful, his energy resonated with the players on the pitch and the supporters in the stands. He made Liverpool one of the best teams in the world. Taking over from such a towering figure was never going to be simple. Arne Slot stepped into a role many viewed as one of the toughest in football:

keeping Liverpool competitive, chasing silverware and doing so with just a single major new signing. There were instances of fortune – like the favourable result against Chelsea and the dramatic win over PSG – but those moments alone don't define an entire season. Slot has the clarity of thought and the ability to assemble a cohesive, effective side. He has a coach's vision, the capacity to see the full picture while managing the smallest details. That comes from his innate football intelligence, a deep connection to the game and an unrelenting commitment to the fine-tuning of his methods over a decade. All of that was essential as he followed in the footsteps of an icon.

Arne Slot has turned out to be an ideal appointment for Liverpool, a coach with the wisdom and confidence to avoid unnecessary changes. His impact has been both impressive and nuanced. Rather than overhaul what he inherited, he built on the strong foundation left by Klopp and elevated the team to another level. That's rare in modern management, where incoming coaches often insist on sweeping changes. While Klopp had aimed for marquee signings like Mbappé, Bellingham, Caicedo and Zubimendi, Liverpool ultimately brought in Szoboszlai, Gravenberch and Endo. Slot inherited a solid and talented squad, but he has significantly improved the performances of players who were previously seen as modest contributors. Gravenberch has been a standout transformation, but others like Gakpo, Szoboszlai and Curtis Jones have also progressed under his guidance. And while Mohamed Salah's incredible season has drawn plenty of attention, it would be reductive to credit the player alone. Slot's composed leadership, tactical adaptability and well-timed substitutions have all played a crucial role in Liverpool's success.

Liverpool under Arne Slot have managed to strike a compelling balance, blending the high-intensity pressing associated with Jürgen Klopp with Slot's own more calculated, positional approach. The result has been dynamic, attacking football that overwhelms opponents with relentless energy, while also embracing a more composed, possession-driven rhythm. A key feature of Slot's tactical management is his ability to distil the game into clear, manageable components. In possession, his players actively look for structural flaws or individual vulnerabilities in the opposition and, once identified, they are quick to capitalise. Slot's strategic clarity has been vital to Liverpool's strong Premier League campaign. His incisive in-game adjustments have often been the fine margin, turning potential defeats into draws, and draws into critical victories.

By February, Arne Slot's Liverpool had done enough to win the praise of the club's former stars. 'This could be a very, very special season for Liverpool,' declared ex-defender Jamie Carragher. Jamie Redknapp, former midfielder, echoed the sentiment: 'Liverpool are probably the best team in the world at the moment. What Slot's doing is phenomenal. He's been fantastic.' By April, the mood around Anfield had shifted from optimism to expectation. A 20th league title, one that would see them draw level with Manchester United at the summit of English football, was within reach. The fans made their feelings known, chanting with growing conviction, 'We're going to win the league, and now you're going to believe us.'

Some critics discounted Liverpool's campaign, suggesting it fell short of historic proportions – brilliant, yes, but not legendary – after hopes of a trophy-laden season narrowed to just the league title. But Arne Slot rightly pointed out that calling it 'just' the Premier League overlooks its true significance. That it happened in his debut season only adds to the magnitude of the achievement. Securing the title confirmed what had been evident for months: Liverpool were the standout team in England. When the moment arrived, the celebrations were spirited and fully deserved – a fitting tribute to a season that was, by any measure, a resounding success.

Arne Slot's impressive start as Liverpool head coach made him a celebrated figure back home in the Netherlands. His early success at Anfield didn't just earn admiration, it sparked a surge of interest in the Premier League, as Dutch fans embraced one of their own making waves on the international stage. Milan van Dongen said on ESPN, 'We honestly think of Arne Slot as the best coach in the world. He already had a big status here in the Netherlands because of what he was able to make of a moderate team like Feyenoord. All the things we saw at Feyenoord we see at Liverpool now but with better players. Normally, we are not the most "proud" of our stars, but the fans of Feyenoord definitely look at what he is doing with joy and pride. We have never seen Arne Slot in crisis. He never lost three times in a row with Feyenoord and he is yet to do so at Liverpool. It is quite special. There is a lot of enthusiasm for how Liverpool are playing.'

VoetbalPrimeur's Lars Teunissen said, 'One hundred per cent there is more interest in the Premier League here because of Arne. I have friends who are interested in the Premier League but would generally only see the highlights. Now everyone is buying a subscription for the Premier League broadcaster to see the Liverpool games. Slot is doing an amazing job. Did we all expect it to be so good? No, but we knew when he was at Feyenoord he made the players look 10 times better. Now you are seeing in the Dutch league that those players are back at a normal level. We knew Liverpool had an amazing manager and now the people in Liverpool are seeing it. He is loved in the Netherlands. A lot of Feyenoord fans hope he comes back one day. But everyone in the Netherlands understands now he will not be working here for the next 20 years because he will win big prizes abroad. Tactically he is amazing.'

Arne Slot downplayed the weight of past achievements, emphasising that each season brings its own unique challenges. He noted that the title-winning Liverpool side of the past faced a different landscape than the one he confronted. Players like Virgil van Dijk, Mohamed Salah and Andy Robertson were chasing a second league crown. But while the squad had experience, Slot reminded everyone that nothing comes easy for a club that had lifted just one league trophy in the last 35 years. 'You can't compare the circumstances because the players who won the league here already did it during a time when there were no fans inside the stadium, and at a certain time they were 25 points clear. You can hardly talk about pressure then!'

The hunger for Premier League glory at Anfield was intensified by the fact that when Liverpool finally ended their 30-year wait, they were robbed of the chance to fully enjoy it. Klopp never had the chance to celebrate winning the Premier League in a full stadium; the 2020 commemorations were held behind closed doors because of Covid. It would be a first for many to celebrate winning the Premier League title in a packed Anfield. Everyone at the club craved the full experience that should come with winning the league – the stadium, the celebrations, the noise, the emotions. Mohamed Salah admitted he and his teammates felt short-changed when their previous successful campaign was concluded without supporters present. He was clear: more than the Champions League, he wanted to win the Premier League, something he had never felt before.

Arne Slot would have been forgiven had his first season ended without silverware. There were disappointments along the way: a Champions League exit in the last 16, a lacklustre FA Cup loss with a reserve side to Championship opponents, and a shock Carabao Cup final defeat. But in the Premier League, Liverpool were a force. Slot's team moved through the campaign with calm authority, pursuing the title with remarkable composure. There was a seamless transition into a new era and that is the greatest compliment that can be paid given the scale of the club and the magnitude of the job Slot inherited.

Jan Everse had two coaching spells at PEC Zwolle while the future Liverpool manager was playing for the club. 'Arne was not so famous when he came to England. I spoke to three or four English journalists at the time and I told them, "I'm sure he's a better coach than Klopp." They looked at me as if I were an idiot. Seriously, they thought I was a complete idiot, like I had just escaped from the ward in *One Flew Over the Cuckoo's Nest*. Yet we have known all along, with many games still to play, they would finish as champions.' What made Arne Slot the managerial genius he is today, this book will tell.

2

FROM BERGENTHEIM TO LIVERPOOL

'Once you have a reputation for getting up early,
you'll never be late again.'
ARNE SLOT'S GRANDFATHER

Driving from west to east in the Netherlands, you leave the metropolitan sprawl behind and enter open countryside. It's flat everywhere, with no mountain or hillock to break the horizontal monotony; the only vertical relief is provided by rows of poplars lining drainage ditches and narrow roads. This is a great place for riding bicycles, something that almost every Dutchman or Dutchwoman does daily. In fact, there more bicycles in Holland than there are people. Separate bicycle paths are a standard fixture, running parallel to roads for motorised traffic, even rural highways. The motorways that run from big cities to the east peter out as you get closer to the regions bordering Germany. A visitor must get to his or her destination over provincial roads surrounded by green pastures with the ubiquitous black-and-white Dutch dairy cows. The pungent smell of manure is a reminder that this is farmland, that Amsterdam, Rotterdam and The Hague are a safe distance away near the North Sea coast. The province where Arne Slot's hometown is located, Overijssel, is named for its location 'across the [River] IJssel' [with a capital J and pronounced 'Ai-sul'], from the perspective of the dominant, wealthy west.

Bergentheim was first mentioned in 1381 as Bergenthem. The name probably comes from Bergenheem, a compound of *berg*, 'terrain elevation or hill', and *heem*, 'place of residence or dwelling'. An odd name, perhaps, since there is nothing resembling a hill around, but then, Dutchmen enjoy adding 'bergs' to place names. Around 1835, local entrepreneurs procured a peat excavation concession. It was a slow beginning: in 1840, the hamlet was home to just 243 people. Soon after, the Almelo–De Haandrik Canal was dug with the purpose of supplying the Overijssel canals with sufficient water to keep the peat barges afloat. Once it opened in 1856, the useful brown commodity could easily be transported elsewhere by ship. In 1905, a railway station was added, but it was closed in 1975 and demolished in 1993, indicative of the demographic ups and downs of this remote area.

Arne Slot grew up in this small village in the middle of the meadows and cornfields. It is a tiny, tidy village a short distance from the German border on a canal as straight as a ruler – as most of them are in the geometric design of the Dutch landscape. The place is peaceful and quiet, and there is little to distinguish the different times of the day. The church bells sound every half an hour to remind the locals that time, indeed, is passing.

Bergentheim sits at the northeastern tip of the Dutch Bible Belt. It is conservative and sober. Whoever zooms in on this eastern enclave sees the Netherlands without wokeism. Unlike in the secularised west and north, religion is still relevant here, with two churches standing sentry beside the canal bisecting the village. Bergentheim native, Hardenberg alderman and Feyenoord supporter Alwin te Rietstap has the lowdown on village realities. 'The Reformed Church alone has more than 1,000 members. And then there is also a PKN church [Protestant Church in the Netherlands].'

The Reformed Church is keeping with the times and has its own YouTube channel. As elsewhere in the Netherlands, secularisation has had an impact here, too – there used to be three churches – but it is still common for people to hang a small picture of Jesus or the Virgin Mary in their bedrooms. The locals are proud of their spiritual and cultural heritage and know that, now as 2,000 years ago, wise men come from the east.

British-Dutch author James Worthy shared a personal view of the local population in his *Nieuwe Revu* column:

> I want to talk to the residents about Arne Slot. Why don't I just call him? I'm a writer and writers never take the easy route. Bergentheim is a village in the municipality of Hardenberg. It has 3,570 inhabitants. The inhabitants here do not say Bergentheim, but 'Banthum'. It is a peaceful village. When you bicycle here, you can see what the houses are thinking. There is a text on almost every home. *Zie niet om. Niet klagen, maar dragen. Doe mar kalm an.* 'Don't look back. Don't complain, but endure. Take it easy.' But the inhabitants of Bergentheim are harder to read. They weigh all their words, but most words seem too heavy for their tongue to bear. I think it is beautiful. Where trust prevails, words are unnecessary. In Arne Slot's birthplace, the back doors are wide open, but the people are closed.

In reality, the situation is not quite as bleak. The locals do have time for a chat, but they first carefully check out a new arrival. They are friendly once they have decided he or she is alright. That is a good thing because now that Arne Slot has put the small village on the map by becoming a successful Liverpool manager, visits from probing English reporters and awed football pilgrims are becoming a regular occurrence.

Arend Martijn Slot is his official full name. He was a student at De Koningsberger elementary school. The school website informs parents interested in enrolling their children that 'the Koningsberger school is an open Christian primary school. All pupils are welcome at our school, provided that the Christian principles are respected. Parents and pupils are expected to make a positive contribution during religious education and the celebrations of Christian holidays.' Rote learning of the New Testament was once a feature of the education programme, as young Arne found out first-hand. He learned psalm verses every week and parts of the Bible were read aloud. 'He especially liked the story of the Good Samaritan,' recalled Jan Ophof, Slot's boyhood coach. 'That one made an impression on him.'

Despite the religious education, Arne wasn't big on attending church. In an interview, Slot said, 'We are religious at home. My parents went to church three out of four Sundays. We always hoped that, when it was ten o'clock, we wouldn't hear them shuffling around. But that childhood made sure that I don't completely let go of my faith, let's put it that way. However, I am not practising.' Former teachers of Arne call him a smart boy who was sociable and popular, who fit well in the group and who worked hard. 'Intelligent, positive, friendly' is the consensus. Former classmate Rik van der Velde also called Arne 'popular with the ladies. They all thought he was a nice boy.'

Like the religious verities that were imprinted on the young Slot's mind, family heritage is never far away. When he became Feyenoord coach, his Rotterdam audience soon became acquainted with some of the wisdom of Arne Slot's grandfather. By the time Slot was guiding his charges around pylons on the Feyenoord training ground, his *opa* had already passed away. The elder Slot must have been a fount of wisdom because his grandson referred to his maxims on a regular basis. 'You can't hate the world because of one person' and other morsels of Overijssel pragmatic philosophy found their way into the minds and hearts of the fans – or, at least, the players. 'Unfortunately, my grandfather is no longer around,' said Slot. The elder Slot's proverb about rising early took some time to register. While church had failed to motivate Arne to get out of bed early, football proved very effective. Today, Liverpool players testify that he is always the first to arrive at the AXA Training Centre, as well as the last one to leave.

Bergentheimers indulge in periodic forays into Germany to get cheaper gas in the village of Itterbeck. *Tank billig* ('fill up cheaply') promises a regional tourist website. On the whole, life was not exciting in the Slot family of six. They occasionally crossed the village borders to go shopping in Zwolle, the provincial capital, a 40-minute drive west. The Bergentheim public infrastructure is limited to two primary schools, a Plus supermarket, a snack bar named Mies, a hunting club called 't Hijgend Hert ('The Panting Deer'), a community centre, the two churches and, of course, the football club. The third of four children in a sporting family, Arne played tennis, but it was an almost foregone conclusion that he would also play football, as one in six of the inhabitants of Bergentheim do. In the Overijssel village, there is not much to do apart from playing sports. On balmy summer evenings, it seems as if the one truly unifying faith in the village is football. It is a very important sport for Bergentheim, confirms Kitty Koiter, deputy director of Arne's primary school. 'It's something you often see in small villages and it also plays a role here. We actually have two major team sports in Bergentheim, and those are volleyball and football. That's why many boys play football. You still see that today.'

VV Bergentheim has an impressive facility located on the edge of a forest, with the unlikely name Sportpark Moscou. Young 'Ban-thummers' have to cycle along the canal to get there. It's only 1.5 kilometres from the heart of the village, a trifle for habitual Dutch cyclists. Children of all ages gather for after-school training at the club, on pitches of surprisingly good quality. There is an old stand, as well as a 4G pitch, where a banner is attached to a fence, displaying the message, 'Green Beast! Green Pride!'

'We have the most beautiful accommodations in the municipality of Hardenberg, which we are part of,' claimed Ophof. 'We have good sponsors,' said chairman Bert Nijenhuis, pointing with pride to the immaculate clubhouse. Nowadays, the club has about 600 members, of which almost 400 are playing regularly. Ophof has a photograph of Arne Slot's team of nine- and ten-year-olds. Arne once was a boy with lush brown hair, demonstrating his deft touches on the ball in a green shirt, white shorts, green socks and wearing the captain's white armband.

Arne's father, Arend, was the headmaster of the village school. He was a natural teacher. 'Just like my mother, my sister and my wife,' said Arne Slot. 'We were not poor, but certainly not rich either. We didn't lack anything, but with four children, we had to watch the money. If my parents bought each of us a Mars bar, they would make us very happy. As in any family, one parent was stricter than the other. For me it was my father.' His father did not just run the school; he had also been Bergentheim's star football player and a former member of the Dutch amateur team. In 1976, his team nearly qualified for participation in the Montreal Olympic Games.

In the elder Slot's day, there was still some stigma attached to getting paid for playing football – especially in the church atmosphere of Bergentheim. 'He played for the Dutch amateur team,' said Nijenhuis. 'But he never became a professional. In those days, it was not so common to go straight into professional football, and father Slot had just graduated from the Pabo (Pedagogical Academy for Primary Education), so he decided to become a teacher.' From the time he was six years old, Arne sat in the dressing room when his father gave instructions to first-team players. Together with his younger brother Jakko, Arne would mine the pages of *Voetbal, leerplan voor de ideale voetballer* (published in English as *Soccer Fundamentals for Players and Coaches*) by football technique guru Wiel Coerver for useful exercises. The elder Slot was proud of his sons' development but always very demanding.

Slot remembered, 'My father almost never came to watch me because he was a trainer [as the manager is commonly called in the Netherlands]. Once or twice a year it worked and we would drive home together. When I asked him what he thought about my game, he could be very critical. I didn't always like that at the time, even though I knew he thought I was a good football player. But he had quite a good view of it and it was certainly good for my development as a player and as a coach. He had a drive to get the most out of his players, and I think they actually performed better the years he trained them. At his level, he was a successful coach. Under his leadership, VV Bergentheim played in the first class of the amateur leagues [the sixth tier of Dutch football], which can be called a miracle. They never made it before or after him.'

Slot's father said, 'Because my wife wanted some time for herself on Saturdays, I often took Arne with me. He sat in the dressing room at every match briefing, very calmly observing everything. I sometimes said: Don't you want to play outside, boy? No, he wanted to experience everything. He was six or seven then. He also sat very attentively next to me in the dugout.' Slot learned some things from watching his father's team talks but developed a rather different style.

'I was physically there sometimes, although I don't think I listened very well. But I saw how it went and found it very interesting. During the matches I sat on the bench between the substitutes. In terms of personality, my father was a Louis van Gaal. His players were really a bit afraid of him, in a good way. For me, tact and fairness are crucial. Just like my father, I challenge a player who makes a mistake head on. I'm not selective, it doesn't matter to me whether someone is captain or a new player. But I always consider: how does that criticism come across? I will never deliberately embarrass anyone. I can certainly be hard, but it shouldn't defeat its purpose.'

In the dressing room, Arne was modest, not the one who always had the last word. 'Not at all,' said Nijenhuis. 'But if he had an opinion about something, he said it, in a polite way. And it made sense. His father always trained for fitness. Today, you can also see that [Slot's] Feyenoord's players are in shape. And everything is done in the form of a match. One against one, two against two, four against four.' Slot's old PEC Zwolle teammate Bram van Polen saw the funny side of coach Slot's commitment to physical development. 'The demand that he wants his lads to be in top shape . . . he didn't have that himself in the past. I don't know if he's ever seen the inside of a weights room.'

Slot stood out. 'His scoring, dribbling, passing, receiving were good. Super. Together with a few other boys, he was part of a good generation,' said Van der Velde, who was in Slot's team from the F's to the C's. Arne was in the under-10 side when he had a trial with Jan Ophof – who was then training the D1, the under-12 team. Ophof said he discovered that his protege was thinking like a coach at the age of nine. 'I was coaching ten- to twelve-year-olds, but his father said, "Can he play with your team?" I said: "Well, prove it!" And he managed it very well, even though he was younger. Technically, he was very gifted. It was the right thing to do . . . Arne was nine years old and he would ask me, "Coach, can we change this? Can we move this player or that? Can we do this, can we do that?" And I kept looking at him, thinking, "Is he really only nine?" I never had another player like him. He was already reading the game as a kid. Even then he was direct, technically very strong. Before he had the ball, he already knew where it had to go. He knew whether to pass it out to the right wing or the left, in a split-second. He would go to sleep with the ball and wake up with it.'

Eddy Eggengoor played football with Slot when they were boys. He thought that the biggest difference between how kids played the game then and now was the unstructured spontaneity that characterised their game time. 'You came home from school earlier. I would throw my book bag in the corner, pick up my neighbour Arne Slot and go play football on the street, in a square, or on a field with a large group of boys. Nowadays you see very few youngsters kicking a ball on the street. All the fields and squares are being built on.' Arne also played football behind the house with his brothers Edwin and Jakko. About his obsession with the game, Slot said, 'If you want to become a professional footballer and you play in the amateurs team, you have to stand out. When I see those six-, seven-, eight-year-old boys playing football now, I sometimes think: they are a hundred times better than I used to be. I usually played with the group above me and I often excelled there too. I did it partly to impress; it probably has to do with wanting to be significant. When we played football at half past eleven, the players from the first team – who started at half past twelve – often came to watch our game. That was a reason for me, as a 13-year-old, to do my best and show something.'

Jakko Slot has fond memories of those early days. At just 14, Arne produced coaching sessions for the VV Bergentheim youth team. 'When I look back at the sessions we used to do with those boys on the training pitch, it was actually ridiculous. The players were 16 years old, two years older than Arne. But Arne knew exactly how he wanted to coach them. It was well beyond their understanding and way above what a coach should pass on to young players. It was top-level stuff already, but we thought it was normal. He is doing everything I always expected from him and even more. Arne was never the quickest player in his professional career, but he was by far the brightest. He has become a famous manager in Europe and can't walk anywhere in the Netherlands without people stopping him for a photo. In fact, they stop me too because we look alike; they think I'm Arne. It happens more and more often. It's quite funny. I am very proud of Arne. What he is achieving is fantastic; he's become a great manager in football. But what makes me even prouder is his personality, how he has developed as a person in every way.'

Football in Bergentheim is a community experience. Because of its location in the east of the country, the village naturally is a stronghold for FC Twente fans. Next in the line of favoured clubs is Ajax, and there are a few stray Feyenoord supporters around. One of these rare specimens is alderman Te Rietstap, who elicits a compassionate response from the locals. 'When I walked around the fields in Bergentheim with a Feyenoord shirt, people looked at me with pity.'

Living in a smaller community is more congenial to maintaining harmonious relationships. Commitment and loyalty are highly valued, and they are part of Arne Slot's DNA. 'I want people to be positive and feel good. It's always nice when they think I'm a good football player or coach, but I think it's even better when they say, above all, he was a very nice person to work with. I have known the people with whom I have worked really well for quite a long time. Loyalty matters a great deal to me. I'm quite easy-going in social interactions, in the sense that I don't first try to determine whether

I like someone or not. When I walk through my old village, I see people and say hi to everyone, because I like to be considerate.' Slot has built an image around his equable temperament, seldom lurching too high or too low. It is a mindset typical of Bergentheim people, who are not inclined towards hero-worship.

Author Ronald Giphart interviewed Slot for his book *Het Beste van Jezelf* ('The Best of Yourself') and asked him how he is able to maintain his core values and moral compass in the rather opportunistic world of professional football. Slot explained that justice and compassion are essential to him. 'For me, humanity is a higher priority than winning a match. During an important team meeting in the Feyenoord training complex, we once saw a father and mother arguing outside in the presence of their five- or six-year-old son. Someone said that we had better continue with the discussion, but I said that I thought it was more important to first see whether the situation involving that child ended well.' Slot is not happy with what he sees as an increasing indifference in modern times. 'You wish you could rewind society 15, 20 years in terms of how we treat each other, but unfortunately that is not possible. We are all responsible for making the world a more pleasant place. It is very clear that football is constantly being used as an example. When I was driving home after a Sparta away game, there was a traffic warden at a road closure, but a man wanted to drive on. The man got out and started fighting. I do see a hardening of society.'

At VV Bergentheim, they still think it's a shame that Arne Slot never played in the senior team. He did play in the youth foursome, and in the national final matches four-vs-four in Zeist (home base of the KNVB, the Dutch FA) he finished fourth with his team. The prize, a beautiful clock, still adorns the cafeteria of VV Bergentheim. After that, he was quickly scouted as one of the talented youngsters and went to Zwolle in 1992–93. The fact that FC Zwolle (the precursor of today's PEC Zwolle) eventually included him in their training programme was a huge experience. 'I had never been on a train before,' Slot said – he was 14. At the time, he was still at the VWO (Preparatory Scientific Education) in Hardenberg and was fanatical about finishing his homework during the daily train journey, just to be able to train and play football as much as possible. He also earned two certificates in preparation for a study in business administration. He was a good student, but preferred to watch football on TV on any channel he could find and practised the game whenever he could. Beyond football, he did what kids his age did at that time. He played PlayStation, listened to the Dutch rock band Bløf, and watched *Friends* and *All Stars*, about the fictional football club Swift Boys. He even read some serious books you don't ordinarily find lying around in a teenage player's room. Pulitzer Prize-winner Frank McCourt's *Angela's Ashes* was on his reading list. He wasn't particularly independent. Even after he turned professional, he still lived at home for some time.

Arend and Fennie Slot kept photo albums about their son for years. His mum is a former kindergarten teacher. His parents were interviewed when Arne got the Feyenoord manager's job. 'Sometimes I really have to pinch myself. I remember well the first time Arne appeared on television. We were all ready for it at home. It's completely normal now when he appears on television. I am so proud of him. I am also proud of Edwin, Jakko and Gerlinde, our three other children. But what Arne has achieved is so special. Almost something magical.' His father added, 'Especially the way in which he has done it. Look how he lets them play. That is football as you want to see it. Beautiful and well developed. Our friends from the Rotterdam area said that, for the next five years, Arne will not be able to walk through the city without a wig.'

While Arne's brothers played at their highest level with the amateurs of HHC Hardenberg, and Eddy Eggengoor and his brother Wilko mainly played in Bergentheim, Arne progressed considerably further. But fame has not turned Slot into a self-absorbed celebrity, as it has some other football stars. The day Feyenoord won the Eredivisie title, 14 May 2023, also happened to be Mother's Day. Fennie said, 'I got a message from him in the morning. "Happy Mother's Day," Arne wrote. On a day like that, that he thinks about it, I thought that was very special. He hardly misses a birthday. If at all possible, he even goes to those of his nephews and nieces.'

As an authentic Dutchman, Slot's father freely offers his opinion on Liverpool's performances when things do not run the way he thinks they should. Even though his son's side topped the Premier League and Champions League tables, he wasn't quite pleased with the Champions League 2–1 victory over Lille. It was an exercise in control, typical of a number of the wins in Slot's first season in England. Slot admitted the more patient approach against the French team may not have been a spectator's delight.

> That is difficult for fans and my father is a fan as well. When I call him after a game, he says, 'Ah, it wasn't as exciting as other games of Liverpool.' I had to try to explain to him that in these games you can easily lose if you are starting to force all kinds of difficult balls, but he's not always agreeing with me then. Nottingham Forest is probably the best in the league if you play these stupid balls – I call them stupid balls – which my father would love to see us playing a bit more. It is a difficult balance of taking the risk and conceding a lot or having control and not creating as much.

The two are close and speak every day.

There have definitely not been many Liverpool games where he has said, 'Oh! I like what I saw!' I think his favourite games would be the ones in which we had a comfortable lead far before the end, because he is always a bit nervous. Every game for us is tight, so I think his favourite would be West Ham away or Tottenham away [when Liverpool scored five and six goals, respectively]. But since he was in the stadium against Manchester City and Real Madrid, I think if you were to ask him now, he would tell you those were his most special moments because he was there with my mum as well. He is an ambassador for his amateur club and they play in Holland at a similar time to us. He has a lot of troubles, so the first half he goes there and then goes home really fast so he can see our game. He is following everything like most dads do. The funny thing is he was always quite critical [when I was playing] so when my son is playing, I am like: 'Oh! Well done! Well done!' I think maybe my son will go on to be critical again.

The well-known VV Bergentheim alumnus returned to the bucolic setting of his hometown in August 2020, the year that Covid-19 appeared, to offer a coaching clinic to aspiring youth. Slot was greeted at Sportpark Moscou with torches burning green, the club's primary colour. On the first day of the training, he explained that good technique is important and taught the children some ball skills. But during his opening speech, he emphasised that having fun in football is the most important thing: the Arne Slot Football Days should become a treasured memory. 'I am happy that, in a summer when we cannot go on holiday or only to a limited extent, I can organise a three-day event for youth aged seven to thirteen in my hometown. When I was young, I went to the streets every day to master Wiel Coerver exercises. My father would show them to me once, and I only came back after I had mastered the exercise. I can remember well that as a young player I was allowed to participate in the four-vs-four tournament at the KNVB in Zeist with some boys from Bergentheim. During those days, I felt what it was like to live as a professional. That made me want more and strengthened my dream of becoming a professional football player.' Jakko Slot's company FrontRow shares responsibility for the organisation of the recurring event. Arne's younger brother said that, for the first edition, the 100 registered children would receive a special kit and a ball. 'We intend to organise this event annually and in several locations in the east of the Netherlands, which makes it extra special.'

The Dutch are firm believers in *nuchterheid*, the sober-minded rationalism that was well represented in their greatest thinker, Erasmus of Rotterdam. Dutchmen think that it is wrong to let emotions gain the upper hand. Football supporters in the Netherlands are a little uncomfortable with Brazilian exuberance, the free flow of emotion in Cameroonians and the patriotic passions exhibited by South Koreans or Russians at World Cup matches. Words such as 'hysteria' and 'craziness' are commonly employed to describe unmitigated outpourings of feeling. Self-control and modesty are highly prized. Showiness is frowned upon, as is flaunting one's wealth. Although being *nuchter* is considered an essential quality in every corner of the Netherlands, the eastern borderlands most fully embody the popular virtue. An Overijssel native is proud of his or her heritage, without thinking it is necessary to shout from the rooftops how great he or she is. For the Bergentheimers, it is important that Arne Slot has remained 'so normal'. Former classmate Van der Velde said, 'When I see him on TV now, I still see that boy from back then, with that Dutch down-to-earthness. A few years ago, one of our former classmates was in the stadium at an AZ match. And then he still spends time to talking with you. Imagine that.'

In Bergentheim – the village of neighbourliness, where the community centre is called *Veur Mekaar* ('For Each Other' – in the eastern dialect), where everyone knows each other and says *hoi* and *ajuus* ('Hi' and 'See you later') – they don't like it when you get too big for your boots. Putting things into perspective is essential. Is Slot the greatest Banthummer of all time? Not really, according to club chairman Nijenhuis. 'Nothing to disparage Slot. But in wartime, we had many resistance fighters. They deserve even more honour.'

'The war hit Bergentheim hard,' said Feyenoord fan Te Rietstap, who is the grandson of one of those resistance fighters and a member of the local committee for the commemoration of the fallen of 1940–45. Twelve members of the resistance were shot on 2 March 1945, two months before the end of the war. 'That is a lot, for such a small village. At school, students adopt war monuments and commit to maintaining them. The war commemoration [on 4 May] is still well attended every year. Maybe that is where my love for Rotterdam comes from: the city that rose up again after [being heavily bombed in] the war. It says something about the mentality. In Rotterdam, and in Bergentheim.'

In an article in the *Athletic*, Simon Hughes analysed 'The Rise and Rise of the Premier League's Frontier Coaches'. He found that in the 2024–25 season, 9 of the league's 20 managers were either born or raised within 50 kilometres of a national border: Unai Emery, Mikel Arteta, Andoni Iraola, Thomas Frank, Oliver Glasner, Kieran McKenna, Julen Lopetegui, Arne Slot and Erik ten Hag (until his October dismissal). Ten Hag was born in the Dutch town of Haaksbergen, just 10km from Germany. Slot was brought up in a village separated from German soil by 12km. (Former Netherlands and Chelsea coach Guus Hiddink hails from Varsseveld, a town 8km from the German border.) Sports psychologist Marc Sagal is quoted in the article as saying:

> Proximity to multiple cultures, including languages and various traditions, can help with adapting to new environments, resolving conflict, and being sensitive to differences. Perhaps from a less obvious perspective, this could contribute to a bit of entrenchment and solidification of a person's identity. In other words, there might be times when, because of so many other influences, there is a desire to protect and preserve one's way of doing things. Border regions often have unique identities that are very separate from the countries they belong to. The desire to preserve one's unique cultural heritage might manifest in football managers as an exceptionally tight attachment to a playing style, football philosophy, or identity.

On the one hand, Arne Slot is an amiable, tolerant and flexible borderland diplomat. On the other hand, he is someone who staunchly believes in his particular analysis, vision and development of football. Taken together, these qualities have enabled him to become one of the modern game's sharpest, most sophisticated and successful strategists.

3

MIDDLING MIDFIELDER

'I would not have put myself in the first eleven.'
ARNE SLOT

No one could have imagined that the world of professional football would eventually reward Arne Slot with a real-estate portfolio that included a beachside apartment in Egmond aan Zee and a monumental 1881 early Art Nouveau villa in the heart of Zwolle. His career as a player was over before it really got started. Dutch sports reporter Sierd de Vos once called Slot the 'Xavi of Bergentheim'. Slot still considers it the biggest compliment he received in his playing career, but it might be a touch generous, given the testimony of former teammates that he was never especially quick or nimble.

Former coach Ben Hendriks gave Arne Slot his debut at FC Zwolle as a 15-year-old. He also made him team captain. In 1995, Slot got into Zwolle's first team as a 17-year-old. It was the beginning of 18 years in the margins of professional football as a gifted but cautious technician, with the through ball his weapon of choice. Slot's playing style was devoid of the dynamism and speed that were to be the defining characteristic of the teams he managed. Although there were few complaints about his abilities and insight, his body looked a bit frail. Slot mostly played at the same tempo throughout the game, without any bursts of speed. Although he recognised the moments for deep runs, he couldn't make them. Due to his limited physical power and range of action, he had to be smart to survive in professional football. He never came anywhere near the level of his dream club FC Barcelona and fell well short of the quality of his childhood idols Marco van Basten and Dennis Bergkamp. Still, he eventually became an effective goal-scoring midfielder.

Typing Arne Slot into YouTube will yield a skimpy selection of footage of his time on the ball. Slot was a stylist, someone who compensated for his lack of physical strength and running capacity with technical finesse and tactical ingenuity. He produced smart receptions and subtle passes. Jan Everse was appointed as Zwolle's manager in 1996. Slot's professional debut before Everse's arrival came in a team that would finish in 15th place in the Dutch second division. He was best suited to play as a number 8 or number 10. Everse saw a 'technical player with a good vision of the game. A lot of people had the idea that Arne was lazy and phlegmatic, that he didn't put much effort into it. But that wasn't true. You just shouldn't expect sliding tackles from Arne.' Slot's start under Everse was not smooth, with many injuries and a lot of sitting on the bench. 'He had some trouble with that, because he thought he was good. He didn't doubt his own qualities. Arne was young and a bit stubborn, so I said, "Invest in yourself, otherwise you will always remain in doubt."'

That message got through. But it took nearly 18 months for him to establish himself in Zwolle's starting XI. 'Sometimes he would get 20 or 30 minutes. He was wondering why he was not playing more. I would say to him, "Arne, you are my best player. But the problem is that when we lose the ball, you do nothing. We cannot just rely on our qualities when we have the ball. It's not enough in modern football. You have to do more. You have to put pressure on the ball. You have to defend. You are a very good passer, but if you only touch the ball 15 times in a game, you do not have value for my team."' Everse remembers seeing a development in Slot's game and told him that he would eventually make it into the team. When Slot took his coach's advice to heart, he grew into an undisputed regular.

Rob McDonald, a striker for PSV Eindhoven and Newcastle in the mid-to-late 1980s, lived in the Netherlands for 40 years. One of his many roles in coaching was in Zwolle, when Slot first forged his reputation. 'The thing I noticed about Arne was not arrogance exactly, but the fact he had so much confidence in himself. I could tell from his face that he was gutted when I didn't pick him for the team at first, but business was business. He had an air about him on the pitch. A player would try to tackle him hard and he would just shoot them this glance. He has had the same attitude as a manager. It is one of "I know what I'm talking about, listen to me".' Former FC Zwolle chairman Gaston Sporre remembered Slot as 'a lad who usually didn't get his clothes dirty, but who had great technique. A proper, neat guy from a good background, who had had a good education. At training camps, he wasn't in the noisy group but kept more to himself.' Slot admitted that, when playing against better teams in the Eredivisie, 'without the ball, I wasn't that good. At a lower level with Zwolle, playing with the ball, I looked much better. I think that as a player I already was a coach. I really am more a coach than a player. Near the end of my playing career, I thought a lot about football.'

At the end of the 1999–2000 season, FC Zwolle were second in the Eerste Divisie, tied with Groningen on 74 points, but with a goal difference of 49 to Groningen's 48. It was a year of great football, and Slot has his own take on the memorable season. 'Staying in people's memories is sometimes just as important as being first. Zwolle came second behind NAC, but people still remember that year, more than the year we won. My idea of how football should be played started with Jan Everse. How we first played a positional game at FC Zwolle, the way we built on that, and what the result was, opened my eyes. Before Jan came, things didn't make sense. After that, good positional play became part of Zwolle's identity. The club is still trying to do that now. I think it's great that as a coach you really leave something lasting behind at a club. It's only when you get older that you start to see those kinds of things.'

Everse is credited with particular influence on Slot's football philosophy. He coached him twice at FC Zwolle, at the beginning and end of his playing career. According to Everse, by the time he returned after an almost decade-long absence, Slot had become an on-field coach. 'He was the best player and was already coaching players around him while he played.'

For five seasons in a row, FC Zwolle failed at decisive moments. Triangles, one-touch football – Zwolle under Jan Everse and his successor Dwight Lodeweges had it all. But when the prizes were distributed, NAC Breda, FC Groningen, FC Den Bosch or RBC Roosendaal got the better of the Overijssel club. That changed with the arrival of coach Paul Krabbe. The start was not promising. He made some changes to the team's game strategy, without wanting to abandon the flamboyant style completely. 'It may all look a bit less spectacular, but we are now winning matches that previously caused difficulties.' The image of the team changed. Eye-catching combination football had made way for new pragmatism.

In 2002, glory finally arrived in their own stadium on the penultimate matchday against competitor Excelsior, who were in second place in the table. The Rotterdam team needed to beat Zwolle, who were defending a three-point lead, to leapfrog them and leave their fate in their own hands. In a bad-tempered and tumultuous match, Excelsior were defeated 1–0 after two players received a red card. The encounter turned especially feisty in the second half with a lot of battles, emotions and serious fouls. In the 66th minute, Excelsior midfielder Gill Swerts was sent off after leaving an elbow in the face of his opposite number Henk van Steeg. Fifteen minutes before the final whistle, FC Zwolle also had to continue with ten men when defender Remco Schol was sent off for a foul on Excelsior forward Leo Koswal. In the 79th minute, Arne Slot scored the decisive goal, setting the sold-out stadium, filled with 6,800 spectators, on fire.

Together with his fellow midfielders Henk van Steeg and Marco Roelofsen, striker Richard Roelofsen, goalkeeper Johan van der Werff and defenders Robert Wijnands and Albert van der Haar, Slot was one of the key players of the squad. 'The foundation was laid by Jan Everse,' he said, after scoring the winning goal. 'He brought in good players and developed our positioning game.' Thanks to the victory over Excelsior, FC Zwolle won the Eerste Divisie title and returned to the Eredivisie after an absence of 13 years. Slot ended his last season, in which he played all 34 competition matches, with promotion to the top league. He spent seven years at the club and scored 50 goals in 164 appearances. The 23-year-old then left for NAC Breda, who at that time played European football.

Arne Slot played for NAC from 2002 until 2007. He spent time on the bench and struggled with manager Henk ten Cate. The Amsterdam native could be merciless and capricious, but Slot did appreciate his professional knowledge and methods. Once again, the non-committal nature of Slot's football emerged. His reputation for playing a spotless game pursued him in the Pearl of the South and he was never universally admired. He didn't cover the hard yards and was said to always leave the pitch without getting his kit dirty. *Juffer-tje Slot*, 'Miss Slot', did not always guarantee the type of masculine football that the Breda supporters liked to see. They thought he was a midfielder who considered every foul a sign of weakness and who in transition moments couldn't contribute much to the course of the match. But, at 24, Slot showed great insight into the game, although he played second fiddle to Alfred Schreuder, six years his senior and the strategist in midfield during the top season of 2002–03. NAC had a good squad and played good football. Besides Slot himself, Schreuder, Rob Penders, Ruud Brood and Earnest Stewart would all become coaches or technical directors.

Belgian forward Bart van den Eede got on well with Slot. 'We became best friends, played a lot of golf together, went to concerts regularly, took the women with us. I was allowed to be there all day at his wedding. Maybe it wasn't good for Arne that he did so much with me because I didn't click with Ten Cate. I used to say to Arne: "Come on, can we stop talking about football for a moment?" He thought that was fine, he also wanted to have a casual chat over a beer. But he wasn't feeling great because he wasn't always playing. Football is everything to him.' Dutch-Moroccan striker Ali Boussab-oun said, 'No "goddamn" ever crossed his lips. As a temperamental guy, I envied that kind of self-control. I saw a coach in him. But Arne had to get used to the street-fighter climate that prevailed at NAC at the time. He was the celebrated man in Zwolle and then you become comfortable. Ten Cate demanded more aggression. Arne had to stretch to reach a new level at NAC and he didn't always play.'

The constant criticism from his notoriously hard-to-please manager disheartened Slot. 'I had to go deeper, every training, every match. We reached fourth place, but I was happy he left, so that I was released from the burden. With hindsight, it was a pity. The way I played back then, NAC need not have been my top team.' Ten Cate did not particularly select Slot for abuse; he was tough on everyone. It was his style. Slot's colleagues thought their new teammate was too restrained and struggled with making the transition from the calmer atmosphere in Zwolle to the tough climate of NAC. One of Slot's hang-ups was his lack of pace, something he has in common with some other Dutch former players who became successful coaches, such as Guus Hiddink and Louis van Gaal. Whatever they lacked in brawn, they compensated with brain. They had to think about football and did so very effectively. Slot's lack of speed would be a blessing in disguise for his managerial career.

Slot said, 'I came from Zwolle, where we already played a good positional game. That made the adjustment easier in terms of football. But that alone was not enough. Henk demanded more from you and he forced it. "Good morning" – that is what I remember. Henk always shouted that when someone made a bad pass. "Good morning, what a bad ball." The basis of my coaching is positional play. I was raised with that by Jan Everse, Dwight Lodeweges and later Henk. I still go back to [training] forms from that time, which you of course adapt to the spaces in which you want to train. My best year as a footballer was under Henk. He was demanding. I never ran as much as in that season. I was often the middle man in positional play, but in between we had to make those runs. I tried to save myself and Henk saw that. "Keep moving!" he shouted. I just thought: "Oh dear, those runs." But you felt yourself getting fitter, and when you get fitter, your level goes up . . . Henk could be very cynical and I don't think that still works with the current generation of footballers. I don't communicate as cynically as Henk did. But the essence remains the same: you try to convince players in a clear way that they have to work harder. I don't quickly tell my players in team meetings what they did wrong or what should have been done differently. Because then the players just look at each other and hardly anyone dares to say anything. I talk a lot, you know. But I'm more into instruction. I tell them what went wrong and how it should be improved. Also, you never take on the weakest player in those kinds of situations.'

Ten Cate was an old-school coach, hard and direct. Slot's approach tends to be more thoughtful and focused on maintaining good relationships, but he does not shy away from confrontation when needed. Some commentators have come to think of him as a laptop manager, someone who coaches his team based on data. 'People think it's just about magnets on a tactics board for me. But data are accessories. In my view, what matters in football management is how you interact with people. You have to have some sense of what generation you are working with. You're constantly busy with the psychology of the players. Mistakes have to be exposed. Of course, you deal differently with every player. One prefers watching the examples of other players, the other rather footage of himself. If you regularly give compliments, you can more easily criticise when it is necessary. I want to convince a player in a nice way that he should do certain things. It is human nature to want to reach maximum performance with minimal means. But I won't give them that space. I won't just say: you have to do this or that. I will come with arguments why it is better for the team and therefore also better for him to demand more of himself. I do that in phases; one picks it up quicker than the other.'

On 6 May 2003, FC Zwolle were fighting against relegation and would get some distance from the bottom three with a victory in NAC's Rat Verlegh Stadium. For NAC, the season would only remain interesting if they beat Zwolle. This way, the Breda team could still hope for European football. NAC coach Henk ten Cate, aware of the precarious situation, conjured up a surprising line-up. Defender Mark Schenning appeared in the attack, with Slot nearby. The strategy proved immediately effective. NAC started with furious intensity and, after just one minute of play, made it 1–0 through

Slot, who scored from a pass from forward Kevin Bobson. The level dropped drastically in the second half. Only in the final 15 minutes did NAC create a number of chances. Twelve minutes before the end, Slot scored again against his old club: 2–0.

Although NAC fans were not always enamoured with Slot's deliberate style, he was appreciated in Breda, particularly for his vital contribution at the end of the 2002–03 season. The last five matches of the season were all won, with the game against RBC Roosendaal as the pièce de résistance. Thanks to a 2–1 victory, NAC qualified for a European spot on the last day of the league programme. In the ninth minute, Slot scored an important goal in the decisive away match with an assist from Alfred Schreuder – the future Ajax manager. From midfield, Schreuder produced a magnificent pass with his left foot to his teammate, who controlled the ball perfectly with his right foot before poking the ball with his left over RBC goalkeeper Wim de Ron: 1–0. NAC achieved a historic fourth place in the Eredivisie, behind PSV, Ajax and Feyenoord, the club's best league finish since 1956. There were celebrations in the dressing room and coach Ten Cate bellowed, 'Congratulations on a great season!'

Slot played his only games in European football in the first round of the UEFA Cup (now the Europa League) in 2003. NAC played two matches against Newcastle United, but were soundly beaten by the superior English opposition. The Dutch side were roared on by an estimated 4,300 NAC fans who had made the trip to Tyneside to celebrate their side's return to the European stage after a 30-year absence. Newcastle went in front when Alan Shearer flicked the ball forward and Craig Bellamy ran on before chipping the keeper. It was the start of a 5–0 rout. Newcastle were less prolific in the return match, winning just 1–0, but the English club's supporters made up for the lack of drama on the pitch. Eighty-seven Newcastle fans were arrested after violence in Breda preceding their team's victory. They had got on well with NAC fans in pubs and bars during the day, but trouble broke out just a few hours before kick-off. There were clashes involving bottles, glasses and chairs. More than 200 riot police, some on horses, rounded up troublemakers. The double loss against New-castle spelled the end of the European journey for NAC.

NAC extended Slot's four-year contract by two years in July 2004. Although he was an experienced player, Slot had to prove him-self again with every new coach. This also happened at the start of the 2006–07 season. Manager Ernie Brandts – the fourth head coach since Ten Cate's departure in summer 2003 – left him out of the start-ing line-up several times, but Slot fought back and enjoyed one of his best seasons.

He took to life in the south. 'In the east of the country, people all have a nice savings account. But here people prefer spending their money, eating out, going to the cafe together. I really learned to enjoy life in Breda.' He was part of the Breda culture for more than five seasons. 'When I listened to the crowd, I sometimes had goosebumps standing on the field. I still look back on my time with NAC with incredible pleasure. There is nothing negative that comes to mind when I think about it. The club started slipping, but that was not reflected in the supporter numbers. That says a lot about the audience in Breda.' Heracles-Almelo hoped they could take the midfielder on a free transfer. Slot said, 'If Heracles maintains itself in the Eredivisie, that club is certainly an option. But there are more clubs that may be interested. They are just not as concrete as Heracles.' In the end, he did not move back east but further west, to Sparta Rotterdam, in 2007. Slot played 167 official matches for NAC and scored 26 times.

Arne Slot played for Sparta for three seasons. Foeke Booy was his manager from the end of 2007 to July 2009. 'When I signed, Sparta was rock bottom. I spoke to all the players very briefly. I told Arne in an exaggerated tone of voice that Sparta was rumoured to actually play with ten men when they lost the ball. It was meant cynically to indicate that I expected more of him when we didn't have the ball. He picked that up very well. He was tactically very strong. He could really put an attacker in front of the keeper and became my extension on the field. In the end, I worked very pleasantly with him for a year and a half and we managed to keep Sparta in the Eredivisie both seasons.'

Sander Westerveld became the most expensive goalkeeper in British football when he joined Liverpool for a fee of £4 million in the summer of 1999. He was Gérard Houllier's first choice and fully justified his manager's confidence by playing a leading role in Liverpool's return to Europe, conceding the fewest goals in the 1999–2000 Premier League season. Westerveld played with Arne Slot during the 2007–08 season at Sparta. 'You could see that he would become a coach. He was a leader, a number 10 midfielder and someone who would change tactics by himself. When I was at Almeria, I was with Unai Emery and he was conducting meetings for one and a half hours, offering all these little details, and then you saw that in the game. Arne is like that, too. He is an intelligent guy and a good analyst. He is not only the manager of a team, he can manage a club and the fans. We still play golf together, so we see each other regularly. Whenever he has a day off, he phones me, "Hey, what are you doing tomorrow?" I am a social golfer who never had lessons. I just want to play 18 holes, but he is a perfectionist in everything he does. He is better than me – I can have my day but it is hard to beat him. That goes for all the games he plays.'

According to the interpretation of Mikos Gouka, a journalist with *Algemeen Dagblad*, Slot ended Marco van Basten's managerial career at Ajax. In May 2009, Slot was a regular substitute at Sparta and the club needed end-of-season points off Ajax to avoid relegation. Slot went to Booy and advised him to start him in the game, telling him how to set up the team around him. 'The next day, the coach did exactly that. Sparta won 4–0 and Van Basten resigned.' It is a good story, but Slot's time in Rotterdam was not an unqualified success. In 2009, Booy was replaced by Frans Adelaar and the 30-year-old Slot no longer featured in the plans of the new manager. Adelaar was of the opinion that 'Arne Slot has simply been surpassed by our young talent, Lerin Duarte for example.' Slot disagreed. 'I won't be written off and certainly not after just two weeks of training. I absolutely do not share the view of the coach. I have had to fight against doubts from managers and the public throughout my 14-ycar career. I am going to fight.' But he was also hampered by an Achilles tendon injury during the 2009–10 season. 'For two months, I had the feeling that Sparta wanted nothing more than for me to leave,' he said. After two seasons, Slot was redundant in Rotterdam and was allowed to depart, even though his contract with Sparta continued for another year. He had played 54 matches for the club and scored six goals.

Heracles-Almelo were looking for an attacking midfielder and the Overijssel-born Slot might have been a good fit. But his disappointing prior encounter with the club complicated things. 'The annoying thing about Heracles is that I chose Sparta two years ago and I think for a good reason, because there were big plans here. Danny Blind came here and wanted to bring in a lot of new and big players. But he quickly left, which means Sparta did not take the step I thought the club would make. Apparently this did not go down well with Heracles. I think that's a shame, because I have nothing against the club. On the contrary, I always had the hope of returning to the east again after three years with Sparta. It's just annoying that it turned out this way because I don't think I did much wrong at the time.'

After their victorious return to the top league, FC Zwolle had again been relegated to the second tier, two years after Arne Slot's 2002 departure. He returned after an absence of seven years, joining on loan in 2009 and on a permanent deal in 2010. 'In the 2009–10 season, I was approached by chairman Adriaan Visser and asked if I wanted to come back to FC Zwolle. Five games had already been played. That season we rose from fifteenth place to a nice third place. After five seasons at NAC and two years at Sparta, I had to get used to the limited public interest in the Jupiler League. [For sponsorship reasons, the Eerste Divisie was named after the Belgian beer brand from July 2006 to June 2018.] In the Eredivisie, you play in front of many more spectators, which is different from Almere City FC or FC Oss . . . But by Eerste Divisie standards, I signed an excellent contract, which included a role for me beyond playing football. That wish was high on my list of priorities . . . Zwolle was a division lower than Sparta. I said that I wanted to come and play for them, on the condition that I would become an assistant coach when I quit. At that time, to be admitted to the professional football coaching course, you first had to have been an assistant for two years. This was my ticket to become a trainer.'

In Zwolle, where his face looms large on the club's wall of heroes, he developed a habit of launching the ball high into the sky at kick-off, something that eventually would gain notoriety as the 'firecracker kick-off'. Dutch TV pundits mocked him mercilessly for it. But what they did not mention was that he was doing it deliberately, wrongfooting the opposition as they looked into the sun. In one year, Zwolle scored seven times within the first 30 seconds. Striker Sjoerd Ars, who played his football not only in the Netherlands but also in Hungary, Bulgaria, Turkey and China, pointed out that Slot did not always pull off his innovation to good effect. 'At Zwolle, I talked with Arne about football all day long. We didn't just talk about clubs, playing systems and tactics, but also about our own input in dead-ball situations. That had some consequences. One time, a kick-off went so completely wrong that [well-known commentator] René van der Gijp couldn't stop laughing. The idea was: lift the ball off the halfway line and then shoot it straight forward, so that we could immediately start battling for the second ball on the edge of the 16 [the penalty box]. It almost looked like match-fixing, because Arne hit it completely wrong.'

At home in the FC Zwolle Stadium, Zwolle defeated BV Veendam. It took until the 45th minute before Zwolle took the lead. Although the team was the better of the two, they weren't sharp with their finishing. Surprisingly, it was defender Albert van der Haar who broke the deadlock with a deflected shot. After the break, another defender, Bram van Polen, decided the match. A good cross from Arne Slot fell behind Veendam's defence. Van Polen made good use of the opportunity and shot the ball into the bottom-left corner from a few metres out. The Zwolle fans saw their team playing well and creating good chances. 'Only in that phase did we show that we can play fantastic football,' said manager Art Langeler.

Former Zwolle players lavish praise on Slot. Jesper Drost was a teenager when he played with him. 'If there's one person who knows a lot about football, it's Arne. You could see that during the rondos [a footballing version of "piggy in the middle"]. He was rarely in the middle. When I arrived at PEC as a rookie, Arne immediately took me under his wing. I couldn't have wished for a better teammate. That social quality is typical of Arne.' Midfielder Jan Wicher Vellinga said, 'You could immediately see that he was a discerning football player. He was always talking to everyone. He was not only critical of himself, but also of the team. In short, he had that analytical side very early. That is why I am not surprised that Arne became a coach. You can see how he is in front of the camera: solid, honest, calm.' Defender Albert van der Haar played 112 matches with Slot. 'I didn't just have a good connection with Arne on the field, but also off. We regularly went out for a bite to eat with our wives. Of course I'm proud of him, although I am surprised that it's going so fast. I didn't expect that. But that's just great – especially how he does it. Self-confident, with some humour and an eye for detail.'

After Slot had become head coach of Feyenoord, Turkish-Dutch winger Mustafa Saymak said that he picked him up after Feyenoord had demolished Zwolle in the first half. 'A good teammate, a fantastic player and above all a great person. That's Arne. I'll never forget his words after we lost 4–0 to Feyenoord. "Cheer up, Mussi," he said. "You have to stay in the Eredivisie." That's beautiful. As if we were still playing together.'

On the FC Zwolle website, captain Slot shared his impressions of the winter training camp in sunny Spain and his prognosis for the second half of the 2011–12 season.

This morning we completed a tough training; this afternoon the first eleven had free time because of tomorrow's match. There is a beautiful golf complex next to our hotel and I spend my free hours there. So far we can definitely speak of a very successful training camp. The training is hard and good, the accommodation and food are excellent, and there are no injuries. The biggest advantage of a training camp in Spain is a cliché, but that is of course the good weather. The first four matches that await us from 15 January will be tough. We play three of those matches outside Zwolle and they are not the easiest away matches. If we get through those games alright, we'll be well on our way. Before the winter break we were in the flow of winning every week. After a number of weeks without games, you have to start all over, in a way. But I expect that even if we have an average second half of the season, we will achieve what we could not achieve last year. I hope that the supporters will come to the stadium in full force from January 20, when we play Almere City FC, to cheer us on and that they will keep the faith, even if things don't go well in some matches. This will give us the needed boost and the opponents will feel intimidated, as most of them are not used to playing in front of such an audience. I also think that we deserve this as a team, after two seasons of both success and great football. During the camp I noticed that all the lads have a great drive to achieve the ultimate goal. The objective of this training camp is clear: FC Zwolle wants to be the best from the start of the second half of the season.

FC Zwolle played well in the second half of the season and were top of the table by the end of March, when they beat AGOVV-Apeldoorn. After 10 minutes, a header from winger Nassir Maachi made it 1–0. Shortly afterwards, it was Giovanni Hiwat who scored the second. Just before half-time, it became 3–0 when midfielder Jesper Drost tapped the ball past the Apeldoorn keeper. There were few chances on either side in the second half. Fifteen minutes before the end, first Joey van den Berg and then Arne Slot missed chances to make it 4–0. Meanwhile, second-placed Sparta Rotterdam, who played with 10 men in the second half, lost 1–0 to FC Volendam.

FC Zwolle could win the title in the 32nd match of the season. With three matches left to play, they were eight points ahead of Sparta and nine ahead of their direct rivals FC Eindhoven. A win over Eindhoven would mean the title was secure. The whole of Zwolle was under the spell of an impending championship celebration, but Arne Slot pointed out that the match against the team managed by Erwin Koeman would be a tough task. 'I don't just assume that we will become champions. First of all, that would be disrespectful to our opponent, FC Eindhoven, who, together with FC Zwolle, are perhaps the best team in the Jupiler League. The score in our away match was 2–2 and we had a very difficult time, especially before half-time. This week there were queues at the main entrance, all people who wanted to buy the very last ticket. The stand that was specially built for this match is also sold out. It gives us a boost, but our focus is still on a difficult match. We lost a championship last year and that cannot happen again.'

In the event, a goalless draw on 13 April 2012 was enough to secure Zwolle the title. After promotion to the Eredivisie, they would play under their former name PEC Zwolle, which they had lost after bankruptcy and club reorganisation in 1990.

The Dutch Eerste Divisie season is subdivided into four quarters rather than two halves, before and after Christmas/New Year, as in the leagues of most countries. According to the Jupiler League website, 'The Bronze Bull is awarded per period to the best team, the best player, the best trainer, the top scorer, and the best young talent. The coaches and captains make a selection of four players from all players in the League who are nominated for the best player of that period. Together with them, the supporters determine which player wins the Bronze Bull for best player. The presentation of the Golden Bull rewards the best sporting performances of the season. The bull symbolises strength, sportsmanship, competitiveness and passion in football.'

Before the winter break, Arne Slot received the Bronze Bull as the best player of the second quarter. At the season's end, the championship medal was hung around his neck and shortly afterwards the Zwolle playmaker could hold up the Eerste Divisie shield. 'This season had an unpleasant start for me. I missed the first six games due to an injury. It was great that the technical staff had put together an eager and talented new squad after the departure of a number of players. Now, a great wish has been fulfilled. You often only experience a championship once in your football life. As captain, holding up the bowl and showing it to the supporters was a first for me. It's been ten years now, but I can still see Marco Roelofsen lifting the 2002 championship trophy. Now it was my turn: a great feeling. Apart from the personal feeling, the championship is wonderful for the club. Our mission to play in the Eredivisie with FC Zwolle has been accomplished. Now the club can continue to build.' The presentation of the Golden Bull took place at Beach Club O in Noordwijk, on 4 May 2012. Both Zwolle manager Art Langeler and team captain Arne Slot received the award.

Slot had a difficult season in 2012–13, when a knee injury kept him sidelined for a long time. This was a reason for Zwolle not to offer him a contract extension. 'I saw it coming, and it didn't make me very happy. I had some hope of seeing some improvement in the coming months and then perhaps continuing for another year. Now I have to think and decide whether I want to continue playing football – and hope that another club will come. Otherwise, I will continue to work at Zwolle in a different capacity.'

Arne Slot ended his career after the 2012–13 competition and was offered a farewell match by PEC Zwolle, the club he had served the longest. The playmaker also received a goodbye gift: a framed match shirt from the club with the number 100 from general director Edward van Wonderen. Slot had scored his 100th goal in professional football in the home match against SC Veendam. He had played 450 games, of which 266 were for Zwolle, and had been a major force in the club's sporting success. In his last three seasons, he played 90 games and scored 23 goals. He became champion of the Eerste Divisie twice with the club.

With a 4–2 victory over ADO Den Haag, PEC Zwolle said a dignified farewell to captain Arne Slot and coaches Art Langeler and Jaap Stam. The Zwolle team managed to keep their place in the Eredivisie. After the win, the newly promoted club ended the season in 11th place and the three club icons were able to say goodbye with a sense of accomplishment. All three continued to work in football, in different ways. Langeler would start as head of youth training at PSV, Stam signed a three-year contract with Ajax as assistant coach, while Slot would continue to work at Zwolle as a youth coach.

4

MANAGER ARNE SLOT

'A born coach? You could say that.'
ARNE SLOT

Managing a football team seems to have been destined for Arne Slot. He realised early that he would become a coach one day. 'I would almost say from the age of six. But around the age of 20, I thought: if I ever stop, I will become a trainer. That was because I think football is fantastic and coaching is a good way to stay involved. I also thought that I could become better as a coach than as a player. Today, people might think it's not that difficult because of course I had a nice playing career. But it wasn't the level at which I work now. I still make use of the fact that I did not reach the absolute top as a player. For example, I say about an opponent's lesser player: "Look, that's a type of Arne Slot. He goes for the ball, but otherwise he doesn't move." Humour is an important factor in building good relationships.'

Although he dreamed of a career as a manager, he realised it would be uncertain because he didn't have an international CV. Slot proved to be a forward thinker. Towards the end of his playing career, he invested in shares. Together with his brother Jakko, he launched a business in personalised captain's armbands and shin guards in 2012. Slotwear survived on the market for three years. 'We considered studying, but decided entrepreneurship is the best study there is,' said

Jakko Slot. 'The intention was never to set up a large company. The goal was to learn more about doing business.' The KNVB initiated a national campaign named No Football Without Respect. To support the initiative and to draw attention to the problems surrounding violence on amateur fields, Arne and Jakko decided to create a special Respect armband for amateur football players. Players throughout the Netherlands could order the armband for €10. Slotwear donated the proceeds to the Foundation Against Senseless Violence.

After retiring from playing at PEC Zwolle, Slot became part of the club's staff. He told the club directors that he wanted to work at the top level. Instead, he was dispatched to a youth team. He also would carry out some scouting work for the main squad. Technical director Gerard Nijkamp was happy with the appointment. 'Next season we want to further invest in the youth academy and the arrival of Arne plays an important role in that. In addition to being a good trainer, Arne is also the face of PEC Zwolle. He has played in both the youth and the first team, and his presence increases the attraction for young talent.' Slot would start as coach of the C2 team. He would also assist Alexander Palland with the B1. Slot said, 'The coaching profession has appealed to me for many years. I am very much looking forward to working as a youth coach at PEC Zwolle next season.'

The transition wasn't easy for Slot. Even though he comes across as a modest and soft-spoken character, he does not lack ambition. 'When I was a professional football player, I mattered. When I went to the bakery or the butcher's, I was recognised and people wanted to talk to me. After I stopped and started training the under-14s at PEC Zwolle, that disappeared and that was difficult for me. It went from "doing what everyone was talking about" to "doing what 10 or 20 parents on the side are talking about and no one else is talking about". That probably has something to do with my upbringing. My father always set the bar very high. I hope that in a hundred years' time my European victories will still be standing and my name will still be mentioned.' His childhood mentor Jan Everse recognised this ambitious streak in Slot early. 'I think Arne thinks very simply in his own interests. That's good because things can end suddenly in the football world.'

In the first half of Slot's first coaching season, Zwolle's under-14s won just once. The results were bad, including 9–1 and 6–0 defeats to Ajax and AZ Alkmaar. But then they started winning, again and again. Suddenly everyone was talking about the team. The difference was Slot. The young Zwolle players would train every morning from 8:30am until 10am. Then they would go to school at the Centre for Sports and Education, across the road from Zwolle's training ground. At 3pm, an analysis of the training session earlier that day followed. That kind of scrutiny was new to the youth-team members, but Slot saw it as essential for getting them out of the rut of defeat.

Max Leeflang, a Zwolle youth-team player, said Slot was the best coach he ever worked with. 'Before Arne, there was no video work in Zwolle. I had never seen it. It was new for everyone. I would ask myself, "Why are we doing this?" It was weird. But then we'd see the results and realise that maybe it helped. He would always say, "Don't play the ball back, always play forward." Every session was competitive. It was the same in games: three versus three, three versus two, two against two. Entire training sessions focused on possession. He wanted intensity and players to feel the pressure of the opponent. His level was too high for the players we had. Some of them couldn't understand what he wanted. It must have been hard for him. He basically wanted the youth system to train as professionally as the first team. After he moved on to Cambuur, I thought, "Arne, please come back . . ." I have had other coaches with long professional careers behind them. They had played 500 matches, but Arne was far better than they were. There was a big difference.'

Slot left PEC Zwolle in May 2014. SC Cambuur general director Gerald van den Belt gave Slot his first significant break in management when he became a part of Henk de Jong's coaching staff ahead of the 2014–15 season, together with Dennis van der Ree. The club did not have a functioning under-21 team and Slot and Van der Ree were tasked with rebuilding the youth team in the next season. Van der Ree said, 'He likes developing young players, but not only them – all of the players. It doesn't matter who they are, he tries to make people better. From the moment I met him, he had a database of clips and we used it in the first team and the under-21 team to develop exercises to train following his principles. He is very good at convincing people of the way he wants to play, but also how to be a professional and train hard, which is crucial, especially for young players. He gives players the feeling that he thinks about everything they say and uses it to help them get better.'

Slot proved to be an attack-minded coach who taught his team to play in multiple game systems in a short period. He was soon promoted to assist Henk de Jong in the first team. In De Jong's opinion, Slot's pace defined him both as a player and coach. 'He wanted to develop himself further and get his professional football coach diploma. He asked if he could do an internship with us. I thought that was interesting because he was unique as a player. Arne was too slow, a bit of a lazy number 10. But this was good for his career as a coach because it meant that, as a player, he had always been thinking three steps ahead. That is why he is special, creative. I like to have that kind of genius around me. I noticed that he had good ideas about attacking football and knew how to develop the requisite tactics and training methods. He makes sure that players know what they should do, but also that they enjoy playing the game. He first coached the youth at Zwolle a bit, then with us the under-21s, slowly growing into the first team and then becoming head coach. Some former players become head coaches too quickly. Take Frank de Boer, Ruud Gullit or Marco van Basten. With a calmer build-up, they might still be at the top now.'

Berend Schootstra experienced Slot in his first two seasons at Cambuur. 'From the start, I told people around me that this was the best coach I ever had. When you saw how he was involved in football and how he helped people one-on-one, I could already see then that he was a great trainer. I was playing at right-back in an away match and things weren't going so well in terms of build-up. At one point Arne said, "Just move into midfield and then we'll see what the opponent is going to do." That very small adjustment changed a lot and we were able to play good football. I enjoyed that even then. It's very special that I got to work with him.' Former Cambuur goalkeeper Harm Zeinstra said, 'It was a great time, in which we played positive and attacking football. Arne was the architect of that. Many coaches have a very good story about football. But with him you could see what he wanted in every exercise during training. I think that's brilliant. We had Young FC Utrecht at home and he said, "If they have the ball in these places" – and he drew it on a board – "then that is a 100 per cent chance for us to score a goal." Within 15 minutes, what he had said exactly happened. That is no coincidence.'

Slot said that at SC Cambuur he developed a rapport with the supporters. 'When we pulled back a bit or had a hard time in the match, Henk de Jong shouted, "I don't like watching this!" He wanted more energy and tempo. But I think this doesn't only apply to coaches. Players also have a lot more fun when they are allowed to play football in a beautiful, proactive way. They feel it just the same. The best compliment you can get as a coach, I think, is when the public comes to watch your team with pleasure. Sometimes we are sitting in the trainers' room after a match and we hear the people walking down the stairs. Then you almost feel, taste the enthusiasm and the energy. Of course that doesn't happen every week, but it does happen often. Those are the moments that make it all worthwhile. Of course it is always about winning, but I think the way in which you do it is just as important.'

As an advocate of using data, Slot made an early impact by telling De Jong to reduce the number of high crosses from wide areas, arguing that few would be productive. 'About one in eighty crosses results in a goal. Besides, it is more difficult to aim with your head than with your feet. Commentators often shout after a header that it was a huge chance, but often that is not the case.' Slot is of the view that a cut-back and low cross offer much better opportunities. Eventually, he converted the Leeuwarden club to his way of thinking.

Arne Slot does not think of himself as an innovator but as someone with a keenly analytical mind and a natural awareness of whether a certain approach is beneficial or not. He is a voracious learner. In Zwolle, he picked up coaching points at the local basketball club Landstede Hammers. As assistant coach at Cambuur, with the league play-offs in mind, he again consulted a local basketball club to find out how a team can manage to play many matches in a short time. He reasoned that, after an MVV–Maastricht away match, players would not be able to perform at their best a few days later after a long bus ride and a sleep-deprived night. Via a sponsor, five large Audis were requisitioned as a speedy and comfortable alternative for the long trip back from Maastricht, in the deep south, to Cambuur's home base in the far north. The players got to bed on time.

'Our fans thought he was crazy at first,' Van den Belt said. 'He is a perfectionist who continuously invests energy in details. He wanted the full support of the home crowd because this could affect the refereeing. So he told me, "On Tuesday evening, invite anyone to the club who wants to come." He spoke for two hours, with a video analysis demonstrating his reasons for asking his players to spend a few more seconds to create a better chance, rather than resort to a high cross. He encouraged the fans to be patient. Afterwards, they were very excited. Arne will do anything to achieve a better result. Anything that's a bad influence, he tries to transform. He doesn't want to ignore a single per cent of his potential influence on a result. You have to stay in control if you truly want to have an influence. Arne always says that the collective, the team, makes the individual look better. That's a very important part of his football philosophy. A scout told me recently, "Never take players from Arne Slot's team. They always look better than they are." When you think about it, that is the biggest compliment you can make a coach.'

When he arrived at Cambuur, Slot was 35. In an interview with *De VoetbalTrainer,* he showed that, even at that relatively young age, he had already formulated many of his fundamental ideas about playing attacking football.

Deep runs are a very effective way to create danger, especially if the starting point, direction and timing of the runs are right. We train a lot on that and I give players clear guidelines on how to go deep. One of the most important instructions I give is that the deep run should always be 'with a run-up'. I don't want a player to be right on the edge of offside, with his hand pointing forward. In that case, you can only start running when the ball is already on its way because otherwise you are offside. So you still have to get up to speed and you can't get in the lead. If you go deep with a run-up, a teammate will register your run better because you are making a full sprint. Then, if the pass comes at the right moment, you cannot be tracked. In addition, it is important that you go deep outside the opponent's field of vision. If you pass in front of him, he sees you and can also start sprinting, or thwart you with physical contact. If you stay out of his field of vision, he will lose you. The moment is also crucial: as a deep player, you have to start running when you think that your 'run-up' will give your teammate on the ball enough time to receive the ball and play deep. The player on the ball then estimates exactly where he has to put the ball. That is quite an art, but if it works, you immediately create a big chance. As a rule of thumb, it is better to play the ball a bit too far than too close because otherwise the defender can intercept the ball and start a counter.

Slot applied the football principles and practices of Henk ten Cate and Jan Everse. 'Good football can be trained, if you can make it trainable with your practice material. Henk ten Cate was incredibly good at that. At Cambuur, I became assistant to Henk de Jong, an underrated coach, and Marcel Keizer. I did the video analyses and was given the task of always starting with the attack. Players had to know from second one that you were an attacking coach. I also experienced a trainer who had players who were not part of the starting team begin certain exercises. These are just a few examples that can contribute to the involvement of all players in the team process.'

He practised playing positional games of six against two, with the rules that Everse taught him in Zwolle: a ball may not be returned to the player who passed it to you and must never be played above the knee. All of it should, of course, be one-touch football. 'That creates dynamism, it forces you to elude cover and everything has to be played with the correct leg.'

Like Ten Cate, he hammers home the principles of the game in team talks, but in tone he is closer to De Jong, thoroughly positive with the firm belief that by putting his trust in them he can help players rise above themselves and build confidence. Slot believes that a more authoritarian style does not work with the current generation of individualists, who are more quickly convinced of themselves and have less respect for authority. As someone straddling the boundary between Generation X and the Millennials, he is not a hardliner who imposes many disciplinary rules. When Slot asks his video analyst to make a compilation of ten match moments, he instructs him to include at least six successful actions and always end with a good movement. That way, he can give a compliment and the player leaves the talk with a good feeling. 'If our striker lacks a bit in self-confidence, you cut the recording at the moment that he shoots and misses the target. But if player thinks he is doing a very good job, you show images of him losing the ball twice.' In the early stages at Cambuur, 'I showed through video images that they were well positioned, that eventually things would come together and that there would be an end product. You really have to believe in it yourself. If you don't, then you are just playing a game with people. But if you believe in it yourself, then you can also convince your players.'

His time at Cambuur stimulated his managerial development. 'I learn a lot from Henk de Jong. One of his most important qualities is that he gives his players the idea that they are invincible. The players also really believe in the playing style. It is an art to achieve that. He doesn't just say something; there is always an idea behind it. One of Henk's strengths is making sure that they have the right mindset after a match, that the lads are feeling good. He once told me that I should spend more time on the strengths of the opponent. So when we have to play against a good team, I show my guys five or six images of what they are good at. Then comes a whole series of images of what they are not very good at and how we can hurt them. It is never the intention that my players get on the pitch intimidated, thinking: this is a very good opponent. The reverse also is not good. If we have to play against the lowest-ranked team and I get the feeling that the lads think they are going to have an easy afternoon, I will show them some data and fragments that suggest the opposite, for example, that they drew against Ajax and AZ. Underestimation never is a good thing. I am constantly trying to figure out how I can best keep my players on their toes. When I show those images and provide a clear analysis, I also demonstrate that the manager did his homework. That's a spark that ignites: I've done my job, now it's up to you.'

Slot was never one to rest on his laurels. 'While others are still enjoying a great match, I'm already looking ahead. In my post-match talk in the dressing room, I try to plant the seed for the next game. I also constantly think about how we can improve further: for example, by finding out how our next opponent exerts pressure and how we can deal with that. I show my players images of how the opponent did not get to play football in a match. Then I show them how we have to do it. Something like that only works if you know exactly how you want to play. You can think of something, but players must also be able to execute it. You have a way of playing and a game plan, and your game plan should not deviate too much from your way of playing. If you never build up, you cannot suddenly expect to build up against the next opponent. Players must stay in their comfort zone.'

In Leeuwarden, Slot made his first acquaintance with Sipke Hulshoff, and the two were to build an enduring and productive relationship. Three years older than Slot, Hulshoff never played the game professionally but is a thoroughly experienced coach. After spending a decade hopping back and forth between the capital cities of the two northernmost provinces, coaching in both Leeuwarden and Groningen, he spent three years with Red Bull Ghana and a summer as interim coach of Al-Arabi in Qatar. In 2014, he followed the Professional Football Coach ('Coach Betaald Voetbal') course and did an internship at Cambuur. He passed the course in May 2015.

Slot and Hulshoff saw how Cambuur struggled through a series of management misadventures. The club made a poor start to the 2015–16 season under Henk de Jong and he resigned in February 2016. Hulshoff was briefly put in charge until Marcel Keizer, coming from FC Emmen, was appointed as De Jong's successor. At the end of the season, the club was relegated from the Eredivisie and Keizer moved on to Young Ajax. He was replaced by Rob Maas, who came from Vitesse-Arnhem. Under Maas, the team had a poor start in the Eerste Divisie and he was fired after just a few matches. On 19 October 2016, the club appointed Slot and Hulshoff as interim coaches.

Cambuur goalkeeper Zeinstra was very positive about the Slot–Hulshoff cooperation. 'Sipke had his Pro Licence, so he was the official head coach as Arne did not have it at that point. They stepped up and immediately had a big influence. The way of playing and training was innovative and fun: high energy, high intensity and with a very clear view of how to play. It was different from a lot of coaches who may want to play the same way – attacking football, pressing high – but they don't train that way. We could instantly see Arne's level of coaching while Sipke was a little bit more in the background, which fitted their profiles and personalities. They really complemented each other. They raised the bar. No training session was similar to the previous one. The overall focus was the same, but there were always different exercises.'

On 5 January 2017, Cambuur announced that Slot and Hulshoff would continue as head coaches for the remainder of the season after 'excellent results and a pleasant way of working'. Under the pair, Cambuur had won eight of the eleven matches in the intervening period, including a historic cup victory over record winners Ajax. Next, Cambuur defeated FC Utrecht on penalties to reach the semi-finals of the KNVB Cup for the first time in their history. After 90 minutes, the score was tied at 2–2, Utrecht having levelled in the final minute through Giovanni Troupée. In extra time, Utrecht missed a few huge chances, after which Cambuur triumphed in a nerve-wracking penalty shootout. The club missed out on a place in the final after losing to AZ, again on penalties.

The Slot–Hulshoff joint venture also helped Cambuur climb from fourteenth to third place in the league. On 21 May 2017, they played MVV in the second leg of the league play-offs after a draw in the first match. After Cambuur forward Martijn Barto scored the first goal, the spoils seemed to have been decided ten minutes before the end. Slot then decided to sit back and defend the lead, switching from playing with four defenders to playing with five and only two strikers, observing that 'Cambuur did well with the 5–3–2 system'. In response, MVV centre-back Steven Pereira made it 1–1 and forward Thomas Verheydt finished the job for the opposition, scoring the final goal of the match.

Jan Bruin, a rare football professional hailing from the northern island of Ameland, was Slot's assistant at the time. He saw a bitterly disappointed head coach after missing out on promotion to the Eredivisie. 'You are often too scared,' Bruin said off-handedly to the novice trainer. The experience played a significant role in the development of Slot's vision for attacking football. He converted Bruin's comment into a rule he uses to this day. 'Just take as much risk as possible, then you will be rewarded more often than when you make a fearful choice. When I think, "Should I bring on a left-back for a left winger?" my thoughts go back to Cambuur–MVV and Jan Bruin. I will certainly lose matches again, but never again from a defensive perspective. We can lose, but we really have to race across the field.'

Without making too much effort, Arne Slot gained the required diploma to become a professional football manager, UEFA Pro. He was in a class with Danny Buijs, Kees van Wonderen and Sjors Ultee, who all also became Eredivisie managers. KNVB instructor Frans de Kat recognised that 'Arne was well ahead, had developed a complete database and a clear vision of how he wanted to play football'. Slot wasn't particularly impressed with the course content, but listening to veterans such as Leo Beenhakker, Louis van Gaal, Peter Bosz and Ronald Koeman made the experience more bearable. 'You had to execute a lot of tasks, many of them repeatedly. You had to make a plan for the year. I had done this for the three preceding years of the course as well, so I got the point. But there were many speakers, among them top managers, and that was fun. Things almost went wrong when I was admitted to the course. I was head coach at Cambuur together with Sipke Hulshoff, he with a diploma and I not yet. So I was actually already a trainer, although I still had to do the course. At the KNVB, you are expected to say six times in every sentence that you come to Zeist to learn. They enjoy hearing that. I sat there during my admission interview with a little too much self-confidence. When they asked what I thought I could learn, I answered truthfully, "Not that much, but I need that piece of paper."'

Slot earned high marks on his final report card for each of the five course components: coaching matches, running training, guiding player development, supporting football technical policy and managing the club network and support staff. 'If I'm honest, I did not learn a lot. That is not a shortcoming of the course, but I believe that there is much more to be learned through practice, by interning with other managers. Before the start of the course, I had already done so many hours of self-study and spent so much time observing other coaches that I had actually already followed my own education. Occasionally during the course someone came by to say something about nutrition or physiology, but I thought: I don't need to know this in such detail if I have specialists in this field available at a club. I like to trust people who know more about something than I do. Because I am ultimately responsible as head coach, I also have to be well informed about these aspects of the profession, but above all I have to ensure that I have the right people around me. To some that may seem arrogant, but to me it has to do with self-confidence. In other parts of my life, I have less confidence. There is more doubt there.'

Slot and SC Cambuur parted ways at the end of the 2016–17 season, and he took the important step from the Eerste Divisie to the Eredivisie. He committed to AZ for three seasons as the assistant of John van den Brom. Gerald van den Belt said, 'It is always unpleasant when someone with a lot of quality leaves the club. On the other hand, we should also see it as a compliment: another person who has developed himself here and is taking a step to a higher level.'

5

AT AZ ALKMAAR

'I want people to think I am a good coach. But my
integrity as a person comes first.'
ARNE SLOT

Ask someone what first comes to mind when they hear 'Holland', and
they are likely to say 'tulips, windmills and cheese'. As it goes with
stereotypes, it's a narrow view of reality but contains some truth. The
Netherlands is the leading producer of tulips, accounting for more
than half of the world's supply – three billion bulbs per year. The country also produces 650 million kilos of cheese annually. In the city of
Alkmaar, 40km north of Amsterdam, cheese trading started in 1365.
In the modern era, each Friday from April to September, the Waag-
plein ('Weighing Square') comes alive with the re-enactment of the
early cheese market, with traders dressed in their classic white cos-
tumes and wide-brimmed hats expertly moving the cheeses to where
they need to go. Around 30,000kg of cheese, mostly of the Gouda and
Edam varieties, pass through the famous square on an average Friday.
At exactly 10am, the market's 'cheese bell' is rung, usually by some
Dutch celebrity or local luminary. Market activities are explained to
buyers and tourists in Dutch, German, English, French, Spanish and
Japanese.

By contrast, AZ Alkmaar is a relative newcomer on the stage

63

of Dutch professional football. The club was founded in 1967 as AZ '67, the merger of Alkmaar '54 and FC Zaanstreek. They take their nickname, De Kaasboeren, the Cheese Farmers, from the local culture. Slot had attracted the club's attention by outlining his vision of football in *De VoetbalTrainer*. In his own inimitable manner, he had explained the team tactics required for playing attacking football. 'Going deep on the contra-side' was one of the items he mentioned. When the ball is on the right side, a player on the left starts a run deep into the opponent's half. In Slot's current view, 'That is nothing new anymore. Every centre-half knows that someone will be going deep.' But in 2017, it was new enough to create some excitement in Alkmaar. Technical director Max Huiberts said, 'We've had Arne in our sights for a while. With more than 450 matches in professional football to his name, he has a well-filled backpack with football experience. Arne is eager to learn, innovative and very ambitious.' With Slot as assistant to John van den Brom, AZ finished third and fourth in the Eredivisie in 2018 and 2019, and lost the 2018 KNVB Cup final to Feyenoord.

AZ had been dubbed 'the Dutch Chelsea' by British commentators in the Noughties for the similarity between the freewheeling banker and AZ owner Dirk Scheringa and the extravagant former Chelsea owner, Russian billionaire Roman Abramovich. Some £600 million came out of Abramovich's seemingly bottomless pockets to fund his pet project in west London. Although the scale of the investments is not comparable, Scheringa, like his Russian counterpart, had an outsize influence on his club's operations. In October 2009, Scheringa's DSB Bank was declared bankrupt by an Amsterdam court and he lost ownership of AZ. Ten days after the court verdict, he announced that he would also step down as chairman of AZ. As a consequence, the club got into financial trouble, which directly affected the sporting results. A decision was made to commit to youth development and focusing on data in order to create a pathway into the future.

On 10 December 2018, the big news in Alkmaar was that Slot would replace Van den Brom as head coach for the 2019–20 season. During his tenure, Slot benefitted from the cultural shift that had taken place at AZ. His intensive use of data and his background in academy coaching and determination to set senior-level expectations for young players influenced his approach to first-team management.

The transition to becoming the main man felt like a logical next step to Slot. 'To be honest, it felt very natural, not particularly special. If it had happened to someone else, you would think: with his CV as a footballer and as a trainer, it is quite a step to now become the manager of a top club like AZ. Some may have thought: this boy is a lucky bird, while I actually thought it had taken a year too long. The annoying thing is that when you know what you can do, you are quickly considered arrogant. I try to avoid that.'

The AZ squad was immediately treated to some Slot-style education. He showed a minute-long clip of players trudging around the pitch after losing the ball. He found it terrible to watch. 'When I joined AZ, they were used to waiting on the halfway line and countering. When we started to apply pressure, there was some resistance, especially when you concede a fair few goals in the beginning. Then you need players who start to believe in it. Wout Weghorst was one of the first to see that if we were to execute it well, it would lead to many more chances for him. So he went crazy. Players have to recognise what is good and what not when we have the ball, or when the opponent has it. That starts on the training ground. Good football runs on certain patterns. Players just have to realise that. For me, attacking football is mainly: what do you do when you don't have the ball? Then we have to go chasing.'

Slot uses this phrase in almost every interview, along with 'Work very hard'. His players have heard these mantras countless times in match briefings. He regularly reminds his group to ask themselves whether they are able to muster the intensity that his playing style requires for the full 90 minutes. In the Slot philosophy, movement and running are the basis for good results.

With Slot at the helm, AZ received plenty of praise for their fresh attacking style and the resulting goals. With 19 points from eight games, Slot got the club off to their best start ever in the Eredivisie. Even Louis van Gaal, who was never outside the top three of the Eredivisie during his first season with AZ, managed only 18 points from the first eight games in 2005–06. Halfway through the season, AZ occupied second place in the Eredivisie, three points behind leaders Ajax. The Alkmaar team also qualified for the last 16 of the KNVB Cup. In short, it had been a good first half-year. Slot achieved these results with attractive football, similar to what he saw at Manchester City with Pep Guardiola and at Liverpool with Jürgen Klopp. 'Beautiful examples. The objective is not to play offensively, but I believe that this is the way to win a lot of games.'

On 7 August 2017, in the match against PSV, AZ winger Calvin Stengs had suffered a serious knee injury that sidelined him for 15 months. 'When I was fit again, Arne emphasised that I had to show my creativity and especially keep the spontaneity in my game. According to Arne, I was sometimes a bit too critical of myself. "It doesn't matter if you have a lesser game sometimes," he would say. I have become tactically stronger thanks to Slot, which allows me to understand the game at a higher level. It may be difficult for outsiders to follow, but one step to the inside or outside can make all the difference. The year before he went to Feyenoord, we won 3–2 in De Kuip. He is a very calm person, can convey his ideas in a simple way, both one-on-one and to a whole group. You always see new players emerge under him who are selected for the Dutch national team, just as I made my debut for the Dutch national team under him at AZ. That is also his quality.'

Ten years after winning the championship in 2009, AZ seemed to be poised to make another challenge for the title. Many Alkmaar supporters went to bed with visions of a victory cruise on the Alkmaar canals. Slot said, 'I live near Alkmaar and everyone is talking about it. But we are only halfway through the season. It is a great compliment that people see it that way. We did not have that six months ago. And it is also right based on how we play and how many points we have scored. The most important thing is that they realise why we have this success. Because we have to keep working hard and even a little harder. We are coming level with Ajax. Two weeks ago, we were six points behind. The fact that we perform so well and also play football so well is great for everyone and therefore also for me. We have very good players who are prepared to work very hard for each other. Every training. Every match.'

The collapse of the roof of their own AFAS Stadium meant that AZ had to play all home games in ADO's Cars Jeans Stadium. On 15 December 2019, they delivered a blow to Ajax during their long-awaited return to Alkmaar, after not playing in their own stadium for 133 days. The return was celebrated as if the championship had already been won. The fireworks were beautiful, the singing spirited, the promise of a home match against Ajax exhilarating and the fight on the field fierce. Ronald Koeman, Co Adriaanse and Louis van Gaal, all three with a coaching history at both clubs, were among the spectators. While AZ coach Arne Slot only had to improvise at the back and found the answer in positioning the diminutive Jordy Clasie next to Belgian centre-back Stijn Wuytens, Ajax coach Erik ten Hag was forced to reshuffle his team. Daley Blind was not available. Sergiño Dest and Nicolás Tagliafico, who had been suffering from aches and pains for a long time, also did not start the game. Ten Hag found the solution in starting places for Klaas-Jan Huntelaar, Perr Schuurs and Razvan Marin. The match was decided in favour of AZ, with the only goal scored in the 90th minute. 'I don't often score with my head,' said 18-year-old AZ striker Myron Boadu, who provided the breakthrough. 'I am happy with every goal, but this is the most important one.'

Slot saw a cagey match, with few chances. 'This is how a top match is played. You need a bit of luck with a set play. If you had asked me beforehand who would score from a corner, Myron Boadu would not have been on my list.' He also had words of praise for Jordy Clasie. 'We are AZ, we want to play football. We would prefer to have a big, strong guy at the back. But if that is not possible, then we want someone who can play good football. And Jordy played fantastic. Of course, it should work; otherwise, you lose credibility. Jordy has football intelligence and is good in the build-up. I want to have good players in my team and make them work hard. Players want to be guided, but they also want freedom. It is best when I can give them the feeling that they came up with a solution themselves. But you also have to motivate them, let them do things that don't come to them naturally. If I would no longer believe that I can influence my players, I would lose my passion for my profession.' From his side, Clasie said, 'I never knew I could be a central defender. I am still a midfielder by origin, but I certainly have no objection to a place at the back. Anything is better than sitting on the bench. I'm not the biggest, so I try to read the game and get things done by being smart. If you lose the ball quickly and often against Ajax, you will get into problems. Then I can be of value.'

At Cambuur, Slot had picked up the idea of the 'enthusiasm team-talk' from Henk de Jong, who was a master of finding different angles on the game to motivate his players. Slot turned it into one of his most effective tools. He made opponents appear smaller than they were and made his own players grow in stature through favourable comparisons. While preparing for the return league fixture against Ajax, he used the example of cyclist Lance Armstrong. Whenever the cyclist did not feel strong, he would beam a smile into the camera and accelerate early on during a tough climb in the Alps or the Pyrenees, just to demoralise his competitors. Slot told his players not to fall for Ajax intimidation: they should not let Armstrong set the pace, but should decide the speed and rhythm of the game themselves. Boadu scored after six minutes, winger Oussama Idrissi added a second goal and AZ won comfortably in Amsterdam. Slot said, 'I think about that more than about tactics. What do I conjure up this time to sharpen them? A manager often gets to the same things in terms of the football. So you have to find ways to reach them.' For the first time in the club's history, Alkmaar had completed a league double against Ajax, winning 1–0 at home and 2–0 away.

Good public speakers know that colourful real-life examples have a significant impact on an audience, often more than logic and arguments do. A football manager should make sure that he has clearly communicated the game strategy to his squad, but he also has to be a good storyteller who inspires his team in order to get the best out of them. Slot pays attention to getting his timing right. 'You can never win a match completely analytically. How you begin and end your team talks is very important. How do you touch them? Before yesterday's match I told the team that they could also see the game as a kickboxing bout where the number one comes into a direct confrontation with the number two. Before such a match, during the staredown, you often see that the number two shouts the loudest to intimidate the number one, precisely because he knows that the other is stronger. So the shouting is mainly an expression of insecurity. I tried to convince my guys that Ajax's bravado in the media also stemmed from doubt and nervousness. That psychological side is very important, and that is why I always try to start and end a match discussion with something they do not expect, for example, that story about two kickboxers.'

Stijn Wuytens saw an outstanding communicator. 'What he excelled in for me was that he had a specific vision and especially how he could convey that to the group of players. That was because of the way he spoke and how he structured meetings. He showed a lot of footage of Napoli and Manchester City, which were his favourite teams at the time. Then he would produce a certain statistic that showed that we were doing things right. That way he always made us believe that we were on the right track, to eventually play football the way he wanted; as all players wanted at some point because everyone would eventually go along with his story. If four different coaches were to make a presentation, I am sure that his would stick the most with everyone.' According to Wuytens, Slot possesses a rare mixture of tactical knowledge and social skills. 'Often it is one of the two. Then an assistant takes over the part that a coach is not so good at. This combination of the two at such a high level, I never experienced that before.'

Marino Pušić is the current Shakhtar Donetsk manager and was Slot's assistant for five years in the Netherlands. They first joined forces in 2019 at AZ. 'You will not see him running to the stands and jumping and that kind of thing. He's switched on, very much focused on the details. He has a lot of deep thoughts about the game, about the development of the game, and is an amazing coach. If you're not running in front of the stands, it doesn't mean that you're not passionate enough. Arne is calmer, he has a lot of passion for the game and he always has nice interactions with the people. He has a lot of feeling for good atmospheres in stadiums and appreciates the fans. He finds it very important to cherish the club and the team. What you can expect is professionalism, 100 per cent. He's a great person. I don't believe a good coach can be a bad person. He's a dedicated coach, working very hard 24/7. Once he's on the pitch, he expects maximal concentration. But the way he trains involves a lot of pleasure for the players to learn his way.'

The 2019–20 season was excellent, aided by consistent performances from youth academy talents such as Teun Koopmeiners, Myron Boadu, Calvin Stengs and Owen Wijndal. AZ won without conceding goals against Ajax, PSV, FC Utrecht and Feyenoord. In different circumstances, Slot might have won the title that year. After 25 games, AZ were level on points with Ajax but in second place on goal difference. With just nine games remaining, the season was suspended due to the Covid-19 pandemic, leaving it to the imagination of what could have been for a club that had won just two Eredivisie titles in their history. No champion was declared and both Ajax and AZ qualified to play in the 2020–21 UEFA Champions League, entering the group stage and second qualifying round respectively. Slot's team was built on a solid defence, conceding just 17 goals in 25 games, six fewer than any other team; 18 of the 25 league matches were won, while five were lost. Under Slot, AZ achieved an average of 2.11 points per league match. No coach with a permanent position performed better at AZ. Georg Kessler, who had been very successful in

Alkmaar between 1978 and 1982, achieved an average of 2.10 points per league match.

Slot's team played refreshingly attacking and entertaining football and got the better of their more illustrious rivals. In away matches, Ajax were defeated 2–0, Feyenoord 3–0 and PSV 4–0. After their win against PSV, there was an exuberant atmosphere in the dressing room. The players had just achieved an unprecedented victory. Slot, master of what psychologists call 'reframing', took the floor and said, 'This may sound crazy, but this should just feel normal. This was a duel like all the others.' A switch was flipped for many: Why is it normal that PSV beat us? Why is it not normal that we beat PSV? At the end of the Covid-plagued and disrupted season, Slot managed AZ to joint first place with Erik ten Hag's Ajax in the Eredivisie competition. The previous campaign, AZ had finished a distant 28 points adrift of Ajax, which demonstrates the transformative impact Slot had on the club. He did it on a shoestring: the budget at AZ that year reportedly was just €25.5 million, compared with Ajax's €110 million.

In John van Den Brom's last year, AZ had met the requirements to play in the Europa League second qualifying round. Under Slot, BK Häcken Gothenburg (0–0, 3–0), Ukrainian FC Mariupol (0–0, 4–0) and Royal Antwerp FC (1–1, 4–1) were seen off successfully in the qualifying rounds. AZ did well in the Europa League group stage, drawing against Serbian club FK Partizan 2–2 twice and demolishing Kazakh outfit Astana FC 6–0 and 5–0. On 4 October 2019, AZ produced a goalless draw in the home match against Manchester United. The visitors failed to register a single shot on target in an uninspired showing. The away match on 13 December was a different story. Mason Greenwood had a night to remember as United dismantled AZ with a barrage of second-half goals. The young striker scored two and won a penalty for another. The Swiss referee was lenient in concluding that United midfielder James Garner had dispossessed Fredrik Midtsjo fairly – the AZ midfielder was booked for protesting he had been fouled – and when the ball ran free to Greenwood, he put it in the net from the edge of the D. With both teams having already qualified for the next round, the only issue at stake was which one would top the group.

Arne Slot was not happy with the course of the match. 'The first 50 minutes I think we played quite well. I had the feeling it was quite a close match and that both teams could score. When you're 1–0 down and you have to win over there it's going to be very difficult. Then the situation with the second goal came and then it was over for us. When you want to have a result at Old Trafford you cannot have a situation like this. Everyone saw it was a foul. We watched it back and it was a clear foul. When you concede a goal after a foul like this, then it's almost impossible for us to win over there.' In the round of 32, Austrian club LASK proved too strong for AZ, drawing 1–1 and winning 2–0, bringing an end to AZ's European journey.

Oussama Idrissi was Eredivisie Player of the Month in both December and January. He continued his strong form throughout the 2019–20 season, proving to be a real asset to his team. He shed some light on what working under Arne Slot had meant to him.

His debut season was incredible. We beat many top teams and Arne made a huge impression on everyone. He would show us videos about how we could solve things before putting on relevant training exercises. He would then ask you to apply it in matches, which he would then analyse. It's the power of repetition, and he would do that many times and in different ways. He makes his philosophy trainable. When we played against a team who sat very deep, we would train on making high runs from deep, which he would sometimes accompany with videos from other teams. I remember Arne showing a clip of Atlético [Madrid] in the quarter-finals of the Champions League, when their wingers had to help in defence but one of them still scored the opening goal. Those things can be really stimulating, because you see what kind of defensive work an Atlético winger is doing while getting on the scoresheet. Those are small details Arne is very good at. He also knows how to motivate players. I remember when we got eliminated from the Europa League by LASK Linz and then had to play Ajax away. Arne said we had to persevere, just like the next bend or next sprint for a cyclist. We beat Ajax 2–0 and were joint first with them when coronavirus hit. We couldn't finish the season, but I'm convinced we would have won the league because we had an easier run.

In the 2020–21 season, AZ struggled in the European competition. By virtue of having a worse goal difference than Ajax, they were required to qualify for the Champions League. Despite a strong start in the second qualifying round, with a 3–1 extra-time comeback against Czech club Viktoria Plzeň, the club lost 2–0 to Dynamo Kyiv in the third round three weeks later, seeing them fall back into the Europa League. In October 2020, the coronavirus threw another spanner in the works in Alkmaar. From the day before the Eredivisie match against VVV-Venlo until the day before the Europa League group-stage confrontation with Napoli, 13 players were infected. Because the required minimum number of first-team players would still be available, kick-off at the Stadio San Paolo would take place as scheduled.

AZ boarded the plane to Italy with just 19 players. At the pre-match press conference, Arne Slot said, 'The past few days have only been about corona. Normally we would have had our meeting yesterday, but we decided to have the players come 15 minutes before training and let them go home without showering. We wanted to rule out 100 per cent that players would still become infected, despite the tests we had already done. But that meant we couldn't have a team talk. If you are lax with the protocols, that would be very bad. But we have an incredibly skilled doctor who has been proactive for months. We are all very upset about this outbreak, but we believe that we have done everything we can to stop it and we are convinced that we have not been lax at all. In addition to UEFA, there are two other bodies that can cancel a match: the local authorities in Italy and those in the Netherlands. Apparently, all three have indicated that we can play.' In addition to managing the problems surrounding Covid infections, AZ needed to get over a bad spell in terms of performance. Four Eredivisie matches had all ended in draws: Zwolle (1–1), Fortuna Sittard (3–3), Sparta (4–4) and VVV-Venlo (2–2). In the games against Fortuna, Sparta and VVV, a comfortable lead was given away.

With their team facing the Italian giants with a significantly reduced squad, AZ fans feared the worst. Instead, a team featuring a number of youth-team players produced an upset, winning 1–0 in the Group F match. With the match mostly played in the Alkmaar half, they struggled for 90 minutes but stood their ground. A goal by Napoli striker Victor Osimhen was disallowed for offside, Bruno Martins Indi prevented a goal by winger Hirving Lozano and a shot by forward Dries Mertens sailed narrowly past the post. AZ chances were reduced to counter-attacks when the Neapolitans lost the ball and the victory came against the run of play. The hero was midfielder

Dani de Wit, who scored the only goal of the match in the 57th minute. Assessing the win afterwards, Arne Slot said, 'This is a historic victory by AZ standards. Also with everything that came with it. We were happy that we could play. We are healthy and the guys who stayed behind are in better shape. The authorities gave the green light for the match and we won.'

In a group with Real Sociedad, Napoli and Croatian club HNK Rijeka, AZ had everything in their own hands. After the win against Napoli and the comprehensive victory over Rijeka 4–1 early in the group stage, AZ were on track to advance, but then lost to Real Sociedad away, played a goalless draw in the reverse fixture and drew 1–1 with Napoli at home. Following these results, AZ needed to defeat Rijeka away to advance. Slot said, 'The chances in this group are very close together. It depends on small things who goes through. You can do all the calculations. We know that we have to get a result, but you don't just win away to Rijeka. We have had to work long and hard together to reach this level. Two years ago, we were knocked out in the preliminary round by Kairat Almaty from Kazakhstan. Since then, we have constantly made steps forward. If you look back to two years ago, we have gone through a very nice development as a club.'

In a sudden turn of events, Arne Slot left AZ the week before the crucial match. His replacement Pascal Jansen saw a disorganised team lose 2–1 to Rijeka, ending their European dream. Napoli and Real Sociedad advanced to the knockout stage at the expense of AZ.

Just six months into his start as AZ head coach, Arne Slot had already been mentioned as a possible candidate to replace Erik ten Hag as head coach of Ajax in case the latter left, a suggestion Slot resolutely dismissed. 'I'm absolutely not concerned with that. I am very happy at AZ. I constantly tell my players not to be distracted and then I have to set a good example.' After the successful Europa

League group-stage away match against Napoli, Slot was again asked about a possible move, this time to Feyenoord. He refused to respond at the time. 'I think if we play as well as we do, almost every player will be in the interest of any club. And if a player were to respond to such questions, I would find it very annoying if it distracted from what was really going on, from what we are working on, namely performing very well with AZ. So let the coach set a good example by not commenting on things in any way until there is something to report. As long as there is nothing, you will not hear anything from us. Nothing from me anyway.'

In what seems an odd holiday custom, AZ occasionally dismiss their managers on St Nicholas Eve. The club fired Ronald Koeman on 5 December 2009. The man who is currently the manager of the Dutch national team had to leave after he lost seven of his first 16 games in charge. On 5 December 2020, Arne Slot was relieved from his duties at AZ. The *Algemeen Dagblad* wrote that the 42-year-old manager had been in talks with Feyenoord about a possible move, adding that the Rotterdam club considered Slot the dream candidate to succeed the ageing Dick Advocaat. AZ decided not to wait for further developments and sacked Slot right away. 'As a club, we have chosen to part ways immediately,' said Max Huiberts on the club website. 'At AZ, we want a head coach for the group who is fully focused on AZ.' Slot was under contract to Alkmaar until mid-2021. 'If you talk to another club without informing the board, then I can understand the anger and irritation. It will feel like a stab in the back for AZ,' NOS Studio Sport commentator Jeroen Elshoff said. 'It is also naive of Slot to think that something like this will not be known. It is a complete shock for the entire organisation. Slot is a coach who is important in everything. He is a key figure in the club and responsible for the playing style. The thought that this happens in a week when a very important European match is on the programme makes it completely bizarre. It is a volcanic eruption.'

Arne Slot clearly did not agree with that assessment. After his highly successful first season with AZ, he had wanted to extend his contract by several years in an attempt to more firmly establish himself near the top of the Dutch managerial circle. The AZ club board instead offered him a simple one-year extension, which Slot rejected. As a result, he was in his last year as AZ manager and judged he was within his rights to consider other options for the following season. A year after the upheaval, Slot shed some light on the difficult episode on the Met Open Vizier ('With Open Visor') podcast of fellow coach Alex Pastoor. 'When a coach is fired, it often happens for one of two reasons. Either the public is fed up with you or the players don't like you anymore. But in my case it must have been the first time in the history of professional football that you are fired while your contract is expiring and you have had a conversation with another club. And I don't think it has happened since. When it came to handling my dismissal, the media often talked about my integrity as a person – at least that's how I experienced it. Look, if I had lost ten times and I had been kicked out, I would have found it very annoying too, because I want people to think I am a good coach or a good footballer. But my integrity as a person really comes first. And I think that was discussed quite at length . . . I understand the disappointment from Alkmaar. We were in competition with Feyenoord and you do not want a coach who goes to the competitor. I just found the experience of being treated like that, with an expiring contract, very difficult.'

Although Slot was suddenly a free man, he would not start working in Rotterdam until the start of the new season. He spent the intervening months playing golf and planning for the move. Slot had been successful at AZ, where he achieved good results with an attacking style of play. 'I have worked with great pleasure at AZ for three and a half years and I am grateful to the club and the players for the development that I have undergone as a trainer. The move to Feyenoord is a very nice next step in my career. When a top club like Feyenoord comes forward, you are not only honoured but also proud that you can take this step.' Technical director Frank Arnesen was pleased that Slot, who was also coveted by other clubs, chose Feyenoord. 'Arne has developed into a successful coach in recent years with a recognisable style of play. His players develop excellently, which is of course very important for Feyenoord. We are very confident that with him the performances under Dick Advocaat's leadership can be continued.'

6

MESSIAH ON THE MAAS

Hand in hand, comrades
Hand in hand for Feyenoord 1
Not words but deeds
Long live Feyenoord 1
FEYENOORD ANTHEM (JAAP VALKHOFF)

Nan Goldin is an American photographer known for confronting social taboos. When she visited Rotterdam, she liked it much better than Amsterdam, which she thought was too cute and looked like a postcard. 'Rotterdam is more real,' she said. 'It's got stomach.' Rotterdam is the second-largest city in the Netherlands after Amsterdam. It is positioned at a strategic location where Holland's 'big rivers' break into multiple branches before emptying into the North Sea. The town was originally founded on the right bank of the Maas, the north side of the river. In 1591, Rotterdam bought a large part of the southern island of Feyen Noort, as it was then called. In 1658, the rest of Feijenoord was acquired. The south side was mainly used for undesirable people and unpleasant activities: people who caught the plague were banished to Zuid; there was a large factory where whale oil was extracted, which produced unpleasant odours; and there was field with gallows where convicts were executed. As a result of dramatic economic growth, by the second half of the nineteenth century, the city north of the river needed to expand. This led to the so-called *Sprong naar Zuid* ('Leap to the South'). Harbours were created, bridges were built from north to south and, in 1877, a railway line opened. There was enough space south of the river to expand, dig and build. Construction was rapid everywhere in Zuid and, a few decades later, Rotterdam had grown into a world port and the population had doubled. People spoke of the Miracle of Rotterdam.

The newly dug harbours and growing industry attracted people looking for work. In the first ten years after the connection with bridges, the population of Rotterdam-Zuid consisted mostly of dock workers. You really were on an island when you went to the South in the past. People from Zuid felt like real Rotterdammers, but many from above the river did not consider the southerners quite up to par. *Op Zuid* ('on the South') still has a slightly negative connotation. These geographic and cultural characteristics came together in the working-class football that has been the standard recipe in the south of the city for years, and the tough workman image has been long associated with Feyenoord. When thinking of Feyenoord, people envisage sturdy dock workers sauntering to the stadium De Kuip – literally 'The Tub'; a united Rotterdam rising from the rubble after the 1940 Nazi bombings; diehard supporters travelling by boat to the semi-final of the European Cup in Lisbon in 1963; and the often fruitless pursuit of arch-rivals Ajax.

By 1962, Rotterdam had become the largest port in the world, surpassing New York City. It kept that status until the beginning of the new millennium, when ports such as Shanghai and Singapore displaced it. It still is the largest seaport in Europe and the world's largest seaport outside of Asia. As tends to be the case with international port cities, the locals have a certain hard-boiled quality. Feyenoord is a club with a clearly defined culture: intense, emotional, with raw devotion from the fans, who collectively are referred to as Het Legioen, 'The Legion'. The supporters of the largest and most successful football club in town are no-nonsense people who are known for their passionate support at matches.

The fighter's mentality of Feyenoord was bolstered during the early years. After the club's establishment in 1908, when football was not nearly as popular as it is today, the founders faced setback after setback but still kept going. The club was forced to change its name several times – from Wilhelmina, to HFC, to Celeritas, to Feijenoord. In 1974, the name was changed once more, from Feijenoord to Feyenoord, as people from outside the Netherlands did not know what to make of the Dutch 'ij'. They also changed locations – from Afrikaanderplein to Kromme Zandweg to De Kuip. Even the club colours were changed a few times, from red-blue-white, to yellow-black-white, to red-white-black.

Feyenoord survived everything, and today their 50,000-seat stadium continues to boil with fan fervour. The hallowed ground is an essential part of the unique Feyenoord culture. People going to a match in Amsterdam say, 'I'm going to Ajax,' but in Rotterdam they say, 'I'm going to De Kuip.' Vivianne Miedema, Manchester City forward and PFA Women's Players' Player of the Year (in 2018–19 while still with Arsenal; she shared the stage with compatriot Virgil van Dijk), grew up a Feyenoord fan and modelled her game on Rotterdam native and former Feyenoord striker Robin van Persie. 'I almost automatically hum along with the club songs, really. By now I've been in quite a few stadiums as a player, but only Anfield comes close to the atmosphere that's generated in De Kuip. Just because of that unique setting, I hope to play one day in "my" stadium for Feyenoord.'

Supporters have the stadium – whole or parts of it – tattooed on their arms or backs. The message is clear: when you are a Feyenoord fan, you are one until death. The supporters demand complete dedication to the cause from their club's players and managers. Arne Slot gave them that, and more. He defied the initial scepticism of some in Rotterdam to become one of the club's most celebrated managers.

On 6 March 2019, Feyenoord announced that Jaap Stam would succeed Giovanni van Bronckhorst as Feyenoord's new boss. The decision typified Feyenoord's brawny style, with the board hoping that the fans would take to Stam: big bald head, don't-mess-with-me image, actions-speak-louder-than-words style. It seemed like a formula for success. He signed a two-year contract and lasted five months. Following a 4–0 defeat to Ajax, Stam resigned on 28 October 2019. Next in line was veteran Dick Advocaat. While at Feyenoord, on 12 September 2020, Advocaat became the oldest coach in the history of the Dutch Eredivisie, at 72 years and 351 days. Not surprisingly, the Den Haag man is someone of the old school. In the Netherlands, his type of manager is often called a 'result trainer', someone with a pragmatic approach designed to grind out wins. With Advocaat as the new head coach, Feyenoord stayed undefeated and climbed the table from the twelfth to third place, only six points behind league leaders Ajax and AZ. They also reached the final of the Dutch Cup.

The supporters were pleased, but then again, they weren't. Image had prevailed over substance. The atmosphere was good, the football mediocre. Meanwhile, there were boardroom intrigues and financial deficits. After two seasons of modest returns, the ever-restless Advocaat left for the Middle East to become Iraq national team coach.

On 15 December 2020, the club announced that Arne Slot – young, smart, well-mannered, understated, persuasive, innovative – would become the club's new coach from the start of the 2021–22 season. He signed for two years with the option to extend his contract for a third year. Then sporting director Frank Arnesen insisted that Slot should be given the chance to take the club down a different track. 'I knew he had it in him, otherwise I wouldn't have signed him, but Arne was of course no guarantee for success. He only had two years of experience at Cambuur and one and a half years at AZ. Feyenoord is very different from AZ when it comes to pressure. You always have to wait and see how a coach deals with that. You have to get good results at Feyenoord. They came quickly, which was a logical consequence of his philosophy and methods. I have great admiration for how he did it in his own way. He is very strong verbally, which means he can explain well how he wants to play. All the players quickly understood that they had to be physically at their best for that style of play. His way of training ensures that the players are in top shape and rarely get injured. The great thing is that Arne and his staff quickly got control of the entire group, even players who weren't part of the starting eleven.'

Impressed with his performance at AZ, Feyenoord had brought in Slot as a kind of miracle worker to reverse the fortunes of the club. Prior to his start Slot tried to temper expectations. 'I don't know if many people agree with that view. Coaching involves pressure and I understand that people expect a certain playing style, and I put that pressure on myself. But that doesn't happen automatically. I've seen Feyenoord play well under different coaches, but the reason they dropped deep last year was that Dick Advocaat wanted it. He thought it suited the team better. Well, that was his right. Every coach has his own philosophy and way of working. My way worked well at Cambuur and AZ. I'm curious to see if it will also work at a big club like Feyenoord. If you apply high pressure, the consequence is that you have to run a lot – probably more than they did last season, when they often dropped to the halfway line. In total, it was a difference of ten kilometres. What I have seen in parts of matches strengthens my belief that these players are capable of performing what I want to see. But the lower limit must be raised.'

Slot does not only advocate a proactive style of play because it makes the game more interesting. 'It is better to choose the football that I aim for because one of the consequences of the philosophy is that players can develop well in it. That was also an important requirement in the discussions with Feyenoord: selling players has been a bit more difficult here in recent years. I am not saying that it is only due to the way of playing, but the lads at AZ have been able to make nice transfers and become internationals partly because of the way we played football. The idea is that 15, 16 players will divide the playing time among themselves and that young talent will be given the opportunity to train with us and then join the main group as soon as possible. You often see that young players can quickly take a step in their development. I think there should be room for that in the squad. Besides, if you have twenty equal players, five of them will walk around with a grumpy face. The condition is that you have a number of players who can play in different positions.'

The Covid pandemic had caused a significant loss of revenue at Feyenoord. The club's board requested that supporters forfeit financial compensation when they could no longer use their season tickets. Advocaat's second and final season had ended with moderate success but also in acrimony. Feyenoord finished fifth, 29 points behind champions Ajax, the same number of points from the top of the table as they were from the bottom three. They barely made it to the qualification matches of the new UEFA Conference League.

Slot got down to work, involving himself in issues he could influence. Together with Frank Arnesen, he paid attention to transfer policies. The assignment for Slot: build a new team with a recognisable playing style while giving young players opportunities so they would eventually go abroad for substantial transfer fees.

The reality at the beginning of Slot's reign was challenging. During his presentation, Slot said that he expected top scorer Steven Berghuis to stay at Feyenoord. That did not happen: the left-footer went to Amsterdam to use his considerable attacking skills in the service of Ajax – a move that did not endear him to the Rotterdam faithful. Feyenoord had scored 43 goals from open play in Advocaat's last season, with the versatile forward involved in 58 per cent of them. He was also heavily involved in the attacks that did not result in a goal. Feyenoord generated exactly 400 shots from open play, with Berghuis playing a part in 63 per cent of those attempts. No player in the Eredivisie even came close to his number – 253. Feycnoord received a modest €5.5 million for Berghuis and had to rebuild.

Feyenoord's highest-paid player earned €1.5 million – less than a third of Ajax's best earners. Slot said, 'Feyenoord pays very different salaries and transfer sums than Ajax and PSV. We have to rely on club love. We can never come close to the salaries that players at top clubs earn. In the past, yes, perhaps the financial position was better. But at some point in the future, we should be able to sign players who have won trophies.' The club had to be creative in the transfer market. Slot had lost his best player but had some money to invest and shape the team to his liking. Early in the transfer window, Guus Til came on loan from Spartak Moscow. Marcus Pedersen (€1 million), Gernot Trauner (€1.5 million) and Alireza Jahanbakhsh (€1 million) were also brought in. Reiss Nelson and Cyriel Dessers came on loan. Ofir Marciano signed on a free transfer. The fact that the club improved on all attacking stats after Berghuis left is a powerful testimony to how effectively Slot transformed his team. He compensated for the loss of individual quality up front through the introduction of modern game principles.

Feyenoord is a developmental club and they are in the business of improving players and selling them on. The Slot factor proved to be highly profitable. The situation in central midfield is a good example. In Slot's first summer at the club, Feyenoord purchased Fredrik Aursnes from Molde FK for €750,000. A year later, on 24 August 2022, they sold him to Benfica for €13 million plus €2 million in add-ons. They replaced the 27-year-old Norwegian by signing 23-year-old Mats Wieffer from Dutch second-tier club Excelsior for a transfer fee under €600,000. On 17 March 2023, Wieffer received his first call-up to the Netherlands senior national team from Ronald Koeman. On 5 July 2024, he joined Premier League club Brighton & Hove Albion, signing a contract until June 2029. With a reported fee of €30 million, he became Feyenoord's most expensive outgoing transfer of all time.

Once ensconced in the bowels of De Kuip, Slot began a process he characterised as 'indoctrination'. In the first team meeting, Feyenoord players were served up video images of the 2021 Champions League final between Manchester City and Chelsea, which was decided in favour of the latter by Kai Havertz. Why were there so few chances despite there being so many good attacking players, Slot wanted to know. The answer was simple: it was because all those attackers also made incredible defensive runs to nullify their opponents. Slot contrasted that with the lack of running Feyenoord had done the season before. He also pointed out that the distance covered compared very unfavourably with his AZ side. 'See? A match without chances,' Slot taught his pupils, 'because these top players did everything possible to prevent giving away chances. We need to develop the same attitude.'

The new manager showed images of the energy and work that

players like Sergio Agüero put in. Slot spoke at length about keeping positions, pressing, chasing the ball and creating chances. Kevin De Bruyne, Riyad Mahrez and Bernardo Silva are brilliant players, he reasoned, but if they can perform so well without the ball, then why would it be impossible for Feyenoord players? Reframing was required once again. It could be done – if they pushed themselves to the utmost. One of the new manager's demands was that his players do plenty of work on the training ground.

The players noticed the impact of Slot's arrival first through muscle aches. He wants his team to be capable of pressing for the full 90 minutes, no matter who the opponent is, with forward-charging full-backs who pull inside, lines that merge together, a dynamic and creative squad that operates at the highest level of intensity, and defenders who play every ball forward instead of wide or to the back. He passed his first real Eredivisie test on 19 September when Feyenoord won 4–0 against PSV.

There is a good reason to put pressure on high up the pitch. 'Opponents will make mistakes when they get tired. And we will as well. So we have to make sure that the high tempo becomes normal for us. Who in the Eredivisie puts pressure early? There aren't many, so most duels are played at a certain speed. If you are able to play at a higher tempo, you force teams to make mistakes that they normally wouldn't make. If you apply pressure well, any team can play far from their own goal, including Feyenoord. Not speed but insight is the basis, knowing what to do at the crucial moments. If players get that, there is nothing to be afraid of. If we keep putting pressure on the ball with Feyenoord, we can feel confident about defending one against one at the back.'

Voetbal International's Tom Knipping was of the opinion that 'anyone who first watches the Disney documentary ["Dat ene word" – "That One Word"] about Feyenoord under septuagenarians Dick Advocaat and [assistant coach] Cor Pot, and then tunes in to a current broadcast of *Studio Sport*, thinks they have entered a different universe'. In recent years, Feyenoord had been one of the league's most defensive teams, especially under Slot's immediate predecessor. Advocaat did not think that a more attacking approach was feasible. He had Feyenoord play in a defensive block with very intensive man-marking duties. Slot disagreed and completely overhauled the defensive playing style. The club wanted him to do it and so did the players. He exploded the myth that 'you can only work with what you have got' and showed that players can change. He replaced Advocaat's man-to-man coverage with zonal defence. He chose to have his team press high-up while also preferring to build up from the back and applying intensive counter-pressing when possession was lost. He gave his team licence to play attacking football, on the condition that they would train harder than ever before.

. . .

A walk from the pitch followed by a natural ice bath in a fast-flowing Alpine stream. In the summer of 2021, Feyenoord went back to basics on the training ground. They were in sweltering Schruns, Austria, close to the Swiss border, for a training camp with two practice matches. Slot made good use of the sessions in the Alps, bringing along a 28-man squad. The manager enlightened the domestic media gathered for the occasion. 'You saw that after an hour, 70 minutes, the well ran dry. That's not surprising, of course, but it can't be that we can only keep up our way of playing for an hour. So the intensity will increase a bit while we work on overcoming the shortcomings. You're talking about coordination, mutual distances. We have time for that now because in two weeks we have to be ready for the first match in the preliminary round of the Conference League.' On another day, a soaked players' group walked into the hotel after finishing an arduous mountain bike ride, which Slot had conceived would be good recovery training after their friendly against FC Zürich. But conditions between the Alpine peaks are unpredictable, and a thunderstorm broke when they had just set off. That meant they had to wait at the top of a mountain because the cable cars didn't descend while there was lightning around. Once back down, they rode back to the hotel over a narrow road with slippery cobblestones alongside a fast-flowing river.

Balancing on a tightrope is what Slot called the preparation. He didn't exhaust his players, but he did push the limits of their performance. 'The goal is not to let them start matches rested. Not yet. But to say that they are too tired, that is not true either. Our specialists monitor that very well. In this phase it is not a problem, although you have to make sure that you stay on the right side of the tightrope.' The sessions were intensive and long as he identified the boundaries of his players' physical abilities. The way he wanted to play required not only dedication and concentration but also certain perspective. 'I showed my players footage of the semi-final of the European Championship this week: Spain against Italy. The Spanish defended very high and conceded a goal. The Italians defended low and also conceded a goal. The difference is the mindset. If you apply high pressure and you concede a goal, everyone says: See, that's not possible. But if you drop back and concede a goal, no one ever says: "Shouldn't they apply pressure?"'

Arne Slot is not known for making a commotion in the technical area at matches. But Feyenoord's new head coach did produce the most noise during the practice match against Bern club Young Boys. His voice echoed across the field in Freienbach on the south shore of Lake Zürich. Feyenoord lost the match 2–0; the Swiss champions were ahead in their preparation. Slot saw good things and elements that needed improvement. 'All in all, I can't be dissatisfied after a week of hard training in Austria. Young Boys was the team I wanted to play against. They bring so much energy, so I was curious to see what we would put up against them in this phase. Well, we struggled for the first ten minutes, but then we got a grip. They put us under pressure, but we put them under pressure too. They were a bit better and further along, so it makes sense. I look at how we did and if you are able to offer so much resistance in this phase of the preparation, that gives me a good feeling. I am convinced that the way of playing as I envision it gives us the best chance of success.'

Iranian winger Alireza Jahanbakhsh explained that challenge was part of the daily diet at Feyenoord. 'No junk food, getting enough rest, consuming little sugar and fat. Every month we focus on something else – for example, not using sugar for an entire month. Everyone at the club participates. Another month there is no cell-phone screen time. We push each other to get better every month. One month everybody got into an icy bath upon arrival at the club, before break-fast: *shock the body*. Then you are wide awake immediately and ready to hit the ground running. We do yoga, meditation, and we have a breathing coach. I pretty much jump out of bed as soon as I wake up, that's how good I feel. We are sharper because of all these elements.'

Former Feyenoord forward Bryan Linssen described how Slot's arrival at De Kuip brought some changes in the Rotterdam club's culture.

From the start, Slot changed the entire style into an attack-ing, forceful way of playing. Arne provided new energy in a pleasant way. We trained very intensively on pressing and I played a very important role in that together with [attacking midfielder] Guus Til. We formed a perfect duo in his style of play. Sometimes he said: 'Just do what your feeling tells you to do as a striker.' Or he called me to the side during the match, said one sentence and then I knew exactly what he meant. We did not only talk about my role in the team. We also discussed things outside of football. He has the advantage that he is still young, so he knows what the younger generation are concerned with. The match briefings were of a very high quality. Arne not only motivated us, but also gave us very detailed information about the opponent. He told us exactly how we had to set up against them in order to be able to play our own game. When what the trainer says comes true nine times out of ten, that gives confidence. In training we had often already executed the entire plan, which is why we believed unconditionally in his approach. When I look back on my career, 2021–22 at Feyenoord will certainly be the best and most enjoyable season.

One of the things Slot changed was the diet, something that wasn't fully appreciated by Linssen. 'At a certain point we went from a full buffet every morning to a half buffet and then to 25 per cent, in terms of tasty things. It was replaced with food which was better for you, but less tasty. Sometimes he would walk past my table in the cafeteria and casually say, "Hey, has someone stolen the vegetables from your plate?" I'm not the biggest fan of vegetables and when I eat them at home in the evening, I don't feel I need to eat them at lunch. So Slot would make a joke about it, but in that joke there was a grain of truth.' Slot's approach created a good atmosphere at the club, which had a positive effect on the players' ability to cope with the increasing physical demands. 'As soon as you play well and the atmosphere in a team is good, it has an impact on the mental and physical state of players. Slot's way of training and playing is fun for the players, which makes them mentally stronger; therefore, they don't get as many injuries. He managed the workload of players well. It's all mutually connected. He makes training and matches enjoyable by the way he lets his teams play. You always want to be part of that because it gives you energy instead of it costing you energy.'

Arne Slot's stewardship at the club is covered in considerable detail by Feyenoord-watcher Mikos Gouka in his book *Kameraden* ('Comrades' – which sounds a little communist but is merely a reference to the much-loved Feyenoord club song). The book explains, in words and images, how Slot's vision of football requires players who are in absolute top shape. Belgian Stijn Vandenbroucke joined West Ham as a first-team physiotherapist in 2009. He was part of the backroom staff under Gianfranco Zola, Avram Grant, Sam Allardyce and Slaven Bilić. At West Ham, outfield players ran more than 10km per game and averaged 50 sprints per match, resulting in ever more strenuous demands on their bodies. By the time Slot arrived, Vandenbroucke was using his considerable experience in the service of Feyenoord.

We have moved away from footballers who are only athletes for two or three hours a day. A football player is now in an environment where he is a player almost 18 hours a day. So much more is involved. Everything is quicker and more intense and more difficult and faster, so the room for improvement you have is becoming smaller. Details are becoming really, really important. I think we all also underestimate the power of social media. Sometimes an angry voice is amplified on Twitter and Instagram. Not every player is built the same way and has the robustness to deal with these mental challenges. If you have personal problems and you don't make it into the team for example, or you have an injury and one thing after another piles up, it just can become too much. You need to think about the total picture – what works and what gives you the best results.

To meet the demands that 'Slot football' makes, Vandenbroucke put in place a Head of Performance team composed of the Australian Leigh Egger and the Belgian Ruben Peeters. Egger worked with Fiji rugby and Peeters was recruited from KRC Genk. Egger explained what was involved in their activities. 'We're busy with so many things pertaining to performance that are non-physical, so, literally, everything you could think of that might influence or maximise the player's performance or potential. We are constantly busy with the lads on the field, off the field, in the gym, in the hotels. Everything from sleep, nutrition, recovery, mental tools, mindfulness, visualisation, breathing, to name just a few. A massive part of our job is getting to know the lads, not being friends with them, but getting to know them and their families – what makes them click so that we can push them to do the things that they might not want to do but that we feel they need to do and the coach feels they need to do.' Egger and Peeters also analysed live data to determine which players had 'overperformed' during a match. These players would receive a tailor-made 36-hour recovery programme.

When a European away match is on the schedule, Feyenoord charter a plane and pinpoint the exact best moment of departure. By cooperating with Rotterdam The Hague airport, passport control, customs inspections and waiting times are reduced to a minimum.

Because of the lower air pressure on board, players wear compression pants; they also make sure they stay sufficiently hydrated. Egger and Peeters required players to do stretch and yoga exercises upon arrival at their hotel 'to break rest mode of the body after many hours of sitting in the plane and on buses'.

Feyenoord appeared on the pitch stronger and fitter than their opponents. Vandenbroucke explained, 'We inspire the guys to develop the mindset of Olympic athletes. That means doing something that our competitors might not be doing. It's not just about the physical aspects, but the mental as well. It's the total package. Team manager Frank Boer also plays a significant role for the newly arriving players.' Boer gets a lot of satisfaction from his work. 'I don't feel like I'm a colleague. I'm just one of their best friends or an older brother who wants to give them advice and uses my network to help them.' At Feyenoord's Training Complex 1908, an 'ecosystem' has been created with partners from outside the club who can help the players improve through a personalised approach. Each player is evaluated to decide what he needs to increase his contribution to the team performance. Sometimes what is required is improved fitness, but a programme may involve anything from mental support to regularly taking ice baths.

'Don't work hard, work smart' is a cliché by now. At Feyenoord they did both. Training hard, recovering smartly and building mental resistance were part of the programme. Players were taught how to better deal with stress and how to manage social media use. They were introduced to the world of meditation, mindfulness, breathing and yoga. The activities were not limited to the club but extended beyond. Players frequented a boxing club or participated in MMA training, as the need arose. A so-called Breakfast Club was created, an idea coming from American sports culture and more particularly from Michael Jordan. The TV documentary series *The Last Dance* was used as educational material, showing the basketball superstar's career, with particular focus on his final season with the Chicago Bulls. What this meant for the Feyenoord squad members in practice is that they worked through some of their individual programmes before the regular training started after breakfast. There was also attention on individual programmes after the team training had ended.

The Feyenoord medical and performance team adopted a biopsychosocial (BPS) approach to player fitness. The idea is that biological, psychological and social factors interact to affect health and wellness. In 2021, the club began producing an 'innerselfie' of each player in an attempt to even more precisely gauge what changes could further enhance and improve performance. Through innovative DNA and microbiome analyses, individualised supplements and integrated menus, the club was able to push the envelope even further. All new arrivals' sweat, urine, stool, blood and saliva were tested. With the so-called multi-omics analysis of Cosmo Group, they produced a complete player profile. Connections between various body systems were analysed and interpreted, and everything was transformed into an applicable programme that helped the player improve well-being and performance. Players were informed about what they should eat, what they should eat less of, and what they should avoid altogether. Catapult training vests were used during sessions to track thousands of pieces of physical data, while each player was given a high-intensity level to hit.

While keeping close watch on a multitude of data and technical details, Slot never loses sight of the purely human dimension. Treating one another in a pleasant and relaxed manner is most important to him. 'You achieve this by setting a good example as staff. When our players see that we enjoy ourselves, that we laugh often and have fun, the rest will go along with it. When I came to Feyenoord, there was quite a grumpy atmosphere. There was a proposal to introduce all kinds of rules of conduct, but I suggested just going back to normal and only intervening or making adjustments when necessary. I am strict with my team when it comes to content, but otherwise I want to be as pleasant a person as possible for the team. A good vibe is crucial. For that reason, we attracted players who were not only good footballers, but whose personalities also contribute to the atmosphere and culture we wanted to create. I'm very much into relationships, for example, by having individual conversations with everyone. That has to do with feeling: that player needs me right now. Sometimes something can feel very unfair to a player, for example, when someone tries really hard and I still can't reward his effort. Then I want to show that person that I really care about him and sympathise with him. That may be important for him to stay motivated. You have to be tough sometimes, but in a human way, and you should always try to offer some perspective.'

He continued: 'Things are different now. Nowadays, players are all basically self-employed. They have their own physiotherapist, their own dietician, they have agents who tell them that they should think more about themselves with a view to a transfer . . . It also has to do with finances. We, or at least I, have not been able to push myself forward when I was a player. But if you can do something these days, the step to a nice contract abroad is easily made. That is what lives in the minds of those players. So the difficult thing about our profession now, I think, is the art of pulling the individual interest into the team interest . . . I think the art is to be tough and clear, but to package it in a way that they do not experience it as being reprimanded. It is a choice of words, nothing more than that. That is something I do think about. Then you need good assistants who know how players react to a coach. I am quite rational and Marino [Pušić, assistant coach] goes more by his feelings, although I sometimes let myself be guided by what I feel. When I drive to the club, I always make a lot of phone calls. What does it mean if we put him in front of him? In the end you come to an agreement based on a sober look, but sometimes also on intuition. Don't underestimate how often we are concerned with how players are feeling, who needs a quick chat with me, Marino, Sipke [Hulshoff] or John [de Wolf, assistant coach], or with the performance coaches. That is an ongoing process. When some guys have to do their runs after the match, I want to know if their attitude is different from normal.'

Something that is often mentioned in conversations about Slot is that he has empathy, knowing precisely what to say to a struggling player. 'He changed Feyenoord's mentality,' Jan Everse said. 'Arne is better than me at managing the emotions of the team. Perhaps I was too critical. Arne is a diplomat. He is very smart. He always first counts to ten.'

Slot provided some background on how he manages individual players in the team collective. 'The trick is that personal ambitions can only be realised thanks to the team. Every player must have some prospect, which is something I also believe in. Players must be able to realise their ambitions within the context of Feyenoord and their position in the group. I think we have done good things in that area. By that I mean that I have seen few dissatisfied players. This has to do with their own ambitions, the fact that they still have the idea that they are developing and have been given sufficient playing time. Playing time, atmosphere and prospects create involvement, and then it also depends on the personality of the players. This always has my attention when composing the squad. You don't always put players in the starting line-up right away, sometimes because of their personality and their attitude.'

Arne Slot was voted Eredivisie Coach of the Season 2021–22 in his debut season at Feyenoord, despite finishing behind PSV and Ajax. He had led the club to their first European final in 20 years. With his wife at his side, he received the Rinus Michels Award from CBV (Coaches Professional Football) chairman Guus Hiddink at the Professional Football Coaches Gala in a posh hotel in the rustic village of Garderen. Slot was chosen ahead of the other nominees – Erik ten Hag (Ajax), Ron Jans (FC Twente), Joseph Oosting (RKC Waalwijk) and Kees van Wonderen (Go Ahead Eagles). The Feyenoord boss said that winning the award was a huge honour. 'It's amazing to be given this award as coach of Feyenoord. To be successful, first and foremost you need talented players who are willing to work incredibly hard day in, day out. I complimented the lads on that more than once last season. I am also privileged to have a high-quality staff around me who are hugely pleasurable to work with. This appreciation is just as much for them. This honour feels even more special when I look at the list of nominees and the coaches who have won this award before me. Not least the name of a great former coach like Rinus Michels, after whom it is named. It is a vote among coaches. I secretly hope that the way of playing also had an influence on this trophy and that it is not just about reaching the final of the Conference League. How am I going to celebrate this? Not very extensively, because tomorrow is the first training of the season with Feyenoord.'

7

FEYENOORD IN EUROPE

'We defend by attacking.'
ARNE SLOT

Kevin Bijlsma from Leeuwarden is the lead singer of the covers band Stageline, with which he performs at fairs and company parties. At the start of the 2021–22 season, the singer, teaching assistant and die-hard Feyenoord fan composed a song about the club's new coach. While weeding in the garden, Bijlsma said he received a revelation when he heard Barry Manilow's 'Mandy' on the radio. 'Oh Mandy, Oh Arne. That was it!' His inspirational ballad was played for the first time in De Kuip before the home match in the Conference League quarter final against Slavia Prague.

> Oh Arne
> Things are going well since you've been waving the
>   sceptre
> Yes, everything's alright
> Oh Arne
> We're ready for a brand new chapter
> Yes, everything is alright
> Oh Arne

The new Conference League had been treated as the ugly duckling of European football. Identified by some as a UEFA attempt to eke out every ounce of commercial potential from its lucrative estate, it was a cup without history, with an awkward name and designed for countries playing little-league football. Others acknowledged that clubs on the periphery of top football have found it increasingly difficult to compete in the two established club tournaments. The C-tournament provides a platform for smaller clubs and football leagues frozen out of participation in the Champions and Europa Leagues. If proof were needed that the Conference League can provide fans with some quality entertainment, the inaugural competition readily supplied it. Slot's Feyenoord reached the final playing some of the most exciting, high-energy attacking football in Europe, losing only a single game on the way.

Feyenoord's European adventure began in the Conference League's second qualifying round on 15 July 2021 in the Kosovar capital Pristina, while visiting FC Drita. It ended on 25 May 2022 in Tirana, in the new national stadium of Albania, in the final against AS Roma; just as in their previous European finals against Celtic (1970), Tottenham Hotspur (1974) and Borussia Dortmund (2002), they faced a strong team. Feyenoord had reached a European final for the fourth time in its history; they had won the first three.

FC Drita, with a budget comparable to that of a Dutch mid-tier football club, kept Feyenoord at bay in a goalless draw in Pristina and started the second half in De Kuip with a 2–1 advantage. A narrow escape led to 3–2 Feyenoord victory. Arne Slot witnessed a poor performance from midfielder Leroy Fer, which almost led to an early European exit. He emphatically supported the player, even after his negative involvement in both Drita goals. 'I am the one who positioned Leroy as a central defender, a position that is not naturally his. So I am responsible.' Although Slot's team dominated, the Kosovar opponents repeatedly cut through the Feyenoord defence and kept pace in terms of shots on target. Questions were immediately raised about whether Slot's tactics, with pressing and maintaining possession, suited a club like Feyenoord. Slot had no doubt. To prove his point, in the next round FC Luzern were overwhelmed in two 3–0 victories.

Slot's team next defeated IF Elfsborg 5–0. In a seething Kuip, Feyenoord immediately pinned their opponents back. The Swedish team distinguished themselves more by their annoying behaviour than the quality of their football. Left-back Simon Strand needlessly shot a ball into the stands after Luis Sinisterra had made it 1–0 and then pulled over a television camera. Feyenoord's Alireza Jahanbakhsh kindly helped the camerawoman pull it back up. Strand escaped with a verbal reprimand from English referee Craig Pawson. Jahanbakhsh scored the second goal of the match and Sinisterra the third and fourth, completing his hat-trick in the 47th minute when he artfully headed in the assist of Marcus Pedersen while falling over. Forward Bryan Linssen wrapped up the rout by making it 5–0 in the 58th minute. Elfsborg midfielder Frederik Holst took out his frustrations on Sinisterra's right calf; he received his second yellow card from Pawson and was sent off. Feyenoord slowed down the pace and suffered a setback when goalkeeper Justin Bijlow got a straight red card after colliding with Elfsborg forward Marokhy Ndione, who had broken through.

'It was excellent, except for the last ten minutes,' said Slot. 'If you win by five goals in Europe, that is impressive against any opponent, also against this one. We have played quite a few matches and it was not the first time that they showed what they are capable of. So I was not surprised. We really wanted to get to the group stage and if you are 5–0 up after one match, you can't complain.'

Feyenoord supporters were not allowed to attend the return match in the Borås Arena, and the team were defeated 3–1. Bryan Linssen added a caveat. 'In the context of realising that we were on the right track, the friendly against Atlético Madrid was much more important.'

On 8 August, Diego Simeone's team flew to Amsterdam for a preseason warm-up. Calling the game a friendly match would do an injustice to Simeone, because in the world of the volatile Argentinian, there is no such thing. Feyenoord, however, stood their ground. Yannick Carrasco duelled with Tyrell Malacia five minutes before half-time and the Belgian kicked his Dutch opponent. Tempers flared. Orkun Kökçü threw Carrasco aside and ended up with a bleeding neck; referee Dennis Higler sent Carrasco off. Simeone ran onto the pitch trying to calm his players down. With a 1–0 lead, the work of Linssen early in the match, the encounter turned into a real test. The Argentinian Angel Correa levelled the score seven minutes before time, but young Feyenoord forward Naoufal Bannis surprised top goalkeeper Jan Oblak in injury time and made it 2–1.

After the match, things blew up again when Simeone took on his opposite number, shoving Slot with both hands against his chest. The implausible explanation offered in the Spanish media was that the Argentine had thought Slot was a mere physiotherapist or assistant trainer rather than the head coach. Slot dismissed the kerfuffle afterwards with a joke but characterised Simeone's reaction as 'slightly exaggerated. I wanted to shake his hand and he didn't want that. I had to laugh about it. If no one had been there, it would have been a bigger problem for me. I wouldn't like to face him one-on-one.

Fortunately, John de Wolf [a 1.88m former centre-back] stayed close by. I told my team in the dressing room: if there is one thing we can learn from Atlético and Simeone, it is that they do not want to lose under any circumstances. Not even in a practice match in Rotterdam. That they can get so extremely angry during such a match, that says something.'

In the group stage of the Conference League, Feyenoord comfortably reached the round of 16, finishing ahead of Slavia Prague, Union Berlin and Maccabi Haifa. In the knock-out stage, the club defeated Partizan, Slavia Prague and finally Marseille. There was something bold, confident and buoyant in the team that Slot forged, though not all European matches were joyous occasions. After winning the home match against Union Berlin 3–1, Feyenoord were penalised for multiple violations by their supporters. They had set off fireworks, blocked stairs and produced 'insulting texts'. The club had to pay a fine of €91,000. The away match in Berlin, which was won 2–1, earned the club another hefty fine, €62,750, for setting off fireworks and 'throwing objects'. According to the Feyenoord website, the club 'deeply regretted' that it had to pay almost €280,000 in fines over the entire European campaign. 'We once again call on the supporters responsible for this to stop the above-mentioned behaviour, which is causing the club great financial and other damage.'

After an exhilarating match against Olympique Marseille in De Kuip, the final score was 3–2. Jorge Sampaoli's team had managed to convert all six of its Conference matches into victories after dropping down from the Europa League, but it was clear from the start that Arne Slot would not be making any concessions to his team's playing style in this phase of the tournament. Feyenoord pinned the French team back as soon as possible. The manager was very enthusiastic about the spectacular match that had produced good scoring opportunities on both sides. 'I think it was a great match to watch. The atmosphere in the stadium made it absolutely fantastic. There were many chances, constant plot twists, and good and beautiful football.' After a lack of interest in the earlier stages of the Conference League, Feyenoord's exploits in the tournament had made people sit up and pay attention. A remarkable number of Dutch media representatives travelled to the south of France for the second leg of the semi-final. According to the Nederlandse Sportpers (Dutch Sports Press), the broadcaster Veronica was there, ESPN sent a contingent of ten people, state broadcaster NOS five, RTV Rijnmond deployed three journalists, *Algemeen Dagblad* and *De Telegraaf* each sent two reporters, ANP – a kind of Dutch AP – two photographers and a reporter, and Voetbalprimeur.nl and *FC Afkicken* also sent reporters.

The happy, positive mood of the first leg of the semi-final starkly contrasted with the grim atmosphere that surrounded the second. The Rotterdam fans were caught in sudden downpours in the fan zone on the beach of Marseille. They eventually broke through the barriers and sought shelter in a nearby shopping centre. The ultra groups of Olympique Marseille played an unsavoury role around the match venue. Men in black hoodies or dressed in dark Marseille shirts and caps went after Dutch supporters. French gendarmes intervened to halt violent clashes between fans of Olympique and Feyenoord in the Vieux Port of Marseille. Iron bars were used in brutal assaults and vehicles vandalised, with police battling to keep the situation under control. The police fired tear gas several times during the day, in the Feyenoord fan zone and around the stadium before the match. Feyenoord were represented in France by slightly more than 3,000 supporters who came to the hostile Stade Vélodrome to do battle with nearly 50,000 Marseille fans. Shortly before kick-off, many visiting supporters were more concerned with their own well-being than with the match. Some of them decided to watch the game on TV from the safety of their hotel rooms.

The Feyenoord team bus had been hit by a brick on the way to the stadium, a journey that was prolonged as police attempted to steer the Dutch team through the crowds of fans and a forest of raised middle fingers. Fortunately, nobody got hurt. Halfway through the long ride, the gendarmerie required the driver to make a U-turn on a major highway so as not to miss the kick-off altogether. It ultimately took the Feyenoord players four times as long as planned to reach their dressing room. A request was made to start the match half an hour late, which was denied. When the team finally arrived at the stadium, the mood in the stands was charged. Alireza Jahanbakhsh recalled, 'Crazy fans, but Slot just started talking so convincingly. "This might be the last chance for Feyenoord to go to a European final. You can make history. You can become the only 25 Feyenoord players to reach the Conference League final." Sometimes I joked with the lads that I thought Arne had to practise his speeches in front of the mirror. It was always so natural.'

The 67,000-seat Vélodrome Stadium is impressive: a magnificent undulating canopy with a view of the mountains behind. The stand where the fanatical Virage Nord (North Turn) fans normally sit was empty by orders of UEFA as a penalty for disturbances in the previous round against PAOK Saloniki. In protest against the closure of the stand, Olympique Marseille supporters prominently displayed their disapproval of the football body. The Virage Sud held up coloured cards making up the words 'UEFA MAFIA' just before the match. The stadium was shown on French TV in just such a way that the text could not be read. It was permitted, as was bringing in boxes full of fireworks.

Adding to the acrid smoke of the fireworks, every now and then clouds of tear gas blew over the field. Feyenoord striker Cyriel Dessers said he felt his eyes stinging at the start of the match and had difficulty breathing. The players could not see each other clearly during the first ten minutes of the game because the smoke was slow to clear. Spectators in the upper sections could barely see the Feyenoord players in their grey away kit.

During the match, the tension was palpable, with time increasingly working in Feyenoord's favour. They stayed alert and did not allow themselves to be drawn into unnecessary challenges when provoked by the opposition. After all the turmoil and the acrimony, the match ended 0–0. The semi-final tie was won and the celebrations were exuberant, starting with those of the manager himself. At the end of the game, he was seen smiling broadly and then jumping into the arms of the staff members around him. A wild and joyful dance ensued, with the bald coach as the radiant centrepiece. Ten months after Arne Slot became manager, Feyenoord would play the inaugural UEFA Europa Conference League final against José Mourinho's AS Roma. It would be played at the Arena Kombëtare (National Stadium) in Tirana, with space for just 22,500 spectators.

The French sports daily *L'Équipe* wrote about the 'end of a dream' for Olympique Marseille. The team looked 'helpless' and was suffering badly from the early loss of star player Dimitri Payet. 'In a Stade Vélodrome that was ready for a European evening, Olympique Marseille failed to transfer the fire from the stands to the field. They came up against a Feyenoord that had enough commitment to reach the final.' *Le Figaro* concluded, 'That's it, it's over . . .' Marseille were 'powerless', judged the newspaper, and described the prevailing feeling as 'so close to the final, but still so far away'.

The Dutch press offered a different perspective. 'In the most threatening setting imaginable, Feyenoord secured a European final for the first time in 20 years,' wrote Bart Vlietstra in *de Volkskrant*. 'Amidst smoke, tear gas, irritating laser lights, deafening drums and chants, tens of thousands of hotheads, more than 90 per cent of whom were cheering on the opposing team, the Rotterdammers kept Olympique Marseille at bay.' Sjoerd Mossou argued in the *Algemeen Dagblad*, 'Feyenoord's success is the success of coach Arne Slot. With just a handful of signings, Slot transformed a listless team into a dynamic unit that dared to rely on its own strength throughout Europe. Like a preacher, Slot passed on his principles of play to the Feyenoord players, until they could recite his commandments in their sleep.' And in *De Telegraaf*, Valentijn Driessen wrote, 'A huge triumph for Feyenoord and the excellent manager Slot. With attractive, fast attacking play according to the Dutch School and bullseye hits on the transfer market, Feyenoord was unstoppable internationally.'

The Italian media had its own peculiar angle on the semi-final outcome. In the Italian *La Gazzetta dello Sport*, there was ample attention on AS Roma, who would be Feyenoord's opponents in the final. 'Delirium at the Olimpico,' the pink sports newspaper headlined. 'Thirty-one years after the last time, Roma will return to the final of the European Cup. On 25 May in Tirana, Mourinho can add the Conference League to his endless trophy cabinet: only Feyenoord stands between Roma and the trophy.' The newspaper also referred to the last meeting between the two teams. In 2015, Roma reached the round of 16 of the Europa League after a confrontation that will mainly be remembered for the destruction in the historic centre of Rome in the first leg. 'Then, the Dutch fans played the leading role in a guerrilla war in the city centre. This time, however, it is being played in Albania and the match is worthy of a trophy.'

On 18 May, the Feyenoord squad were heading to Lagos, on the southern coast of Portugal's balmy Algarve region, for a mini-training camp to recharge for the last and most important match of the season. From Portugal, they would travel directly to Tirana. It would allow them to escape the madness that engulfed Rotterdam and the surrounding area in the run-up to the final. The relative familiarity of the Cascade Resort would help, as it had already been the stopover for Feyenoord and the Dutch national team on earlier occasions.

Only 4,000 tickets for the final were available to Feyenoord supporters, of which 3,000 were reserved for those who had attended many away games. The remaining 1,000 would be reserved for staff, partners and sponsors. The news about the lack of tickets led to desperate reactions from fans who absolutely wanted to be in the stands at the game. A club statement read, 'Feyenoord is disappointed about the limited number of tickets available for this historic match for fans of both finalists. A great match like AS Roma–Feyenoord, the very first final of the Europa Conference League, deserved a bigger stage with tens of thousands of spectators from both clubs.' UEFA incurred the wrath of Feyenoord and its supporters by unexpectedly starting the sale of the remaining 8,500 tickets. Apparently, people knew about it in Italy, but not in the Netherlands. As a result, the majority ended up in the hands of Roma fans.

Feyenoord supporters were brimming with confidence. That José Mourinho had lost only three of the 21 finals he had managed meant little to them. Supporters were on their way to their meeting with destiny and emerging in the most unlikely locations. Photos appeared on social media of fans who had been travelling for 30 hours by car and were still not in Albania. The locals in Tirana were likewise caught up in final fervour – most of them, however, in support of the other side. The main building of the University of Tirana was adorned with a gigantic yellow banner with red lettering – Roma FC's club colours – picturing Mourinho on a scooter. The Portuguese celebrity was warmly welcomed to Albania: *Benvenuto a Little Roma Mister Mourinho.*

In Rotterdam, the Stadhuisplein town square was full of beer-drinking supporters on final day, and large groups of fans were gathered at gigantic screens on the Binnenrotte and Willemsplein and in other strategic locations in central Rotterdam. Although kick-off wasn't until evening, Dutch ESPN started its broadcast at noon. The sports channel was straining to give minute-to-minute updates, even when there was nothing newsworthy to report. In De Kuip, 48,000 men, women and children would be watching a huge four-sided 'jumbotron', sitting on the turf in the centre circle. They were singing along when the Rotterdam Philharmonic Orchestra performed the Feyenoord classic 'Hand in Hand Kameraden'. About 4.5 million Dutch people were seated in front of their televisions. The first torches were lit, both behind Feyenoord goalkeeper's Justin Bijlow's goal and at home on the Stadhuisplein. Everyone associated with Feyenoord was overwhelmed with emotion; it seemed the only one who was in control of theirs was Arne Slot.

Given that both Roma and Feyenoord came into the contest having already secured Europa League football for next season through their domestic league positions, it was all about the glory in Tirana. The Dutch club were not clear favourites, but their performances had made a bigger impression in Europe than those of AS Roma. However, there was no sign of that before half-time. Feyenoord, aiming to be the first Dutch club to win a European competition in 20 years, since their 2002 UEFA Cup triumph, failed to really test Rui Patrício in the Roma goal. After Nicolò Zaniolo produced a skilful finish in the 32nd minute to make it 1–0, the Italians held off a spirited comeback from their Dutch opponents, who were twice denied by the woodwork after half-time. Roma centre-back Chris Smalling made a couple of crucial blocks in the early stages of the second half when Feyenoord were at their best, keeping out Cyriel Dessers, the competition's leading scorer. Feyenoord were denied an equaliser when Patrício tipped Tyrell Malacia's superb strike from 25 metres onto the bar soon after centre-back Gianluca Mancini inadvertently hit his own post while trying to make a clearance.

The stats told the story of the difference in style. Feyenoord had 67 per cent of the possession and 13 shots on goal to Roma's 33 per cent and 9 shots. Roma received four yellow cards to Feyenoord's one. No matter how carefully Slot had prepared his team for a European final and tried to find strategic weapons to turn the match around, it was not enough. For the manager the match in Tirana was a crash course in international top football and an inescapable baptism of fire. José Mourinho won his fifth European trophy. The cameras constantly zoomed in on the Portuguese, theatrical as ever, repeatedly exploding in angry outbursts or demonstrating mock-amazement. A few metres away, Slot was limited to playing a secondary role in the shadow of one of the greatest showmen in professional football.

Slot was dismissive of their opponents' performance. 'It wasn't football. It was mostly slowing down and whining after they went ahead 1–0. I knew that ahead of time. I told myself beforehand: I am not going to get involved with the refereeing because we won't win that game anyway. I see Mourinho constantly moaning to the fourth official, to the referee. You won't believe how often he does it, incredible. He gets away with it because of his status. Any other manager would have been sent to the stands a long time ago. But he does it so cleverly. When he feels that the fourth official is fed up with him, someone else comes off the bench. The physiotherapist, the assistant, the club doctor. And it works. When we're not awarded a well-deserved penalty right after half-time, the question is justified whether this was the consequence of that.' With some hindsight, the Feyenoord manager said, smiling, 'Maybe I should put a bit more pressure on the fourth official in the future. When you see that happening continuously from the other side, throughout the match, you hope that your calmness will eventually be rewarded. That turned out not to be the case.'

José Mourinho said in the post-match press conference, 'We struggled in the second half, our opponents played well and they forced us to make defensive changes. Congratulations to Feyenoord.' In his match analysis, commentator Sjoerd Mossou came to the conclusion that 'Feyenoord not only lost to Mourinho and the often sublimely defending Italian opponent. Above all, they succumbed to their own stage fright before half-time, when they never got into their own game. In the final phase, the Rotterdam team never really got into their rhythm, paralysed by the Portuguese king of the anticlimax – and his cunning team.' Feyenoord, with players an average 23 years of age, were much less seasoned than their opponents, who skilfully exploited their lack of experience. Cyriel Dessers, Reiss Nelson, Orkun Kökçü and Gernot Trauner did not even come close to their usual level for long stretches of the game. The atmosphere had been cheerful and full of confidence all day, but the end was deeply disappointing. Against Roma, Feyenoord needed to do what they had done all season: be themselves. But that proved not to be possible in the final.

In typical Arne Slot manner, calm and restrained, the manager analysed where exactly it had gone wrong. 'You know that you will never get ten chances against an Italian team. Certainly not if that team is also led by Mourinho. We certainly created our chances after the break, but then we also have to be a bit lucky.' He addressed his players immediately after the match in the dressing room in Tirana. 'I told them that I could not take away their disappointment. But I also said that it was a privilege to be able to work with this team every day this season. There has not been a single day that we have not enjoyed being on the training field this season.'

It had been Feyenoord's longest-ever season – 54 competitive games, of which 19 were in the Europa Conference League, including qualifiers. Their previous record was 51 in 2001–02, when they had won the UEFA Cup. Their loss, although bitterly disappointing, was not a cause for shame or even embarrassment. Their second-half performance was infinitely superior to their showing before the break, yet ultimately they didn't have the guile to get the better of a street-smart Roma side. Owen Hargreaves, of BT Sport, said, 'Feyenoord pushed and dominated the ball, but defensively Roma were so good. Let's be honest, they were the better team.' Mourinho was the first coach to win all three current men's UEFA club competitions – UEFA Champions League (Porto 2003–04, Inter 2009–10), UEFA Cup/Europa League (Porto 2002–03, Manchester United 2016–17) and UEFA Europa Conference League (Roma 2021–22).

There was thunderous applause from the travelling Feyenoord support at the end of the game as a thank you for the wonderful series of matches in Europe that the players had put on the field. The final was not a fitting conclusion. Yet, the Feyenoord of Arne Slot had attracted the attention of the world well beyond the Rotterdam environs.

• • •

The income generated by their Conference League achievements was €24 million, less than the starter's bonus awarded to clubs participating in the group phase of the Champions League, which is

€30 million. Nonetheless, the funds were very welcome at the cash-strapped Rotterdam club. Feyenoord had the considerable advantage of not having to struggle through an extensive preliminary round of matches in the summer months of 2022. They had been admitted directly to the group stage of the Europa League, which included a hefty starting fee. They were drawn in a group with FC Midtjylland, Sturm Graz and Lazio. All teams ended with eight points, but Feyenoord finished the group stage in first place by virtue of a superior goal difference.

They impressed in the Europa League group stage by demolishing Austrian outfit Strum Graz 6–0 in De Kuip, four of the goals coming in the first half. Some critics downplayed the win as coming against European minnows, but Slot was pleased with the performance because 'that team is on the rise in Austria'. Feyenoord had been defeated 4–2 by Lazio in Italy, but by beating the Roman team in Rotterdam in a thrilling battle, they qualified for the last 16 of the Europa League as group winners. 'Lazio commits suicide in the Netherlands,' headlined *La Gazzetta dello Sport*. 'They thought they could get out of De Kuip unscathed, but that turned out to be impossible. Santiago Giménez's goal in the second half was the punishment Lazio received for missing chances and the disastrous defensive performance, which ultimately decided the match.'

After the match, a big party broke out in De Kuip. At the post-match press conference, Slot said, 'It is very special and beautiful to see the interaction between players and fans. I think it is wonderful for this group, in which just six of the 21 outfield players are the same [as the previous season], that they can deliver such a unique performance. We did everything we could today. We also needed a good goalkeeper, but this is a wonderful 1–0 victory. The focus was mainly on the goal, but I certainly wouldn't want to forget where the assist came from. Because that was also from a substitute. In the end it's great for those players, it's great for the supporters, but as a coach I also think it's quite nice when two of your substitutes are involved in a goal. It is a very special moment for the club because the last time that we reached the last 16 at this level was in 2002. And that after the last transfer summer, when almost everyone left. I think that is a very good achievement.'

Feyenoord reached the quarter-finals of the Europa League after a huge victory over Shakhtar Donetsk. Slot's team bulldozed the Ukrainian top club aside 7–1 in the second leg. It was the biggest victory of a Dutch team in the last 16 since 1979, when Ajax defeated Omonia Nicosia in the European Cup 10–0. Arne Slot also achieved a special club record. He surpassed famous Feyenoord managers Ernst Happel and Bert van Marwijk with the most European victories. Slot, in just his second season at Feyenoord, had won 15 of his 27 European matches. He said, 'We were very effective tonight and also scored a lot with shots from distance. I saw a great many good things. Despite the result, I think Shakhtar showed in the first half-hour that they are better than many people think they are. You would be doing us an injustice by saying that our opponent was incompetent.'

The war in Ukraine cast a shadow over the match. Slot said he had thought about each Shakhtar player, wondering whether they had lost a family member or had someone serving at the front. Croatian Igor Jovićević, the Ukrainian team's coach, felt the same way. 'Our soldiers are dying and we are playing football. How you have to deal with that isn't something they teach you at a coaching course. It's very difficult to train well during the war. We often have to travel to away games for 24 hours by bus because flying is impossible in Ukraine now. I really don't want to make all kinds of excuses: Feyenoord deserved to win. But the situation isn't easy for us.' Shakhtar's consolation goal led to applause from Feyenoord supporters in De Kuip, an expression of sympathetic support for the Ukrainian team and its fans during these difficult times. Slot was proud. 'I thought that was a very special moment. Our fans showed themselves from their best side in that respect too. It was special to hear afterwards that the people of Shakhtar felt very welcome here.'

Sometime after the 2022 Conference League final defeat, Slot said, 'I didn't watch that match again. Too painful? Actually, yes. I see things that we should have done differently. It's very difficult to win a prize, and we were really close. We had chances. Look, if we get AS Roma in the Europa League, I'll definitely watch that match again. But I'd rather not.' Of course, after the Europa League round of 16, Feyenoord *were* drawn to play against AS Roma – again – in the quarter-finals. Prior to the match Slot said, 'The Dutch media asked me a lot of questions: "Do you think about revenge?" . . . and then the headline is "He wants revenge". But of course if you've lost a game, whether it's a final or another game, it's quite normal for a professional sportsman that you want to win the next time . . . I do not think that it's the emotional burden that makes it hard to play against Roma. What makes it difficult is that they have a very good organisation and very, very good players.'

At home in the Kuip, Feyenoord defeated Roma 1–0. The away match in the Stadio Olimpico spelled the end of Feyenoord's journey in Europe that season: Roma won 4–1 after extra time. After the match, José Mourinho, being his usual combative self, yelled at Arne Slot, 'You shouldn't watch Manchester City and Napoli all the time. You should look at us. Go home.' When asked about his encounter with the riled Portuguese, Slot replied, true to form, 'Mourinho was a little upset. Did I respond? No, we had just lost, AS Roma was through, and then you just take your loss.' When his peace and sanity had returned, Mourinho later admitted that Slot was 'a great coach'.

Two matches against Diego Simeone's Atlético Madrid over the span of two years illustrated what Slot had accomplished at Feyenoord. The first meeting of the two, the friendly win in Rotterdam shortly after Slot's arrival, would set a benchmark for many competitive results. The second, a narrow 3–2 away loss in the Champions League on 5 October 2023, demonstrated that Feyenoord's trajectory was still on the way up. Despite the defeat, Slot's team imposed its attacking football on their opponents, which was reflected in their seven shots on target, a number last bettered against Atlético in the Champions League only by Real Madrid in April 2015, when they recorded eight attempts on goal. By the time the second match against Atlético was played, the global footballing world had come to see what Slot was all about: high-pressing and an emphasis on attacking football, regardless of the opponent. The legion of Feyenoord supporters had fallen in love en masse with the bald man from the eastern hinterlands.

8

DUTCH CHAMPIONS

'Our habits decide our future.'

ARNE SLOT

In 1970, Feyenoord became the first Dutch club to win a European trophy. A European Cup, three league titles, a KNVB Cup and a UEFA Cup were won in De Kuip within five years. Success had become a habit. This was an era in which only the very best was good enough at Feyenoord. The illustrious history is treasured in Rotterdam-Zuid. Winning the UEFA Cup in 1974 was the last gasp of a seemingly unassailable top European team. In recent times, success has been much harder to come by: in the first two decades of the new millennium, Feyenoord won the league just once. Yet, the self-image of being a 'top club' proved to be amazingly persistent. The present is measured by the standards set in the past, but performances have rarely lived up to these towering expectations.

The pressure of expectation has been counterproductive, resulting in disappointment and frustration. Usually, the Rotterdam club has had to yield to their competitors to the north and south: Ajax Amsterdam and PSV Eindhoven. The two have dominated Dutch football since 1999: PSV won 10 and Ajax 9 of the 23 titles. There is also the financial reality. In 2010, Feyenoord came close to bankruptcy, which was only averted when a group of fan-led investors, the Friends of Feyenoord, intervened. The disparity between the 'top three' is considerable. Ajax's overall revenue reached €189 million by 2022, compared to Feyenoord's €87 million. To this day, Feyenoord have never spent more than €8.3 million on a transfer. For a long time, there was a reflexive conservatism, a tendency to play it safe. There has been talk of a new stadium for some time, but no new ground has been broken. Slowly, a need for change was recognised.

The new multifunctional Training Complex 1908 was designed exclusively for the first team of Feyenoord and came into use in June 2018. Within the complex there is a large fitness and training area, a spacious dressing room and a room for video analysis. A sizeable portion of the building has been dedicated to the sports medical facility and a performance research department. There is an auditorium, relaxation rooms and various wellness facilities for the players and staff. MoederscheimMoonen Architects were responsible for the building design. Erik Moederscheim explained that 'prior to the design process, we carried out intensive research by visiting the facilities of various international professional clubs together with Feyenoord. From there, we developed a programme which responds to the constraints of the site as well as meeting Feyenoord's spatial requirements.' The result is that the facilities are placed organically in the building, with the first-team dressing room at its heart. The players are close to the wellness and sports medical facilities, the players' lounge, the corridor towards the outdoor fields and the central staircase leading to the restaurant above. The interior is designed in such a way as to create an environment that stimulates concentration and focus; a lot of light colours and natural materials were used. The glass facade gives the complex a contemporary appearance and many of the spaces have a direct view of the fields. The football pitches are of a high quality. Various surfaces have been created with warm-up and goalkeeper zones. These are all equipped with the latest technology, which enables optimal monitoring of the players.

With the new facilities came a need for a new manager with fresh ideas. Although Arne Slot generally has a friendly disposition, he plays the game by his own rulebook. That often leads to a review of entrenched patterns and a call for innovation – something that would seem inimical to a firmly established club culture. With his train-as-you-play mindset, Slot was precise about what he did at the 1908 grounds. For instance, he concluded that in sessions on days immediately after games, the players should work in a space no larger than 40 metres. If they played in bigger areas, it meant they had to accelerate more; sports medical science proved that running above 20km/h risks more muscle injuries.

On 2 July 2022, the club lost 7–0 in a pre-season friendly to Copenhagen, with their Danish opponents accusing them of not taking the game seriously. It was not the match-up Copenhagen manager Jess Thorup had hoped for. He had wanted a serious test against the Conference League finalists. The Feyenoord faithful at the well-attended match were in shock. Ironically, the Copenhagen team went on to endure the worst start of a season ever and Thorup was gone by 20 September. Meanwhile, in Rotterdam, things ran a different course with Feyenoord going on an almost unprecedented winning spree. What Slot engineered at the club was startling. The Dutch daily *NRC* called him 'the transformative coach that Feyenoord needed', perhaps the most important one in 30 or even 50 years. Part of Feyenoord's path to victory was a very much new-look team. Slot took the team with him at all times. Newcomers were smoothly integrated. Mats Wieffer, for example, developed himself from a decent performer in the second-tier Eerste Divisie to an vital cog in the machine that won the national title. He turned into the director of pressing, winning balls and finding solutions. Slot's decision to give Orkun Kökçü the captain's armband was a vital move.

Feyenoord once again went to a training camp in Austria, this time in Saalfelden. It is a beautiful location, wedged between the mountains, and with the short-cropped pitch in great shape. A high fence prevented balls from the adjacent driving range landing on the wrong greens. Just before noon, the players descended from the Hotel Gut Brandlhof to the field nearby. Arne Slot wanted to size up his team in some peace and quiet. About a dozen supporters made it to Austria, but they had to be satisfied with watching the training from the public road. The premises were also off-limits to the media. Everyone had to wait until Saturday's friendly to see whether Feyenoord had made progress during the week.

When the players had the afternoon off, they could spend time as they pleased. They informed team manager Frank Boer whether they wanted to play golf, go cycling, sailing in Zell am See or challenge themselves in a climbing zone. Feyenoord concluded the training camp with a game against Red Bull Salzburg. The match against the Austrian champions was played at Salzburg's Anif sports centre and tickets for the encounter were available for just €13. The match finished 2–1 in Feyenoord's favour.

Every new season starts with the Open Day, known as the Feyenoord Festival. The highlight is the arrival of the new players. Since 1995, Feyenoord newcomers have made their entrance with a helicopter landing in the De Kuip. Sjaak Troosts, the initiator of the tradition, is said to have been inspired by the example of AC Milan. Silvio Berlusconi bought the club from beleaguered president Giuseppe Farina in February 1986. On 18 July Berlusconi and his newly acquired team arrived at the Arena Civica in three helicopters to the sound of

Wagner's 'Ride of the Valkyries', aka the *Apocalypse Now* music. The weather in Rotterdam being a bit more unpredictable than in Milan, it is always exciting to see whether the helicopter can actually land. There were no problems in 2022.

Feyenoord lost several key players in that summer. They had attracted international attention and went abroad for considerable sums. Luis Sinisterra went to Leeds United for €25 million, Fredrik Aursnes went to Benfica for around €13 million, Tyrell Malacia left for Manchester United for €15 million and Bournemouth paid about the same amount for Marcos Senesi. Sales raised around €70 million, while the players had cost Feyenoord a fraction of the amount. It was a club record, but also a sum that Ajax collected that summer for only one player, Lisandro Martínez. Just over 40 per cent of the money was reinvested as Feyenoord pursued financial sustainability after too many years of fiscal mismanagement.

Arne Slot demonstrated that he was keenly aware of Feyenoord realities. 'The fastest and cheapest way to earn money is by developing your own youth. The recent sale of Tyrell Malacia is a perfect example of that, and the academy should be proud. Everyone knows that the club is working hard to take the next steps in the youth academy. It is inevitable that we will reap the benefits of that. That is essential for a club like Feyenoord. In an ideal situation, besides the regular trajectory in which you bring in youngsters to the youth academy as early as possible, it is also possible to bring in a number of boys aged 15, 16 or 17 from other clubs every year. I call them lateral entrants. If that works well, the youth academy gets a huge boost. If you don't do that, you end up in a situation where you have to bring in players to the first team from outside more often. That is, of course, a lot more expensive than getting young top talent from other professional clubs and developing them further yourself. The overall level of the youth training will also increase immediately, which is, of course, also good for the youth players who are already part of the training.'

A good example of what Slot was talking about was team captain Orkun Kökçü. A youth product of FC Groningen, he joined the Feyenoord youth academy in 2014. He made his Eredivisie debut against FC Emmen on 9 December 2018 and contributed a goal and an assist after coming on as a substitute. In 2019, he extended his contract until 2023. The 2021–22 campaign marked the start of Kökçü's transformation. The Turkey international had never fulfilled his talent but realised if he wanted to survive in Slot's high-speed game, he had to become fitter, better and more versatile. He was at the heart of the great victories in Slot's first two seasons. Kökçü lifted the Eredivisie trophy in Slot's second season, and within a month his transfer to Benfica had earned Feyenoord a fee of €25 million, plus €5 million in add-ons. The sum represented a record signing for the Portuguese club and the league, surpassing Darwin Núñez's transfer from Almería to Benfica in 2020, and Feyenoord's biggest sale since Luis Sinisterra's transfer to Leeds United.

In an interview with Turkish broadcaster TRT 3, Kökçü expressed his belief that his former boss defined his career. 'When my former coach Arne Slot took over, I had a big breakthrough in my performance in his first season. That year, we made it to the finals of the Conference League, but unfortunately we lost. Still, I think my performance that season was very good. I actually wanted to be transferred in the summer; some of the big clubs in the top six in England were interested in me. We had serious talks about transfers, but they didn't happen at the last minute. The following season, Arne Slot made me the team captain, and this responsibility increased my performance even more. We became champions at the end of the season and I was chosen as the Player of the Year in the Netherlands. In the middle of the season, we started to hold transfer talks with various clubs including the English Premier League, Serie A, Bundesliga and Benfica. When I realised that Benfica was seriously interested in me, I made an evaluation with my family. Instead of staying on the bench in England, I decided to go to Benfica because I thought I could play regularly there and improve my performance even more ... Arne Slot is like a father. He made me who I am. He's the best coach in the world.'

In 2022, in came no fewer than 17 players in one transfer window for just €30 million. Feyenoord brought in new players such as Dávid Hancko, Sebastian Szymański, Quinten Timber, Mats Wieffer, Danilo, Javairô Dilrosun, Santiago Giménez, Oussama Idrissi and Igor Paixão. Two of those players, midfielder Timber and defender Hancko, cost €6.5 million each, which meant just €17 million was spent on 15 players. Giménez was signed for €4 million from the Mexican top-flight club Cruz Azul. He was not the only player recruited from markets that many Dutchmen turn their noses up at. Feyenoord signed Paixão from Coritiba, a winger who had played in the Brazilian second division during the previous campaign, as well as bringing in Wieffer from Rotterdam neighbours Excelsior, in the Dutch second tier. Of their 12 permanent signings, not one was aged 24 or over.

Giménez was 21 when he signed and playing for Feyenoord was his first experience of European football. Physiotherapist Vandenbroucke said, 'We came to a conclusion that we needed a few months to get him up and running. Arne agreed and he is the only manager I've ever worked with who would do that. It meant accepting we could not play him from the start of the game because we needed the time to put more into him to get the output in the later stage of the season.' They analysed his running style and noted he needed more 'control around his trunk and pelvis' to avoid injuries and physically compete at the highest level. The observations were based on screenings of the player's movement patterns, in-game and on the training field. Consequently, Giménez started only five games in his 2022–23 debut season before club football paused in the November for the Qatar World Cup. After the tournament, he started 20 of Feyenoord's final 21 Eredivisie and Europa League matches, scoring in 12 of them and finishing as their 20-goal top scorer.

Integrating all these new people, arriving from different clubs and speaking different languages, into a team was not an easy task. Paixão was a promising new arrival and the speedy Brazilian made an immediate impression on his new teammates. But Slot had a hard time getting his message across. 'When I shout "Go, go, go!" he doesn't understand what I mean. When we call "Press, press, press!" it's the same. You have to be really good to still make a difference. The only way to give him the chance to improve himself is to give him game time – besides giving him language lessons of course.' Slovakian Dávid Hancko explained how Slot worked with central defenders. 'When I first joined Feyenoord, I didn't understand everything the coach said. He sometimes spoke so quickly, but by listening and watching carefully, I started to understand. Now I only need two words to know what he means. For example: I am able to see very quickly how our opponent is pressing. I wasn't really concerned with that before, but since I've been playing at Feyenoord, the first thing I try to recognise is whether the opponent is pressing with numbers 9 and 10, or with the wingers. I know exactly where we can find the free man, how we can get an advantage.'

Slot said, 'Feyenoord fans want to see good football. That is what we will be aiming for again next season. I often hear that as a coach I have succeeded in getting the most out of the groups of players I work with. But I also combined that with results. Cambuur reached the semi-finals of the cup tournament and almost got promoted. AZ went into the winter break while being active in Europe, and when the season was cut short by corona, the club was still level with Ajax. At Feyenoord we reached the final of the Conference League and we took more than two points on average in the Eredivisie. But if fifth place turns out to be the maximum attainable next season, I don't think they will pat me on the back in Rotterdam in sheer joy.' Feyenoord won four of their first five league matches, and in the home match against FC Emmen (4–0) all goals came from newcomers: Timber, Giménez, Jacob Rasmussen and Szymański.

The successes of 2022 created excitement among the fan base, but Slot tempered the expectations. 'We have to become champions, win the Europa League and the cup. That's Feyenoord. Whether you have two or sixteen new players doesn't matter. But we'll have to be there in the second half of the season. That's crystal clear. So far, we had the programme on our side. In recent weeks, we played teams from the bottom half of the Eredivisie. What I got from the first half of the competition was that we are difficult to beat. I think that is a Feyenoord quality. But we also made concessions to our style of play. Just six players remained from last season. We had to build a new team. Fifteen men joined. At Feyenoord, the team makes the individual better; it is not a group where the individual makes the team stronger. We have sometimes adapted and won some ugly matches. But that all had a purpose. The long winter break gives us time to develop our own style.'

Because the squad contained relatively few players who would be involved at the World Cup in Qatar, Slot could continue training after a short holiday while other teams had to wait until their key players returned from the tournament. During the winter break, the foundation was laid for the successes that would follow in the second half of the season. Feyenoord again were in Lagos, well settled at the top of the Eredivisie table. The squad prepared for the restart of the competition for six days.

Inclement weather put the trip in jeopardy for a time, but they were assured by the local management that the drainage system of the training pitch at the Cascade Resort was in good working condition. The worst storms had passed by the time the players set foot on Portuguese soil. Every now and then there was a downpour, but it was dry for most of the training camp. In the Estadio Algarve, they beat Strasbourg 1–0. They concluded the week in Portugal with a practice match against Stade Rennais. The French team proved too strong and defeated Feyenoord 2–1.

One of the visitors to Feyenoord's training camp was sports psychologist Dan Abrahams. He was lead psychologist for England Golf, as well as a former touring professional golfer and PGA golf coach. He built up a reputation for his work in both golf and football and has published several books on his art. He has worked with Manchester United and Newcastle United, as well as individually with players such as Gareth Bale. Like Slot, he has his own jargon, speaking of a 'high-performance mindset' when players have to put on a 'game face'. He identified Slot as a coach who is willing to

> challenge perceived notions about Dutch football. Arne is someone who hits that sweet spot between open and closed minded. There's a topic in sports psychology called professional judgement and decision-making and Arne was very competent, utilising what people had to say when it was of value but knowing what to shut out. He's got a strong bullshit detector. I found him caring towards his players. He was

connected to them. He's very much an individual coach as well, helping players develop. He would take a lot of time. English management hasn't fully embraced that kind of caring model.

Another January visitor was scientist Karl Marius Aksum. The Norwegian is a UEFA-licensed football coach with a PhD acquired while working on 'Visual Perception in Elite Football' and a Master's degree in coaching and psychology. He is interested in how football players learn and develop. He is a dynamic presence on X – formerly Twitter – and expressed his reservations about the position game that is essential to the Slot paradigm. When he and Slot engaged in some lively debate, Feyenoord staff thought that Slot had converted Aksum to his view of football. Aksum himself appreciated the encounter, saying, 'Slot likes to listen to the ideas of other people and he likes to be challenged. He is open and willing to consider how things can be improved further and involves others in that process.'

Feyenoord began 2023 at the top of the table, but Arne Slot was unimpressed. 'It's not on my mind at all. I'm never focused on the table, especially when we've played only 14 games. Once we have reached round 32 I will pay more attention to it. But we still have to go such a long distance and we still have to improve so many things. It is pleasant when you're at the top of the table rather than 12 points behind. But it didn't put me in a hallelujah mood over Christmas. For one and a half years there has been a very positive mood around Feyenoord. That is particularly pleasant. Feyenoord has made progress and some of it has come much quicker than we could have wished for in our dreams. But we still are in a – terrible word that – process in which we have to keep considering the transfer value of our players. We must still rely on players' love for the club.'

Feyenoord versus NEC Nijmegen on 9 February 2023 could be remembered as one of the craziest football matches ever. Both teams gave everything during the round of 16 KNVB Cup tie. The Rotterdam side advanced to the quarter-finals thanks to a penalty shootout win at De Kuip. Feyenoord excelled in attack, having 50 shots in the match, with 27 of their efforts on target. With this number of shots, they surpassed Atalanta's European record of 47 in a single match. NEC keeper Mattijs Branderhorst made 23 saves in an absolutely stellar showing. He easily beat the English Premier League's save record, standing at 14; David de Gea, Vito Mannone and Tim Krul all reached this mark during an English top-flight match. Visiting side NEC went ahead after 30 minutes. A smart move saw defender Calvin Verdonk open the scoring. Striker Pedro Marques then doubled NEC's advantage just before the break. The visitors appeared to be heading through to the last eight, but a wild injury time proved their undoing. First, centre-back Philippe Sandler received a red card for a handball that denied a goal. The subsequent penalty was calmly converted by Feyenoord captain Orkun Kökçü. Slot's team brought themselves level with a few minutes of added time to spare when forward Igor Paixão scored, diverting a header into the net. Despite playing with ten men, NEC regained the lead in extra time thanks to midfielder Jordy Bruijn. The advantage lasted just two minutes before Feyenoord's attacking onslaught brought them level once more. Fans at De Kuip thought they had finally made it through when winger Javairô Dilrosun made it 4–3 with an absolute stunner. But NEC fought back once more, with Bruijn getting his second for a 4–4 draw, forcing penalties. Feyenoord were perfect during the shootout, scoring all five while NEC missed one.

At the conclusion of the exhausting encounter, Arne Slot expressed mixed feelings. 'I am not sure how happy I should be with this win, but I am pleased with the mentality we showed. I just gave my players a pat on the back. At the break, I was less satisfied.' Goal-keeper Branderhorst obviously had reason to be proud. 'Man, man, what a delightful match! It had everything. At some point I thought: bring on that penalty shootout.' Orkun Kökçü expressed amazement when reviewing the post-match statistics. 'Did we really have 50 shots? Well, that's what Feyenoord is famous for: being the first in everything.'

Arne Slot's Feyenoord were expert at tempting opponents to take risks in the build-up. As in the first season under Slot, they won the ball far from their own goal more often than any other Eredivisie team. Feyenoord scored no fewer than 12 times after gaining posses-sion deep in the opponent's half. Where rivals PSV and FC Twente retreated when they failed to exert high pressure effectively, Slot's team stayed as high up the pitch as possible with their back line. In the Eredivisie, no team intervened as little around their own penalty area as Feyenoord. Given that the style of play was so demanding, it was impressive that the squad suffered so few injuries, a direct conse-quence of Slot's training-ground methods.

De Klassieker (The Classic) is the match between Feyenoord and Ajax, the main football rivalry of the Netherlands. It is the Dutch equivalent of Liverpool–Manchester United, of Barcelona–Real Madrid. The competition between these two clubs goes beyond the football rivalry itself and is rooted in the long-standing contest between Amsterdam and Rotterdam. It began when the two cities first received their city rights in the thirteenth century. Amsterdam is the Netherlands' capital city and is renowned for its art and cul-ture, including sophistication on the football field. The 'Venice of the North' is the city of Rembrandt and Spinoza, of Rinus Michels, Johan Cruyff and Total Football. Rotterdam is Europe's largest port and its cargo transportation hub. The 'Gateway to Europe' had to be recreated from the ground up after heavy Nazi bombing in the Second World War. Rotterdam people are proud of their work ethic and disdainful of Amsterdam showiness. There is a saying that reflects these sentiments: 'While Amsterdam dreams, Rotterdam works.' The inhabitants differ significantly in both attitudes and cultures, which is clearly reflected in their football traditions. The game is seen as a clash between the artists of Amsterdam and the workers of Rotterdam. Ajax's style of play has long been a source of pride for the supporters, and one of irritation for Feyenoord fans. The Rotterdam supporters feel that those hailing from Amsterdam suffer from delusions of grandeur.

Before the 19 March 2023 instalment of The Classic, Ajax boss John Heitinga asserted that his team had more individual quality and was therefore 'the natural favourite'. Slot does not think this is a smart way of approaching an upcoming match and has his own way of dealing with the opposition. He made light of the comment, saying that the manager just showed his 'sense of humour'. 'I will not do anything to incite an opponent. I always try to soften them up. Radiate respect to others, while with my own players I do everything I can to put them on fire. I try to send them onto the field with the thought: if we just do what we agreed on, we are not going to lose this match.' The Ajax bravado had been the subject of discussion in Feyenoord's dressing room. Mats Wieffer, a sober-minded easterner, was not perturbed. 'I wasn't particularly bothered by the words coming from Amsterdam. But some other players were.' One of those was Orkun Kökçü, Feyenoord's energetic captain. 'Man, they do talk a lot! But we show it on the pitch. No words, but deeds.'

Feyenoord took a giant step towards the Dutch league title with a 3–2 victory over their old foes in a feisty match at the Amsterdam

Arena. They took the lead early in a seesaw game. Ajax equalised shortly thereafter and just before half-time scored again. After the break, thanks to canny tactical interventions by Slot, Feyenoord drew level and then scored the decisive goal just before the final whistle. Lutsharel Geertruida headed into the net from close range to give Feyenoord their first league win in Amsterdam since 2005 and open up a six-point lead at the top of the table with eight games to play. The away victory was celebrated in Rotterdam as if the gates of paradise had opened. In the aftermath, Slot quelled the excitement generated by the victory with typical calm rationality. 'Winning against Ajax brings expectations. I immediately got working on our next match against Sparta because everything has to be right again. I did not want our own photographer to take a photo of the euphoric mood in the Feyenoord dressing room after the match against Ajax. I said, "A small club would do that, but Feyenoord are too big for that." And I concluded by saying, "Guys, this is very nice, but the objective is not to win against Ajax. We have a higher goal. So let's not pretend that we are already there." And so I try to plant another seed to motivate them for the next match.' Yet, with the win, Feyenoord had struck a major blow. They never relinquished the advantage they gained over their arch-rivals.

Journalist, broadcaster and Ajax supporter Henk Spaan thought it was an unequal match-up. 'If you look at the compositions of the Ajax and Feyenoord squads, you see that Ajax has the better play-ers in terms of transfer value. But Slot made Feyenoord into a team that Ajax has no chance against. Feyenoord is not replete with great players, but taken together it is an incredibly strong team, a kind of fighting machine. That is Slot's accomplishment. If Slot were to leave, Feyenoord would have to go back to the drawing board. If he is wise, he heads out the door, because winning the championship twice in a row seems very unlikely to me. Moreover, important players such as Giménez and Kökçü will leave. I don't think it is a good idea for Slot to go to Ajax. That is not a smart move, you will just get a lot of hassles. Maybe we will see him at Ajax one day, but first he has to do a club in between.'

The KNVB Cup semi-final in Rotterdam on 5 April 2023 against Ajax was not a collector's item, and not just because Feyenoord lost 2–1. In the 62nd minute of the game, Ajax midfielder Davy Klaassen was struck on the head by a lighter thrown from the stands in section Z. He got hit after he had made what turned out to be the winning goal, and had blood running down his head and neck. 'There was some sort of altercation which I tried to calm down. All of a sudden, I felt something hit my head. It just hurt at first. That quickly changed into anger. I thought to myself: is this really happening?' The match was suspended for 30 minutes and Klaassen was substituted. Arne Slot spoke of 'shame' after the match. He also thought the incident had deflated his team, which otherwise would have been capable of a comeback. 'It wasn't the first incident. These people are not helping us. What happened tonight is terrible, a black page in the history of the club. During the warm-up the Ajax players had all sorts of things thrown at them. As far as I could tell, there weren't any lighters then, mostly cups of beer and other things you shouldn't be throwing on the pitch.' Feyenoord general director Dennis te Kloese backed his manager. 'There is no excuse for this. The field is sacred. Players should feel safe when they are on the pitch. An apology on behalf of the club is in order. This does a lot of damage to the club.' Section Z remained vacant during the subsequent Europa League encounter with AS Roma.

In 2023, the concept of 'the Arne Slot phase' was introduced. In rapid succession, FC Utrecht, FC Groningen (twice), PSV, AZ,

Shakhtar Donetsk and Ajax witnessed how Feyenoord could salvage a match in the final minutes with one or more goals to achieve a draw or victory. Fitness is one of Slot's non-negotiables, a basic requirement to play good football for the full 90-plus minutes. He wants his players to collectively run 120km in a match, a large part of them at top speed. Late in games, the superb fitness of Feyenoord players paid dividends. This quality was not lost on their opponents. AZ wing-back Milos Kerkez saw how his team had to sit very deep in the final stage of their encounter with Feyenoord: 'Not everyone was active at the end, had the spirit and energy to win the match.' Slot was rightfully pleased with his players' do-or-die attitude because it demonstrated 'the Feyenoord DNA. It says a lot about their character that they can still muster the energy. Everyone in the organisation, particularly the [staff's] physical experts, is committed to constant improvement. But the key is the players: they have to do it.'

• • •

Cock van der Palm was a Rotterdam-born singer and lyricist. He was best known for writing songs about his favourite football club. The most popular of these is 'Feyenoord, Feyenoord (What Are We Going to Do Today?)', composed in 1992. He based the melody of the song on 'Daisy Bell (Bicycle Built for Two)', which was written exactly a century earlier by Harry Dacre. The song is a club hit, played and sung along to at matches in De Kuip.

> Feyenoord, Feyenoord, what are we going to do today
> We're going to win, the only question is by how much

On 14 May 2023, Feyenoord won 3–0 against Go Ahead Eagles and thus claimed their first national title since 2017 (exactly six years earlier to the day), with two matches to go. They became champions for the 16th time, in a boiling Kuip. Long before kick-off, the championship fever was palpable in Rotterdam. Hours earlier, the red and white of Feyenoord shirts were visible throughout the city. Championship ecstasy combined with mild May weather encouraged fans to take a dip in the fountain at the Hofplein – a time-honoured tradition – which had been specially cleaned for the occasion by the municipality. Supporters unrolled the largest banner ever displayed in a Dutch stadium: 1,100 square metres of white fabric, 550 metres long – almost the circumference of the stadium – emblazoned with lines from the club song in huge black letters. The supporters' association organised a crowdfunding campaign to pay for the enormous banner.

After 15 minutes, the championship party got going when Oussama Idrissi made it 1–0 after a pass from Mats Wieffer. When all the supporters went crazy after this opening goal, Arne Slot stood with his hands in his pockets on the sidelines. The big release only came when Santiago Giménez doubled the margin with his 15th league goal. That goal delighted Slot because the attack came straight from the Training Complex 1908 textbook. Then, early in the second half, Igor Paixão provided a match highlight. With his back to the goal, the Brazilian turned away from his opponent with his right foot and then curled the ball into the top corner with his left: 3–0.

Slot admitted that he had been in considerable turmoil. Winning the match and the championship was a personal breakthrough. 'I think that as a coach you first have to win a prize before you can find some peace for yourself. I may have seemed calm at first, but my family can tell you that the past two weeks have not been a lot of fun at home. The tension builds when everyone just assumes that you will make it. When it's your birthday, you know with certainty that the party will go ahead. Today, we also had a party here for everyone, but we first had to win. I'm also wired in such a way that I can imagine all sorts of disaster scenarios. If you win a prize, you're in a different league of trainers than if you don't win a prize. And winning the national title at Feyenoord is really next level.'

He had witnessed Feyenoord becoming champions six years earlier, on TV at home. 'I thought, if you get to stand there, it doesn't get any better than that. Once you're actually there yourself, it's pretty unreal, I have to say. The feeling that we've actually pulled it off still has to sink in a bit.' He readily shared the credit with his staff. 'They play a tremendously important role in this success. I am convinced that every player will say that every staff member was incredibly valuable this season. As the head coach, you get all the attention. But this was a good moment to focus on them. I think it is beautiful to see that everyone comes to the club with great pleasure every day and to see the interaction between staff and players and players among themselves. I saw that confirmed again today.'

Prior to the famous Feyenoord–Ajax clash, goalkeeper and PSV icon Ronald Waterreus was asked to create a best eleven composed of all available Ajax and Feyenoord players. Without batting a eye, he answered that he would pick only Ajax players. His comment was not appreciated in Rotterdam. 'Apparently, people did not understand the irony. With my comment, just before The Classic, I just wanted to emphasise the power of Arne Slot. He makes the difference. Now that Feyenoord has won the title, I still think exactly the same way. More than to anyone else, the success of Feyenoord is the success of Slot. It cannot be denied that he has created a completely new dynamism in Rotterdam-Zuid, with the championship as the crowning achievement. The title belongs to him. Of course, it also belongs to the rest of Feyenoord.'

Arne Slot won the Rinus Michels Award for best coach of the Eredivisie for the second year in a row. Besides Slot, Ron Jans (FC Twente), Pascal Jansen (AZ), Joseph Oosting (RKC Waalwijk) and Maurice Steijn (Sparta Rotterdam) were nominated. 'I am refreshed and we still have a week to go before we start again,' said Slot at the presentation of his award. 'Actually, I'm saying something that isn't true, because the past two or three weeks I've been pretty preoccupied with the new season. Last season, we dealt with the difficult side issue that [technical director] Frank Arnesen was struggling with his health. On top of that, we lost 15 players. Now we may lose two or three. That's impossible to predict in football, but it will remain calm in my head because from next week I'll be working full speed with my staff to get the team playing as well as possible again.'

Feyenoord became champions with two games to spare, having spent virtually the whole season at the top of the table. They had only lost once in the Eredivisie back in September, when they let in a late goal for a 4–3 defeat at PSV Eindhoven. (Their second defeat of the season came in their meaningless final match against Vitesse.) They took the Eredivisie by storm, earning 42 points away from home, the club's highest tally in their history. They also scored in 31 consecutive Eredivisie games, their longest streak since 1961. Feyenoord finished seven points ahead of second-placed PSV. Winning the title in Rotterdam is redemptive. Winning it the way Slot did was cathartic.

9

FAMILY MAN

'The best gift is family.'
MOTTO POSTED IN THE SLOT HOME

Arend 'Arne' Martijn Slot's last name is an invitation to sideline commentators to display their cleverness. In his Zwolle days, the wordplay ranged from the disdainful 'Slot machine malfunctions' to the laudatory 'Slot be with us', 'Honour be Slot' and even 'Slot is God'. The English media assured doubters that the Dutchman would 'Slot right in' as soon as the news of his relocation to Liverpool broke. There were creative suggestions for what songs Liverpool fans might be singing about their new manager: 'Slot in the Name of Love', 'Feeling Slot, Slot, Slot', 'Slot is Love'. And when Liverpool went on a relentless run of wins: 'It's beginning to look a Slot like Christmas' and 'Best of the Slot'. The Dutch word *slot* has several meanings: 1) lock; 2) castle; 3) conclusion or end. Amsterdam locksmith and Ajax fan Michel Vrachtdoender said, 'Slot should have become a locksmith, like me. Or he should have been with Ajax.' *Tot slot* or *slotwoord* in a book is the epilogue. And Slot normally makes sure that, after everything has been said, he has the last word.

While the pronunciation of the surname poses no challenge to English speakers, Arne is more complicated. It's not Arnie, as some Britons have assumed. It also isn't Arnay, as others have proposed, and also not Arn. It's like 'Arn-uh', with the second syllable sounding like someone deciding whether to have eggs or porridge for breakfast. The Dutch 'r' is a problem for non-native speakers. When Slot was asked in his first Liverpool interview how his name was properly pronounced, he conspicuously rolled the 'rrrrrrr' – maybe to discourage his interlocutor from trying? The Dutch are a bit heavy on their consonants, but the people in Bergentheim, Slot's hometown, are inclined to swallow some of them whole, so that his name sounds more like 'A'ne' when pronounced by the lifelong locals. Arne is derived from Arnout, an old Germanic name that means having the power of an eagle, ruling like an eagle. Slot's birth name is Arend, which literally means 'eagle' in modern Dutch. He was named after his father. The name suits Slot, who, despite his sociable character and sunny demeanour, is a deliberate, eagle-eyed and ambitious leader.

Since he was young, Arne has been together with Mirjam, who was born in a village 30km south of Bergentheim named Enter. This territory is called Twente and the locals are known as Tukkers. They are often characterised as a little suspicious of strangers, frugal with money and just as sparing with words. So it may not come as a surprise that Mirjam Slot is a little camera-shy and tends to stay in the background. Like some members of her husband's family, she is a teacher by profession. She spent most of her time teaching at a primary school in Ommen, a town further north and about five times the size of Bergentheim. Arne and Mirjam were married in 2009. Their daughter Isa is 17 and son Joep (pronounced 'Yoop') 15. Slot regularly talks about his wife in interviews. 'My wife thinks I don't work that hard at home,' he said, laughing, in an AZ video in which he was filmed at home. 'But I say: you can't work hard everywhere. If you are already doing that at AZ, then home life should provide a bit of balance and equilibrium.' Family is important to him. 'I like to be involved in the interests of my children. My daughter plays tennis and my son plays football and if possible I'm there.'

When Slot became head coach of AZ in 2019, the family moved from Zwolle into a new home in Limmen, a small town 10 kilometres south of Alkmaar. His son played football at the local club, VV Limmen. A replica of the Zwolle Peperbus appeared on the sideboard in the living room. Peperbus is the nickname of a late Gothic tower in Zwolle belonging to the Basilica of Our Lady of the Assumption, which the locals think looks like a pepper shaker. It is the defining landmark of the city where Slot fine-tuned his footballing skills, and he is the type of man who remains true to his roots. In 2020, Slot also bought an apartment in Egmond aan Zee, the same distance from Alkmaar as Limmen, but, as the name indicates, located on the North Sea coast. According to website BekendeBuren ('FamousNeighbours', which tracks the real-estate activities of Dutch luminaries), he paid €385,000 for the place. 'Perhaps it is an investment object for Arne. He is able to rent out the apartment, which has a beautiful view of the sea, to tourists.'

A football manager at a top-flight club is very much under public scrutiny, and opinions about Slot's every move are expressed daily through traditional media outlets and hourly on social media platforms. This inevitably affects his family life. The impact of Slot's sudden removal as AZ coach at the end of 2020 was considerable. On the Met Open Vizier podcast, Slot spoke about some of the turmoil he and his family went through. 'Of course I found the dismissal unpleasant, but I wasn't even that bothered by it. But I was bothered by what happened next. It was as if everyone understood why I was ultimately dismissed. By everyone I mean in particular what I saw in the media. I found that very difficult. And then I haven't even mentioned what it does to your family. Especially to the children. I had moved to Limmen from Zwolle when I became head coach at AZ. Limmen is a town just below Alkmaar. This being the first chance I got as head coach, I wanted to do everything as well as possible. So I moved to reduce my travel time. My daughter just started secondary school in Limmen and my son was still in primary school. If you are dismissed in that region and the people near Alkmaar have the perception that I am a snake and a member of the NSB [Dutch party collaborating with the Nazi invaders during World War Two], it has a big impact on your children.'

Slot used the Alkmaar experience as learning material. When he signed for Feyenoord, he and Mirjam decided not to move the family to Rotterdam. Slot occupied an apartment in the city centre, but his wife and children moved back to Zwolle. 'I began working for a national club. If things would go badly for Feyenoord, they would also suffer from it in the Zwolle region. But I think it would be a lot less than in Rotterdam if they were at school there. In Limmen I ate at home every evening and I heard a lot from the children. In Rotterdam less. That was a consequence of the dismissal in Alkmaar.'

Guus Hiddink once said that 'football is the most important side issue in the world'. Arne Slot is at least as infatuated with the beautiful game as his eastern neighbour is, and he also knows there are things in life that are more important than football. He is driven to achieve, but he will not put the well-being of his family at risk. 'I have always said that I was too young to become head coach, considering the age of my children. Everything really went too fast. After Feyenoord, the logical next step is going abroad. My children still have three years of high school ahead of them; you don't just pull them out. It is not insurmountable, in the end you just adapt. But it does play an important role in my decision-making.'

Especially when considered in the context of the world of

professional football, with its moral relativism, wealthy men and beautiful women, romantic dalliances and frequent divorces, Slot is a traditionalist. He is faithful to his wife and devoted to his children. They are central in his life. He is famous for his coaching expertise, but his family clearly matter most. He enjoys spending time with Mirjam, drinking a glass of his favourite Italian red, Amarone della Valpolicella. He keeps his work and private lives separated, not just socially, but geographically as well. That requires, for a man who is so much in the spotlight, some effort and sacrifice. He spends most of his time with his team in one town, while his family live at some distance in another.

Slot is associated with Rotterdam because of his achievements at Feyenoord where he won the Eredivisie title. Yet it is in Zwolle where he started his coaching career and had two spells as a player, and where his wife, son and daughter still live. While at Feyenoord, Arne Slot had a comfortable pied-à-terre in Rotterdam, away from home and family back east: a beautiful apartment on the Maasboulevard, in a high building next to the Nieuwe Maas river, with great views of the Noordereiland (North Island) and the iconic Erasmus Bridge, the Kop van Zuid (South Bank) and the Maritime District. The sun could be seen setting over the city with its distinct skyline: the piercing Euromast tower and the zigzag of avant-garde architecture. From one of the bedrooms the floodlights of the Feyenoord stadium were visible. It was a modern three-bedroom apartment, with space and amenities to comfortably accommodate Slot's family on weekend visits. But those didn't really happen much.

Arne Slot is a master of his craft. His passion for the game is so intense that, in his last season at Feyenoord, he intimated that coaches like him, the real 'football nuts', are precariously balancing on the edge of burn-out. Questions were raised about his health, especially when he was seen coughing on the touchline for an extensive period of time. 'On a Sunday evening when we haven't won, I'm sitting on the couch by myself, knowing that my family is at home in Zwolle without me. Sometimes I think: what kind of poor life is this? And when I watch a match abroad on TV and there is a shot of a father with his son in the stands, the thought pops into my head: I could have done that with my son today. If you aspire to such a one-dimensional life as a football player or football manager, where all your time is taken up by your work, especially on the weekend when other people are doing fun things, you have to be very, very driven.'

Slot does not have many opportunities to see his son play football, but when he does, he is impressed with his quality. 'I also think sometimes that he could be a little more fanatical on the field, just like my father used to think of me. But when I go look at him, I don't bombard him with advice. Sometimes I just give a thumbs up. By the way, my son can really enjoy playing football. I sometimes say that he is unlucky that his father is a coach at Feyenoord. If I had more time to train him, I think he would have had a good chance of getting into the youth academy of a professional club because his technique is fantastic. But when he is daunted by something, it doesn't always come out. He's got that from my wife. My daughter is more like me. She thinks she's pretty good. She is not easily bothered by things.' Family time is at a premium. During Euro 2024, he was in the stands of the Cologne stadium with his son, watching Belgium play Romania. With his daughter, he has spent a few days at season's end on Ibiza, the family's favourite holiday island.

'I hear from my wife, when she watches a match at home with the children, that they are completely involved. It is extraordinary how much emotion it causes. My father also watches everything, and I mean everything – in terms of reactions, analyses, you name it. When things are going well, it's fine. But I also notice that when things aren't going so well, that man is completely stressed. I feel that pressure too. What I notice most about the difference between AZ and Feyenoord is not so much what is said or written about it by the media, but that you are recognised as the Feyenoord coach everywhere. I don't have too much trouble with that myself, but my daughter would never say her name is Isa Slot. She limits it to Isa. That is a dimension that people sometimes forget. That is not a sad story or anything, and we are used to it, but your family didn't choose that of course. My wife also says that when she comes to Feyenoord, she feels that people see her as the wife of the head coach. She doesn't always like that. My daughter has a picture of us together on the front of her phone, but when she went on holiday with a friend, she changed that photo. She has no need to be seen as "the daughter of . . .".'

Feyenoord head coach Arne Slot waited patiently in his car for an hour or so until his daughter and her friends resurfaced after a night out at the Black Box. He slid down a little in his seat to avoid recognition in enemy territory. The Amsterdam concert hall, formally named AFAS Live and located near the Johan Cruyff Arena, was the site of a concert featuring Surinamese-Dutch rap artist Jonna Fraser. Isa Slot is a fan. Papa Slot apparently isn't. But even if he had wanted to see the performance, they wouldn't have let him in: only those aged between 12 and 17 got tickets to the We Are The Future Festival. One ambitious goal was making the biggest number of simultaneous selfies ever: 6,000 – everyone present in the concert hall. There is no available evidence to show that the challenging project was successfully completed.

'My wife always thinks she is more nervous than I am. I believe that's true, but that is because when I see that the match is going according to the way I planned it with the staff and the lads, it gives me the peace of mind that we have done our prep work well. You can still lose, of course, because of an unfortunate moment or an individual action, but those are aspects of football that you as the manager have no influence on . . . It is also about the dynamics and opportunism. You don't know where you will be working next year. In this profession you never know for sure. As a technical director, that is different, but for a manager, the short term still applies. At AZ we were having a great time, and in one day everything was different. That's difficult for my wife and that's why I think those matches are so intense for the family. Winning is so important, also for them.'

When it came time to say goodbye to Feyenoord, Slot was serenaded in De Kuip and his son Joep was part of the celebrations. 'There has not been a day that I have not felt the appreciation in Rotterdam, but of course not as extreme as today. That is a very special experience. The nice thing was that my son was among the supporters. He had one wish in the three years that he was here: to be among the hardcore. I had already seen a few videos of him singing along loudly. Maybe he had been singing along with the songs every time. His dream came true to watch Feyenoord among the hardcore.'

He continued, 'I always say that I'm quite good at losing. That may not be a logical statement coming from someone who likes to win. My wife and children are really nervous during every match and they ask why I'm not. The answer is: if we play very well in a match against Ajax, we can still lose due to bad luck. I can make peace with that, especially if we have shown what we can do. Attractive, attacking football, by daring to take risks . . . But I do really take it home with me. I notice it and always say: the pleasure of winning is much less than the misery of losing. If we lost on Sunday and we have Monday off, then that day is just one big drama. If you have won, then it feels normal, and you are already worrying about how to win the next match. Strangely enough, I sleep much better after a defeat than after a victory. Apparently, I am so tired after all the whining and fuss that I sleep better.'

Life has been good to the Slots. Arne got a very sizeable raise after his successful first year as Feyenoord's manager. The club realised that they had to give their hero some incentive to resist the charm offensive and the financial temptations coming from some English Premier League clubs after they began taking note of Slot's managerial skills. He earned as much as €4.6 million in his last year, which would make him the best-paid Eredivisie manager ever. Coaches such as Louis van Gaal, Erik ten Hag and Peter Bosz received considerably less. The photogenic Isa has an Instagram account where she regularly posts pictures of the family's latest forays into foreign lands. They show that the Slot family love to travel. In one year, they visited Madrid, New York and London.

When Arne did move to England, the Slot household didn't have to think about it for long. Mirjam, Isa and Joep would not be moving to Liverpool anytime soon. Jürgen Klopp resided in a lavish villa in Formby, a coastal town just outside Liverpool, close to the city but in peaceful greenery with a golf course nearby. One of Merseyside's most expensive areas, Victoria Road is often referred to as the region's Millionaire's Row, thanks to its huge mansions and celebrity neighbours. Over the years, it has been home to players and managers alike. Slot would not be occupying the residence that was originally owned by Steven Gerrard before becoming home to Brendan Rodgers and then Klopp. Others might have been tempted to move into the mansion with its three living rooms, seven bedrooms, games room, swimming pool, two-storey gym, solarium, jacuzzi, sauna and cinema. Slot wasn't. Liverpool put the £4 million property up for sale after he turned it down. With his family in the Netherlands, he initially stayed in an apartment during the summer, before moving to a house in the county of Cheshire, just south-east of Liverpool. But it is no more than a stopover: he spends most of his time in his room at the AXA Training Centre.

Family, friends and football – these three are most important to Arne Slot. They should not needlessly be mixed up. At the top of football, and certainly in the Premier League, there is almost no time to spend time with family. The work schedule is too intense. 'I think that almost every coach of a top club is on the verge of being overworked. Being a head coach is a very tough job, certainly at a top club with so many opinion makers in front of you every week.' He uses the word deliberately: opinion makers. Journalists no longer just report on events, they now are 'news analysts', he believes.

Be that as it may, Slot has gone about his business in a quiet way. He works long hours at the training ground, eats most of his meals at the club and takes home a pre-cooked dinner when his schedule is tight. Slot doesn't really go into Liverpool itself. He only knows the trendy areas second-hand from photographs – for example, Albert Dock, the beautiful scene next to the Mersey with its many restaurants. 'They say that it is not easy for players and the technical staff to walk around there quietly or have a bite to eat. I did not do that often anyway, but here not at all. No problem. I often get a meal from the club, eat it at home and watch football on television.' He does not have many out-of-work interactions and is usually last to leave Liverpool's training ground. He may finish the day playing padel with his assistants Sipke Hulshoff and Johnny Heitinga and the performance lead Ruben Peeters, but once home he is on his laptop again. During international breaks he spent time back home with his family. They came over from the Netherlands when Liverpool faced Real Madrid and Manchester City. 'It's great here. They've given me and my staff a very warm welcome and the facilities here are fantastic. But privately it's a bit of a switch. The fact that I'm on my own definitely has an impact. Liverpool is also a completely different city than Zwolle. Apart from that, I don't have any other relatives living here now. It's not difficult, because I'm constantly busy. But there are times when I would have liked to stop by my brother's for a cup of coffee, or my parents'.'

10

WALK ON, WALK ON

'Football is a very simple game, if you understand it.'
ARNE SLOT

Victor Orta was known as one of the better technical directors in the Premier League. The executive who is currently sporting director of La Liga club Sevilla used his business acumen in the service of Leeds United for six years. When he fired manager Jesse Marsch in February 2023, the Spaniard had already made a list of possible successors. He was looking for a manager with an attacking mindset. After Rayo Vallecano's Andoni Iraola had declined, his attention turned to Arne Slot. Feyenoord's general director Dennis te Kloese knew that Slot had come onto the radar of big English clubs. 'I haven't heard anything from Leeds, not officially and not unofficially. I also know Leeds as a proper club, so I don't believe they're doing anything behind our backs. The transfer of Luis Sinisterra also went in a very clean, proper way.' The former Feyenoord winger had plied his trade at Leeds since the summer of 2022, so Orta had a reliable source of information on someone who could be an excellent replacement for Marsch.

Slot never made a secret of his ambition to manage a club in the Premier League. He extended his contract with Feyenoord in 2022 until 2025, but it included a clause that allowed him to transfer to a club in a bigger league without penalties. The attitude of Slot's agent

Rafaela Pimenta had been a cause for irritation in the Feyenoord boardroom. The former right-hand woman of the late Mino Raiola, 'the world's first female super-agent' is influential at top European football clubs. The blonde Brazilian is a self-assured businesswoman, committed to etiquette and always impeccably dressed. But once she is seated at the negotiating table, she demonstrates a relentlessness that also was a trademark of Italian-Dutch dealmaker Raiola. Slot remained affiliated with Pimenta and the One agency when Raiola unexpectedly passed away in 2022. Her client base is worth many hundreds of millions of euros. Manchester City striker Erling Haaland is considered the superstar of the agency, of which Pimenta was already a co-owner years before Raiola's death. Matthijs de Ligt had his multimillion-euro transfer to Bayern Munich completed by the Brazilian. The tough-minded football agent and former lawyer made sure that Feyenoord regularly received signals from the market. At different times, Brighton & Hove Albion, West Ham United and Crystal Palace had shown interest in Arne Slot.

News reports speculating about a possible Slot transfer to Tottenham Hotspur emerged in the British media, accompanied by claims that Feyenoord had priced him out of a move. Slot did not mention the name Tottenham himself, but when Pimenta spoke to Te Kloese she was told that Slot would not be coming to London. Slot said, 'There have never been any negotiations between any club and Feyenoord. Rafaela opened the conversation with Te Kloese by saying that I would stay at Feyenoord no matter what. In the end, we reached an agreement for one extra season at Feyenoord. And the clause that I could leave for a fixed amount disappeared. After winning the national title, I wanted to take the time to investigate how I felt – towards Feyenoord, towards interested clubs. Then I read and heard a lot of untruths. At one point my family said: "Maybe you should just tell people what you told us, because it's getting really negative around you on social media." I provided that clarity by making a statement. Feyenoord wanted to announce my contract extension in a nice way.'

Micha Jacobs put it a little more bluntly in his *Panorama* column.

You say no to a snake pit in the Premier League where there is no honour to be gained. You simply remain loyal to the club you made champions and with which you want to reap the rewards in the Champions League. Of course, I do not believe for a second that Arne Slot only stays in De Kuip for sporting reasons: the bag of money that is waiting for him is apparently historically large by Rotterdam standards, thanks to his Brazilian agent Rafaela Pimenta, who takes good care of herself and her clients. A smaller bag than in London probably, but still large enough for Slot to have made his pile. I actually think that is the smart thing about Slot. By staying in De Kuip for at least another year, he assures himself of a number of things that many Dutch managers can only dream of: experience in a European tournament, a chance to become champion twice in a row, perhaps a historical double and, in any case, financial security. It is a package of opportunities that is not available anywhere else, not even in the Premier League. I completely understand why he stays in De Kuip.

Slot decided to postpone an adventure in the Premier League for at least another year. Thus ended two weeks of speculation and gossip, not least fuelled by his own press conferences, where equivocating answers gave the impression to some that Spurs were making a serious attempt to sign him. Slot clarified the issue by saying he would simply stay at De Kuip. 'I have heard a lot about the interest of other clubs. I am grateful for the appreciation that was expressed, but my wish is to stay at Feyenoord and continue to build on the foundation that has been laid in the past two seasons. There are no transfer talks going on, there have not been any and the discussion was exclusively about a possible extension. All talks with Feyenoord are only focused on that. I am looking forward to the new season at Feyenoord.'

Late in May 2023, Slot put pen to paper on a new contract, signing until 2026. 'I'm not done here yet,' he said after the announcement of his new deal. 'We have had a great season with Feyenoord, with the championship as a wonderful reward for all the hard work that has been put in, but I really want to continue building. We are going to play in the Champions League, which I've never done before as a player and as a coach, and there is a national title to defend. Enough to look forward to, so I am proud to be and remain in Rotterdam as Feyenoord's manager. The club is in a real good place. Sometimes you also have to cherish what you have. There's more to life and to football than only winning a prize. It is also the way you work. You're not easily in a place where you can work like we can here and be happy, profession-wise but also family-wise.'

There had been considerable activity in Rotterdam in terms of incoming transfers for the new season, but it could not be compared with the previous year. Ramiz Zerrouki came from FC Twente, while Thomas van den Belt and Thomas Beelen exchanged PEC Zwolle for De Kuip. Bart Nieuwkoop returned after a short detour through the Belgian Pro League, German goalkeeper Timon Wellenreuther was signed from Anderlecht and Calvin Stengs was reunited with Slot after their time together at AZ. Japanese striker Ayase

Arne Slot in action for
PEC Zwolle during a
Dutch Eredivisie match.

On the touchline as
AZ Alkmaar's assistant
coach, gaining tactical
insight early in his
managerial career.

Feyenoord head coach Arne Slot with assistant Robin van Persie at the Rotterdam Kuip.

Celebrating Feyenoord's Eredivisie title alongside top scorer Santiago Giménez.

Arne Slot lifts the league championship trophy from the Rotterdam City Hall balcony.

Clad in Feyenoord's traditional green robe, Slot celebrates the 2023–24 KNVB Cup win at De Kuip.

An emotional embrace with captain Orkun Kökçü following Feyenoord's title-clinching victory.

Joined by family on the pitch, after delivering Feyenoord's first league triumph since 2017.

Popular with the fans – Liverpool's new head coach makes an instant impact.

Double Dutch: Liverpool head coach Arne Slot and captain Virgil van Dijk share a victorious moment after an important win over Chelsea at Anfield.

With Mohamed Salah during a Champions League clash against Real Madrid.

Slot reacts on the touchline during Liverpool's Champions League second leg against Paris Saint-Germain.

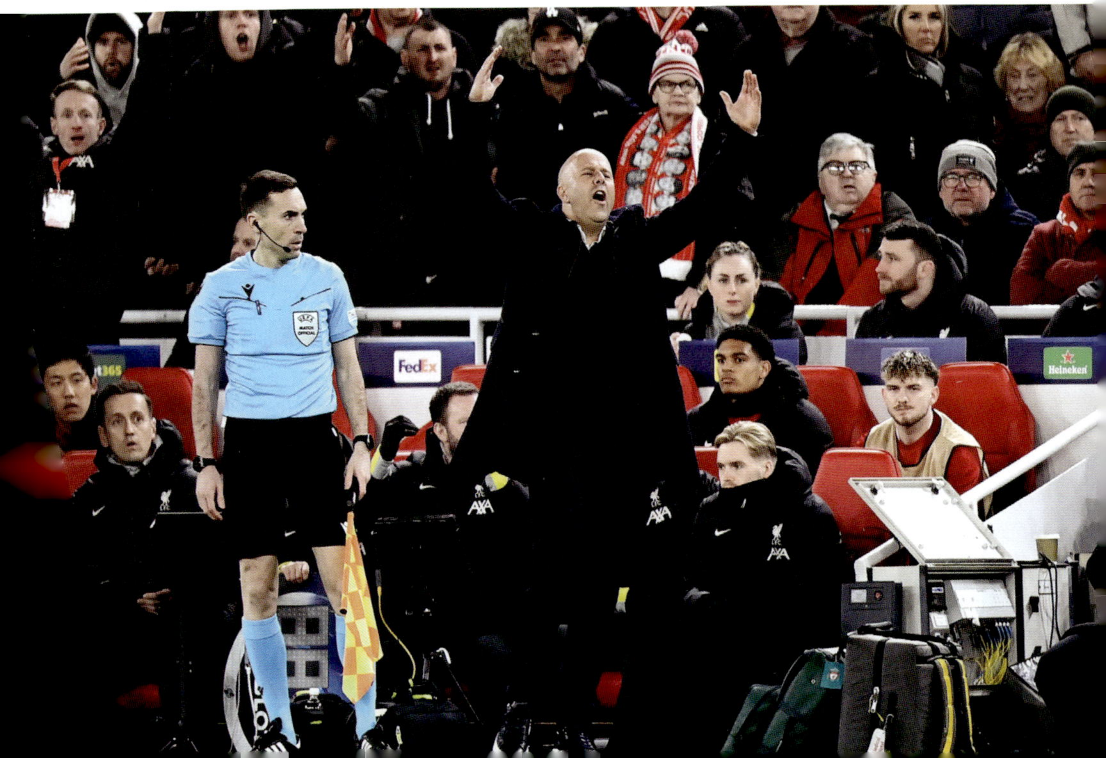

Overseeing training at the AXA Training Centre in Kirkby.

Slot celebrates Liverpool's Premier League victory after the decisive win over Tottenham at Anfield.

Liverpool seal the Premier League title as players and staff unite in triumph.

Jubilant Liverpool coach and players lift the Premier League trophy.

Ueda was brought in as a replacement for the departing Danilo, and Ondřej Lingr and Yankuba Minteh came on loan. After weeks of negotiations with Dinamo Zagreb, Croatian winger Luka Ivanušec completed a transfer in the last week before the window closed. Slot commented, 'I've said it a hundred times and I'll repeat it again if asked: Feyenoord is currently only able to sign players who can become good after they've been with us for a longer period. Mats Wieffer, Quinten Timber, Dávid Hancko, Quilindschy Hartman, Calvin Stengs and Santiago Giménez are important players, but none of them were so from day one. Players need three or four months to get used to the way we train and work. That's the consequence of our salary structure. We can't afford to sign a ready-made player who will immediately strengthen us. Last summer, Georginio Wijnaldum trained with us for a while to keep his fitness up. Then you can see ready-made top quality straight away. Not that we could sign him: he went to Saudi Arabia.'

For the second consecutive season, Feyenoord defeated Ajax on a visit to Amsterdam. Santiago Giménez scored twice in the opening 18 minutes and Igor Paixão put the visitors 3–0 ahead after 37 minutes. A sign on the big screen at the Johan Cruyff Arena reminded spectators that the 'lighting of fireworks is prohibited', but the message fell on deaf ears. De Klassieker was abandoned in the 56th minute, after home fans threw flares onto the field. There were riots afterwards around the stadium, with hooligans forcing their way into the main entrance and confronting the police and mobile units in a manner not seen in Amsterdam for a long time. Feyenoord's players and staff had to stay in their dressing room until it was safe to leave. There were no Feyenoord fans at the match. Beleaguered Ajax coach Maurice Steijn said, 'It is a jet-black day and this [fan response] makes it even worse.' Feyenoord boss Slot said, 'It is especially annoying that this match ends like this. The chance for something very beautiful is taken away from us. We understand the decision that has been taken, but we do not feel a sense of victory.' The game was resumed three days later behind closed doors. Giménez completed a hat-trick to wrap up a 4–0 win. With Ajax adrift in the league, Steijn was sacked soon after.

During the February outing against Almere City, Arne Slot was at home in bed with whooping cough. He watched the match on television and kept in constant telephone contact with assistant Sipke Hulshoff, who was in the dugout in Almere. With the score tied at 0–0 for a long time, Slot introduced Yankuba Minteh as a 'long-distance substitute'. Ten minutes after the Gambian got on the pitch, he made it 1–0, before scoring the second towards the end of the game.

On 7 April 2024, Ajax visited De Kuip. It would be a memorable afternoon because Feyenoord defeated the team of new coach John van 't Schip by a historic scoreline – 6–0. Feyenoord's superiority was spectacular. Almost all of the goals came from high turnovers – winning the ball within 40 metres of the opposition's goal. More could have followed. The reigning champions recorded 30 shots to Ajax's one as they scored three goals in each half to earn a famous win. Igor Paixão and Yankuba Minteh got a brace each for the home side to go with goals for Dávid Hancko and Quinten Timber. The six-goal success was a record margin of victory for Feyenoord against their biggest rivals – topping a 9–4 win in 1964 and a 6–1 win in 1960. The victory created a jubilant mood in the port city. Feyenoord had beaten their Amsterdam rivals by a 10–0 aggregate league victory. Commentators speculated that the chance that another Feyenoord coach would be able to improve on this accomplishment would be small. The win consolidated second place in the table for Feyenoord, with 69 points from 29 games, nine points behind leaders PSV Eindhoven. Ajax were in sixth place with 45 points.

In the 2023–24 Champions League, Feyenoord were drawn in a group with Atlético Madrid, Celtic and, again, Lazio. They won the home games against Celtic and Lazio but, despite showing good form and impressing the media with their play, they failed to pick up a single point in either of the matches against Atlético. Arne Slot had his own take on the developments. 'For the first time in my career as a coach, I have lost twice in a row this season, against Atlético Madrid and PSV. Not nice, you never get used to it, but I can handle it, losing. If I know that I have done everything I could beforehand, if I know that we as a staff have prepared the players well, it still can happen. The disappointment, if you can call it that, is more that our good play, which was not rewarded, is insufficiently recognised because of this. Football is discussed as black and white and mainly focused on results. I sometimes have a hard time with that. I still believe that we have made quite an impact in the Champions League. The proof is the attention given to our players, who have become more valuable, but also in the way the foreign media spoke and wrote about us. I think that at Champions League level that kind of treatment was limited to Ajax for years.'

Feyenoord ended the group stage in third place and qualified for the knockout round of the 2023–24 Europa League, where they again faced AS Roma. A few weeks after Mourinho was fired, Arne Slot's team once again failed to beat their old nemesis. The home game ended in a 1–1 draw. At the return match in the Stadio Olimpico, more than 67,000 supporters were on hand to cheer on new manager Daniele De Rossi's team. Because away fans were not welcome in Rome, the club was able to fill the away section with their own *Romanisti*. According to the calculations of *Corriere dello Sport*, this meant space for an additional 5,000 supporters. The extra tickets were sold out in no time. 'It will be a thrilling European evening, with emotions that Roma has already experienced in recent years,' the newspaper predicted.

Despite the overwhelming Italian support, Feyenoord managed to eke out another 1–1 draw after goals from Feyenoord forward Santiago Giménez and Roma veteran Lorenzo Pellegrini in the first 15 minutes. After extra time, the score was still tied. The penalty shootout ended 4–2 in Roma's favour. In the post-match news conference, Arne Slot said, 'I don't like losing. I don't like being eliminated, and even less by the same club because then a feeling of hurt pride comes into play. Playing 1–1 away at AS Roma is a great result. I think we were well organised again. If you look at why we were eliminated, it has a lot to do with [the first leg] last week. Unfortunately, due to the circumstances, we couldn't start with our best eleven. We could and should have made the difference then. If you can survive in Rome, you must be at a certain level, and then you can go far in the Europa League. With our way of playing, we can keep pace with a club like AS Roma. But it's just not enough every time.' The Giallorossi had eliminated Feyenoord from Europe three times in as many seasons.

• • •

Wembley, the home of the England national team, was built in 1923 and was used until 2000, before the 'new Wembley' was opened in 2007. The 1923 FA Cup final was the inaugural match in the original stadium. The official number of people in attendance, those who paid for a ticket, was 126,047, but unofficial estimates went as high as 150,000. The tradition has continued since then. In England, cup trophies are lifted at Wembley; with 90,000 seats, it's Europe's second-largest sports stadium after Barcelona's Camp Nou. All FA Cup and the EFL (Carabao) Cup finals are played at the ground. By contrast, the Netherlands do not have a designated national stadium for football, and the Dutch national football team plays primarily at the Johan Cruyff Arena in Amsterdam. Today, holding the KNVB Cup final in Rotterdam's De Kuip has become a celebrated ritual. A generation ago, the cup tournament was an afterthought in Dutch football culture. Many players turned up their noses at it and the football association did little to give the tournament any prestige. The final match of the tournament often changed venues, mainly for commercial reasons.

In the late 1980s, the then KNVB director Jan Huijbregts saw the light. 'I was at the Cup Final at Wembley last week. That's a completely different event. For some reason we haven't managed to make the cup tournament a tradition.' Huijbregts took action and in 1989 submitted a request to then mayor Bram Peper of Rotterdam to make De Kuip, at that time already a leading stadium and often host of the cup tournament, the permanent location of the cup final. Peper agreed in early 1990 and a tradition was born. There are some critics of the custom who suggest that Feyenoord have a continuous home advantage at cup finals. They point to the fact that the winning percentage of the Rotterdam team has been marginally higher since 1989 (seven victories in nine finals) than that of the traditional competitors PSV (seven out of eleven) and Ajax (nine out of thirteen). The football association does not agree. The KNVB insists that the cup finalists are always treated equally. 'For example, clubs are always allowed to bring the same number of supporters and all other conditions are the same for the two teams. Any home advantage of Feyenoord in the final is thus ruled out as much as possible.'

After losing four cup finals, the last one in 2000, NEC Nijmegen travelled to De Kuip determined to write history on 21 April 2024.

The 17,500 NEC fans in 160 buses and countless cars caused some traffic delays on the highway to Rotterdam. Feyenoord fans were well represented at home. The enormous green and white banner with the text 'Destroyer of Dreams' clearly showed their intentions. In his first cup final as head coach, Arne Slot led Feyenoord to victory in a tumultuous conclusion of the KNVB Cup tournament. He had seen his players put in better performances during the season; this time it was mentality that made the difference. After fireworks caused a fire in a channel behind the goal and a long interruption due to poor visibility as a result of smoke, Igor Paixão scored the winning goal in the second half. Gambian winger Yankuba Minteh's red card 20 minutes before the end – two yellows within a minute – meant it was a battle of survival inspired by Timon Wellenreuther, Thomas Beelen, Lutsharel Geertruida, Dávid Hancko and substitute Gernot Trauner.

After the previous season's national championship, it was Slot's second major prize with the Rotterdam team. 'It was a strange afternoon. The first half started slowly, certainly from our perspective. In the second half we got out well. Of course, I'm happy with this prize. It's not the joy of a title, nothing can compare to that. But it is a crowning achievement in a season in which we were very difficult to beat. In 2024 we haven't been beaten yet and we've continued to develop. It's not a top or great season. Then we should have retained the title. That would have been possible if PSV hadn't been so ridiculously good.' Feyenoord's 2.4 points average per game was identical to their title-winning campaign, reflecting their consistency over a long period. In Peter Bosz's PSV, they simply were up against the most prolific chance creators across Europe's top seven leagues.

No football historian seems to know exactly what prompted the shape of the KNVB Cup winners' trophy. That mattered little to the players of Feyenoord, and the on-field celebrations revealed how happy the players and staff were with the Pine Cone. They proudly held it up at the victory celebrations on the Binnenrotte in Rotterdam. Of course, it was not the grand occasion as when Feyenoord were crowned league champions on the Coolsingel, but there was happiness all around. Coming in second in the league was disappointing, but the cup victory was a considerable comfort. And never before in its history had Feyenoord managed to qualify for the Champions League two years in a row without preliminary rounds.

Slot reflected, 'Yes, I could very well become a kind of Arsène Wenger at Feyenoord, although you don't see that much these days. Diego Simeone is an exception to the rule. If you walk into the stadium in Madrid, you see a bust of him. This year is the first time that I have lost two games in a row, Atlético Madrid and PSV. That is still quite a lot of wins, but I heard that fan sentiment was starting to change a bit. You can also consider that a compliment; it is a result of what we have achieved together here at Feyenoord in recent years. Only when you, as a coach, really get the feeling that people are starting to like it less should you draw your conclusions. I don't think that point has been reached yet. I am still very happy at Feyenoord and still get satisfaction from the challenges we meet here and developing the players and the team. After every home game, when I'm in the coach's office and hear the supporters happily walking down the stairs because they have been entertained again, I get that confirmation.'

Although Slot was very successful as Feyenoord manager, his activities at the club were not nearly as prolonged as those of his famous French colleague at Arsenal. In late April it was widely reported that negotiations with Liverpool were at an advanced stage. Slot said on Feyenoord's website, 'It is certainly not an easy decision to close the door behind you at a club where you have experienced so many wonderful moments and worked successfully with so many wonderful people. But as a sportsman, an opportunity to become a head coach in the Premier League, at one of the biggest clubs in the world, is difficult to ignore.' Keen to avoid creating any unwanted distractions before Feyenoord's final against NEC, Liverpool had waited until after that victory before opening talks with the Dutch club a few days later. Slot's old contract stipulated that he could have been released for a fixed sum of €5 million in the summer of 2024. But in his new contract, running until 2026, that clause had been removed. Chief executive Dennis te Kloese proved to be a tough negotiator, resulting in a compensation package of around €11 million (£9.4 million). An official announcement was delayed until after the end of the season, allowing both Slot and Klopp to first say their goodbyes to the home fans. On 20 May, the transfer was officially confirmed: Arne Slot would be the new head coach of Liverpool FC.

In his 100th Eredivisie match, Slot oversaw the meeting of Feyenoord with PEC Zwolle, the club where he had spent two phases of his playing career. After 31½ matches that season, Feyenoord had already improved on the number of goals scored during their championship year – 81. After goals by Ayase Ueda and Luka Ivanušec, that total was surpassed. The crowd seemed to have made peace with the idea that Feyenoord had been outperformed by PSV. Slot was the second-best performing coach in the club's history. With an average of 2.28 points per game, only legend Ernst Happel had done better. It was Slot's last match in a sold-out Kuip. He would manage Feyenoord for two more games, one of which would be in De Kuip against Excelsior on the final day of the competition, when a number of sections of the stadium would be closed due to a disciplinary sanction, so the Zwolle game was used as the best moment for a heartfelt farewell. The last 15 minutes of the match were completely dominated by the attention lavished on Slot. When Santiago Giménez scored to make it 5–0, the entire Kuip got to its feet and applauded the extremely popular manager. The crowd serenaded Slot by singing en masse, 'Ga staan voor Arne Slot' and 'Arne bedankt' – 'Get Up for Arne Slot' and 'Thanks, Arne'. In a nod to Slot's future club, 'You'll Never Walk Alone', the Liverpool anthem, was also played.

Slot felt a little uneasy during the extensive tribute. 'When they start singing something like that for the fourth, fifth or sixth time, you think "hmm". You are aware that everyone is looking at you at that moment. Sometimes it is uncomfortable when you are not on the field yourself. When you play football, you are used to it.' Slot joined in the post-match celebrations more emphatically than usual. He was pushed onto the field by his players. 'I have never done that in the past three years and it is not really my style. From the first to the last day – which is still to come – I felt the appreciation of the fans. It was massive, impressive. They chanted my name and that is a reward for the last three years. It was very special. I could play it down, but that would not do justice to the feelings I had. It was really very special. That only Sipke Hulshoff and I were being sung to is too much of an honour. We worked very hard on everything with many other people. That enabled us to serve up three years of great matches to the fans. As head coach, you are in the limelight when things are going really well, and when things are going really badly, they shout at you to get lost. I'm very happy that Sipke has now also received appreciation, but there are another 10, 15 staff people.'

Arne Slot was in the dugout for the very last time as Feyenoord coach in the match against Excelsior, a 4–0 win. 'Beautiful. I think the banner turned out well. Sometimes it seems my head is just too big, but I think this is about right. I also got a farewell from the players, who said nice things and showed a video. I think the most enjoyable thing is when they say something about me as a person. Of course I like to hear that they learned something from me, but if something on the human plane follows afterward, I think that's the best thing. I am incredibly grateful for the memories I made at this club. I want to thank my wife and children, as well as the great staff, including the management. I owe the players the most gratitude because they gave everything for the club. We felt the support from the fans from day one. Thank you very much, and much success.'

Arne Slot changed Feyenoord. Under him, hope made way for expectation among the supporters. Positive transfer results every season became the rule rather than the exception. Where the club never really stood for a style of play, Slot gave Feyenoord a new identity: attacking, energetic and attractive. They reached Champions League football twice in a row, beat Ajax for the first time since 2005 and did so twice in one season. After almost 150 matches, a Conference League final, a national title, a KNVB Cup and more than €120 million in transfer income, Feyenoord finished second in the Eredivisie behind PSV, with 84 points. In three full seasons as Feyenoord manager, Slot never lost consecutive league games. He won back-to-back Dutch 'coach of the year' awards. He was treated as a demi-god in Rotterdam.

Slot was honoured by Feyenoord fans in his final match in charge with a banner that read 'Walk on, walk on', a reference to Liverpool's famous anthem. Almost simultaneously, in another port city 500km to the west, Jürgen Klopp encouraged the crowd to chant his successor's name: to the tune of Opus's 'Live is Life' – one of the songs the Anfield crowd had adapted for the German – 'Arne Slot' resounded across the stands.

11

THE SLOT WAY

'Being able to convince players is what sets one coach apart from another.'
ARNE SLOT

It sometimes seems the Dutch feel they invented football, perhaps because they are quite good at it. They take considerable pride in the innovations of the legendary Johan Cruyff and the invention of Total Football by FIFA Coach of the Century Rinus Michels. They are inclined to believe that their way is the only way because these ideas and methods laid the foundations for the modern game. The resulting tunnel vision can be an obstacle to necessary adaptation and renewal. In the fairly recent past, it was not uncommon to hear commentators in the Netherlands complain about the 'muscular and brainless' football played in the United Kingdom. In this view, the English game was a form of rugby: punt the ball to the front and have the team run full throttle into the opponent's half. Although a number of Dutch players have made good use of the opportunity to shine in England, history has shown that Dutch managers have found it difficult to shape teams there in their likeness. Furthermore, although many speak decent English, that does not mean they are great communicators.

In the Netherlands there has been a particular way of playing the game for decades, with the 4–3–3 formation adhered to almost as an article of faith. In training there is particular focus on positional play, with coaches frequently interrupting sessions to make corrections. Louis van Gaal gained notoriety for moving his players around the pitch like pawns on a chess board. As a creative player, Robin van Persie felt it was like a footballing straitjacket. Central defender Ramon Leeuwin played under Erik ten Hag at Utrecht and Arne Slot at AZ. 'We had to get used to Erik in the beginning. His way of training was very tactical and training was often stopped – sometimes you felt like a PlayStation figure.'

In the Netherlands, both coaches and players openly react to things when they are not pleased. Straightforwardness is so intrinsically Dutch that there's even a word for it, *bespreekbaarheid*: 'speakability'. The assumption is that everything can and should be talked about. There is the sense that people have the right to say whatever they want and be as direct as they want. If other people don't like it, they are at fault for getting offended. Mention this to a Dutchman and he is likely to suggest that the way people interact in the Netherlands – on and off the pitch – is *gewoon*, 'normal'. In an interview with the *Athletic*, former Liverpool winger Ryan Babel referenced the 'Dutch ego' and an attitude of 'we are not going to adapt, we always try to play our way. If you go to a completely different league, culture, different set of rules then, yeah, sometimes you need to adapt and be realistic. And the step from the Dutch Eredivisie to the Premier League is simply very big. Coaches need to adapt to the Premier League. The Premier League won't adapt to a foreign coach.' Dutch managers also have had difficulty getting to grips with a football culture where one loss is a setback, two a worry and three a full-blown crisis.

Spanish, Italian, French, Portuguese and German coaches have managed Premier League clubs and a representative of each nation has either won a league title or a Champions League crown. Ten Dutchmen, however, have failed to achieve the same feat. Former manager Martin Jol did quite well in England, managing 259 Premier League games with Tottenham and Fulham. Jol said, 'You have to know the culture in England and that has been a problem for Dutch coaches. My big advantage was that I played in England [for Coventry City and West Brom] so I knew the dressing room, knew the mentality and knew the situation when you lose or win games.' Ruud Gullit won the FA Cup in 1997, Chelsea's first trophy in 26 years, but he misjudged his next job at Newcastle United by placing club icon Alan Shearer on the bench. The words 'arrogant' and 'blunt' appeared in player assessments once he was booted out of St James' Park. Guus Hiddink featured in two caretaker stints at Chelsea, three months in the 2008–09 season and five months in 2015–16, steadying the ship after the respective dismissals of Brazilian Luiz Felipe Scolari and Portuguese José Mourinho. Current Netherlands national team coach Ronald Koeman was very effective at Southampton, finishing in seventh and sixth place in successive seasons. He became a footnote after he moved to Everton and was fired two months into his second season. Dick Advocaat lasted half a year at Sunderland. At the time of his resignation, Sunderland were in 19th place in the relegation zone. He finished with a record of four wins, six draws and nine losses. Even Louis van Gaal, for all his managerial skill and tactical acumen, went down rather ingloriously at Manchester United, with some commentators suggesting that his press conferences were more entertaining than his football.

Frank de Boer won four successive Eredivisie titles with Ajax, the first manager ever to achieve this in the Dutch league, but he was sacked just 77 days into a three-year contract with Crystal Palace.

Formerly a great player, he had high ideals but little awareness of any need to adjust to his environment. Then there was René Meulensteen, who spent 13 years at Manchester United, nearly half of which were devoted to supporting Alex Ferguson's first-team training. Meulensteen's Fulham stint was over in a blur of 13 league games. The experience of Erik ten Hag at United was the most recent in this series of disappointing showings. While he was spectacularly successful at Ajax, his accomplishments in Manchester were modest: EFL and FA Cup victories in two consecutive seasons. After a string of poor results, not entirely his fault, he was dismissed at the end of October 2024. Bert van Marwijk, the former Netherlands manager, wrote in *De Telegraaf,* 'For Dutch coaches, it could be very important that Slot becomes immediately successful. There is a discussion about the influence of Dutch coaches because they have not done well, and there are more German and other foreign coaches running around in England for a reason.'

Jan Everse, Arne Slot's mentor at PEC Zwolle, acknowledged that Dutch coaches have a stubborn streak: the more they are told they can't do something, the more they try to prove it is possible. At the same time, he called Slot a 'diplomat', a title one does not readily associate with Gullit, Koeman or Van Gaal. Slot has the potential to buck an unfortunate trend of Dutch managerial failure in England. He said, 'I've been watching football for a long time and I think this was an era where everyone looked at the Barcelona of Xavi, Iniesta and Messi and the rivalry that was there with Real Madrid and Cristiano Ronaldo. I think when that ended, the new rivalry in European football was because of Jürgen Klopp and Pep Guardiola. I think it was a fantastic era for anyone who loves football to watch the games. They both brought out the best in each other. Klopp did a great job with Liverpool.' In *Wij Gaan Winnen* ('We're Going to Win') – an analysis of Feyenoord's 2022–23 championship year by Bart Vlietstra and Willem Vissers – Arne Slot says:

> There are two people who have genuinely enriched football during the last decade and who have never disappointed me: Messi and Pep Guardiola. Messi can do anything. Guardiola's teams always play good, dominant, and well-thought-out football. It's outrageous how he manages to accomplish that wherever he goes, each time with different players. An 18-year-old back joins in passing the ball as if it's nothing. Of course, he has good players, but they really aren't much better than those of Real Madrid or Juventus. Very close behind is Jürgen Klopp. Manchester City–Liverpool is the ultimate in viewing pleasure.

It is widely known that Arne Slot is a disciple of Pep Guardiola. 'If I were to ask you who won the Champions League five years ago, you wouldn't know the answer. But when I talk about Pep Guardiola's FC Barcelona, you know exactly what I am talking about. Guardiola gives me the ultimate pleasure in football. I certainly don't want to compare myself to Pep, but he is a control freak, just like me. I watched Guardiola going on a rampage against the referee. I am also accused of doing that occasionally. I sometimes wonder: Why? Why did he react as if he had been bitten by a snake to a refereeing mistake? I think it has to do with perfectionism. When I look at myself, I try to win a match the week before it is played, by conveying the tactics as perfectly as possible in the training and preliminary discussions. That is why the frustration is great when a referee makes a seemingly small mistake to your disadvantage. You know that it can have an incredible impact and can simply undo all the work you have done. Putting down the ball ten metres further, getting a silly ball on a player's arm and conceding a penalty. That is extremely frustrating.'

'I'm curious who told you we play 4–2–3–1,' Slot said at his unveiling in July, making clear that assumptions about his preferred formation were wrong. 'Maybe that one should go to get his licence or analysis a bit better.' There are parallels with Pep Guardiola and Roberto De Zerbi's approach, particularly in build-up. Defenders are encouraged to play short passes to midfielders, who then find the space out wide for the full-backs or wingers. Guardiola and De Zerbi are among the managers he is most inspired by, but Slot is also known to also admire Jürgen Klopp, Mikel Arteta, Marcelo Bielsa, Jorge Sampaoli and Luciano Spalletti. He has also shared ideas with Klopp's assistant coach at Liverpool and fellow Dutchman Pep Lijnders. Slot visited Lijnders' home when he was starting as a youth coach a decade earlier, and they exchanged ideas on how the game should be played for hours. Lijnders considers Slot the best Dutch coach of the new generation: someone who is tactically smart and an innovator, with a clear playing style, and the personality needed to effectively manage a team.

Guardiola's style is a combination of positional play ideas, pioneered by Johan Cruyff, and the pressing, counter-pressing and counter-attacking football of Germany and England. The combination translates to the three phases of play – in possession, out of possession and transition – which is the best way to understand Slot's own vision of playing. Referring to his role model, Slot said, 'Guardiola disproves the idea that there are no more systems. He plays 4–3–3, which in reality turns into 3–2–4–1: three in the build-up, two controllers for the defence, two on the inside, wingers on the outside and a deep striker. He wants those positions to be covered at all times, and I see that also when I look at Spalletti's Napoli. Spalletti is right with his statement about having the courage to do what you have to do as a team. Suppose we can hardly get through the deep defence of our opponent and then they do put high pressure a few times. Those are precisely the moments, especially for top clubs, when you can finally play in space. That's what the long ball is meant for in my view: to let your attackers attack in larger spaces. They don't get that chance that often because they normally play against teams that drop back en masse.'

Half-spaces are the vertical strips on the pitch between the centre and the wide areas/wings. The five strips are of a similar size. A player who is on the ball in the centre should be able to reach all the strips within the range of his passing ability. The half-spaces are close by and both wings are easily reachable. He has several options in terms of range: a large part of the playing field is directly accessible with one pass. Google Earth showed that Guardiola, during his time as coach of Bayern Munich, marked the training field with chalk lines in such a way that the half-spaces became visible. These lines divide the field in the left wing, left half-space, central axis, right half-space and right wing. The extra lines on the field are a form of communication; they subconsciously increase the players' orientation. This kind of spatial awareness is important for players on a Guardiola or a Slot team. In Slot's football vision, there is no lateral division of the 'opponent's half' and 'own half', but only a vertical distinction between 'the ball in the axis', the centre of the pitch, and 'the ball on the side', the wide areas. Due to the ineffectiveness of classic wing play, Slot strives for combinations through the centre. Like Guardiola, he is committed to an attacking formation with only one player per flank. At Ajax, Ryan Gravenberch always went to the left to pick up the ball. At Liverpool, in nine out of ten cases it is in the centre. Slot understands that most managers, like him, want to play through the centre. That is why Liverpool under Slot sometimes offer opponents an apparent option to escape the pressure through the middle. In reality, it is a trap to win the ball in an attractive position.

Apart from Guardiola, Slot believes there are few people who can teach him a lot about football. 'Not about my way of playing attacking, attractive football. That style of play is more suited to a team at the top of the table than to a club at the bottom. I don't want to make any concessions on the way we play, unless someone can convince me, but that doesn't happen often. It rarely happens that someone comes up with an idea that I haven't already thought of myself . . . I often discuss this topic with the lads. I ask them the question: How did we become successful and how can we continue to be successful? And also: Why do other teams drop points and we don't? I am an advocate of regular change, not so much in personnel, but in your tactics. Pep again is an example. He always comes up with a new trick. Sometimes a full-back on the inside, then building up this way or that way. I also believe that you have to trigger players regularly with something new. The basic idea in terms of behaviour and playing style always remains the same. But then we adapt the cooperation between the full-back and the winger, and a few weeks later we fill in another position differently.'

Slot has his own peculiar jargon. He urges his players to 'squeeze' immediately after losing possession. The intention to regain possession is the most important thing after the transition. Slot calls this 'chasing through the ball'. He means pushing for the extra metre when applying pressure. Do you chase an opponent at full speed to retake the ball or do you slow down a bit, giving the opponent space to escape? In his coaching sessions, Slot insists his players do the former. 'I try to show players that if one person doesn't partici-pate for a moment, the whole field is open. But if you are alert, you make it easy for everyone.' He wants them to profit from an *overtal*, 'surplus number'. The central zone between the midfield and the opponent's defence is called the 'hotzone' by Slot, for lack of a better term. According to his explanation, many successful attacks originate in this area, which is why he attaches a lot of importance to it. Slot always tries to position at least three players from his team in this space, so that his team have a numerical advantage. From the hotzone, the aim is to get into the 'scoring zone'. That is the section in and around the penalty area from where most goals are scored. Everything happens at sprint speed. This applies to pressing, but also to 'closing back', as Slot calls the return to the defensive shape in your own half. Then the team defends purely in the zone, with extremely small spaces between players, waiting for a good opportunity to develop forward pressure again.

Players initially respond with bemusement to these idiosyncratic instructions, but according to Slot, 'it's not higher math', and sooner or later the penny drops. But it does take some getting used to. During Slot's time at Feyenoord, a drone perpetually hovered over the training ground to film every aspect of the training. The coaching staff scrutinised the images and made a selection of the most useful ones to dish out to the players. Slot's sessions are intensive and long, and he seeks the limits of his players' physical ability. 'The difficulty lies in constantly carrying out your tasks with the highest intensity. It is always about outnumbering the opponent. When you have the ball, you want to create a surplus situation and get it out quickly. If you don't have it, you have to make sure you don't get left behind. And if that does happen, you have to sprint back like crazy to eliminate the opponent's surplus. That's why you always have to move with the ball to be able to create a surplus everywhere on the field.'

Slot told everyone about the book *Intensity* by Pepijn Lijnders, calling it 'the best football book I ever read'. This look behind the scenes at Liverpool was another incentive to stay with the proactive way of playing. At Feyenoord, Slot asked his players to press all the time. It seemed exhausting but, after a few weeks, it became second nature. 'If you apply well-organised pressure, an opponent may make mistakes. Losing the ball often results in an opportunity for us. I hope that I let my teams play so dynamically that we are difficult for opponents to analyse.'

He believes that a certain style of play is becoming increasingly common to all the best teams. 'I greatly appreciate the intensity with which Jürgen Klopp allows his teams to play, often with the same players for years. But you would be doing them a disservice by saying they base their way solely on energy and pressing. I don't think City plays with much less energy and that Liverpool is simply on top of the ball. What you like is personal to everyone. I find it striking to note that there is a similarity between the teams that are at the top in Europe. I want to play the way I think a lot of managers in football want to play at the moment. I think most of them want to have the ball more than the opposition. And if you want to do that, you have to press the other team high and you have to have a clear idea when you have the ball. You see that a lot in modern football. I think a few years ago it was a bit more balanced – some managers liked to defend and some liked to attack. But now you see, especially at the top clubs in every country, that they prefer the style of play where their team has the ball a lot.'

Carteret Analytics provides detailed manager assessments to Premier League, EFL, Bundesliga and MLS clubs. They assessed Slot and compared his style of football to that of Klopp's, using quantitative metrics indicating strengths and weaknesses. 'Slot has similarly high levels of possession, but the build and transition through the phases – from defence to attack – is much slower.' Where Slot also differs from Klopp is in how heavily his team commits to the press when out of possession. Klopp's Liverpool used their full-backs to move in aggressively on their opponents, which allowed for more attacking players infield to burst forward, should they win the ball. Slot's press is more restrained. His teams play with a 4–4–2 without possession, which means the responsibility to move forward lies with the midfielders. Slot's shape is more structured and guarded and is designed to limit the risk of opponents playing through the press – a problem Liverpool encountered more regularly under Klopp.

All training ground work is related to the attacking style of play. There is always pace and energy in the exercises. 'I hope that players will later say that they just enjoyed training,' Slot says. Still, he plays a 'run-like-hell game' of six against six with goalkeepers to develop fitness, on a field that reaches from one penalty area to the other. At the same time there is a recognition of the risks involved with such an intense style of training. Slot works closely with his data and fitness teams: when they tell him a player's numbers are dropping or they are in the 'red zone', he will ease off. The demanding attention to detail is a constant theme. Slot works hard on the mental side of the sport. He convinced his Feyenoord players that the more games they played, the stronger they would become.

In meetings, he relays this vision to the players and stresses that, by being fitter than their opponents and outworking them, his team can win even if their quality drops. To build such physical robustness, pre-season preparation and conditioning throughout the season are very important to Slot. One of his core beliefs is that players should never stand still on the pitch, that they should always be on the move. Leigh Egger, one of Feyenoord's performance leads, said, 'The training sessions are constantly changing. They hit the sweet spot of overload, tactics and physical demand. It makes our job in performance easier, because the players really want to train all the time. You see it also with the substitutes, who may have every right to be disappointed at not playing, but our training availability is so high because the sessions are stimulating and really fun from a footballing point of view.'

Bryan Linssen, the former Feyenoord striker, remembers how Slot would show his players game compilations of several attack-minded teams in Europe, with the majority of the clips coming from the Etihad Stadium.

I remember him showing things from Napoli as well, but it was especially clips from Guardiola, like how they played and how they pressed. I remember one particular clip of Raheem Sterling in the Champions League final between Manchester City and Chelsea of 2021. You see him sprinting back 70 metres to make a defensive action, which prevented a goal. It showed us that as a forward, football is not only about attacking and that the star players also track back 70 metres to help the team, before they go up the field again to make an attacking move. Slot showed us those things to illustrate what he wanted to achieve with us and how fit we had to be in order to achieve it. We went from a pretty defensive playing style to an offensive one under Slot, which was about taking initiative throughout the whole match and pressing high everywhere on the pitch. We trained on that from day one. That meant the intensity automatically increased, which obviously required a certain fitness level.

Slot has developed an impressive football media library with a lot of documentation and images that are helpful to developing game insight. Visitors with some interest in football should anticipate that he will open up his laptop to share his latest discovery. An interview may last three or four hours. Slot believes in science. At Feyenoord, he became interested in maintaining his players' circadian rhythms. His performance experts suggested that players should adapt their lives to revolve around upcoming kick-off times. Slot changed the schedule, making sure that they trained at the same time they were playing the next night, enhancing their metabolism. If his team was due to play a game at 9pm on a Friday, then Slot and his staff would make clear to the players via a text message that they shouldn't be asleep at that hour on Thursday evening but should be active, to avoid their circadian rhythm making them flat on matchday.

According to Slot, tactics and practice methods are not unimportant, but they are not the central part of being a manager. 'How can you convince players and how do you approach them in such a way that they play to their strengths and keep doing that? In my opinion, that is the most important thing about being a coach. Coming up with game tactics is something that almost all managers can do these days. And connecting a few nice training ground practices to that is a matter of a moment in the current era, with a targeted internet search. Managers who submit reports on their football vision at the coaching courses almost always arrive at the same conclusions. We can write and think about game principles for hours, but I think that in the end it is a matter of how you manage your players. There is an image of me always moving magnets around on a board – a little to the left or right – because a player has to move a little more in that direction. But it's really a matter of: I may or may not substitute that player, but how will I deal with him tomorrow? What will I do with him? The way you deal with your players makes the difference.'

In *De VoetbalTrainer*, Slot explained that he gives his players considerable freedom within his preferred game method.

I never give my players fixed assignments, in the sense of: the striker moves to the near post, the winger to the far post, and the attacking midfielder comes on the penalty spot. All situations are different and players have to anticipate them. With rigid tasks you deprive players of their much-needed freedom. But they always have to be positioned in such a way that it can lead to a scoring opportunity from a cut-back. Of course, players have to look at each other. If all three arrive at the penalty spot, it takes just one opponent to guess their intention and all three are covered.

Arne Slot rationally and carefully considers his options and then makes a deliberate choice. He is not someone who forces his style on his team. He steadily convinces his players of the rightness of his views through information, illustration and education, or his so-called indoctrination. He believes that managerial control should not be exercised by imposing discipline from the top but through the power of reason and persuasion. 'I am very forceful in the way I play because that is my world, but I see myself as someone who does not impose himself on an organisation. In my experience, attitude can be regulated by the composition of the team, staff and the perspective you give players. Being able to convince players is what distinguishes one coach from another. My meticulous preparation is the signal to my players and staff members to also prepare well. I sometimes hear from colleagues that other trainers shout and swear at others. I have never done that. They must have the feeling with me: I have to give everything I have, because he does it too. But in harmony.'

It is important to be fully aware of players' sensibilities. 'Do you start a practice form with your substitutes instead of the first eleven? So that the substitutes will think: okay, so we are not the fifth wheel on the car. If you as the manager can ensure that everyone works together, that all players are willing to continue working hard and enjoy coming to the training sessions, then you have already achieved a great deal. I am not going to scrutinise every player a scout recommends. My time is better spent on working with the players I already have. I'm also not going to tell [the groundsman] which way the grass needs to be cut. We have many young, ambitious people who want to continuously improve things and should get the space to do so. They know a lot more about many things than I do. When I know I am good at something, I am not nervous, also during a team meeting. I always want to be able to clearly explain my choices to myself; for example, why someone is not lined up. To the players I also almost always do that. It is easy to be clear when you know exactly what you want. I always say: there is one person in the world who would make me a bit nervous if I had to talk about football and that is Pep Guardiola. Then I would be afraid that he knows even more about it than I do. Of course I won't say that I know more about football than all those other coaches, but I do know about my own way in which I want to play football. I'll never be nervous explaining that.'

Slot's greatest quality is his ability to communicate. He believes only 60 per cent is the idea itself and 40 per cent is how clearly it is explained. His ideas are successfully projected onto the pitch because his thoughts are clear and his words are carefully chosen. He never asks his players to do things they can't do. 'I don't have any illusions for a second that I can make players better individually. But the team can do more to make an individual come into his own.' Just before Slot's arrival at Feyenoord, the club hired Matt Wade as the club's head of sporting strategy. Wade said, 'Slot operates very democratically, but is always retaining control. He is a brilliant communicator, and consultative, but also clear at the same time. He is quite cautious, quite introverted, but very rule-based and principled, which means everyone knows where they stand. And he is not paranoid, which allows freedom for specialists to operate.'

Slot rolls up his sleeves at team talks to let his group know that he is about to start and begins his speeches in a somewhat softer voice to increase their level of concentration. He approaches his squad in a civilised and positive manner. He knows that handling players these days requires more tact than before and a different tone. He understands that he is working with a generation that is more easily convinced of itself and less resilient. It is no longer the hard school it used to be for young players. He looks with concern rather than bitterness towards the smartphone generation and demonstrates empathy and care. 'It's much more difficult nowadays to play football. Social media, being judged by everyone; it is more negative than it was in my day. And these guys now need to be so much fitter – really top athletes. Yes, a big chance to earn a lot of money, but the pressure is higher than it was 20 years ago.'

He continues, 'Times change, players change too. But I think that applies to society as a whole. Coaches from 20 years ago had it easier, although that also applies to police officers, teachers, mayors and so on. Everyone in a managerial position had it easier. Because people simply listened much better. I think we have gone a bit too far in giving freedom. I have noticed that life and therefore also football has become much more individualistic. In the past, you looked at the team; now individual bearing and performance pay off. I don't think that's so strange: one good year of playing well and you can become financially independent ... When I was still playing myself, the coach had an opinion about my game and when I came home, my father also had something to say. Now players have agents, mental coaches and three or four other guides who hang around a lad. They all want to see things that they think can help the player on his way to a transfer or something. All this sometimes complicates things quite a bit for a manager. It makes this profession much more than just moving magnets on the board. You have to keep an eye on a lot – for example, the hierarchy. What does it mean if I choose him? How does he react to that? I keep an eye on that. I am really not going to explain every decision, but as a coach you do have to know what is going on in your group. Mutual relationships are incredibly important. What do you have to do together with your assistants to turn the group into a good group? That is management and that is not easy.'

Bryan Linssen said, 'He will call you over to explain why he has made certain choices. He is very honest and that is what players appreciate. When he doesn't play you, he will still treat you the same. Some other managers are more like, "Okay, you're not playing this weekend, so you're not important for me now, I don't need to talk to you." Slot isn't like that. He treats everyone the same, regardless of whether they're playing or not. That's his human side and that's just nice. He is a very normal and social person with a good heart.'

Oussama Idrissi worked with Slot at AZ, and later at Feyenoord.

Everyone knows their place because he is transparent. To motivate the starting eleven is not so difficult but he is really good with players 12 to 25 in the squad. You have many different characters in a team and he always knows how to trigger the guys. He is up for a joke and brings a certain relaxation into the squad, but he can translate it into a performance-oriented mindset. Arne is a really nice person off the field, which was highlighted to me last season. On the day we played Ajax in the Dutch Cup semi-final, my wife was about to give birth. I was in doubt whether to be with her or stay with the team, but Arne convinced me to put family first and luckily I was on time for the birth of my child. In the end, I still played the match as well. I noticed how Arne also helped players who had off-field issues and managed that well, giving them the right amount of freedom. On the pitch, he knows when to give compliments, when to put an arm around a shoulder.

In an interview with *Feyenoord Magazine*, Lutsharel Geertruida explained why he doesn't appear in front of the camera. He has a stutter and indicated that he was not ready to give interviews on television. 'Appearing in front of a camera is still too early for me. I've had this since I was four years old. There are a few triggers that make me stutter: a camera, the pressure and unknown people. I mainly have it when the focus is on me. But with friends or family and in the dressing room, I have it less. And when I sing, I don't have it at all.' It was a speech coach who helped Geertruida improve his delivery of words, but Slot who gave him the guidance and confidence to become a vocal force in the Feyenoord team. He also turned him into a leading voice in the dressing room.

Midfielder Orkun Kökçü needed to physically adapt to increase his acceleration over the first few yards, even getting a gym installed at home. He would regularly receive text messages from Slot asking for updates on his progress. Kökçü and Slot developed a strong bond. During Feyenoord's championship year, the captain suffered from 'a small trauma', as he would later tell *de Volkskrant*. 'It was because of a recovery that I didn't quite hit the mark during Ramadan. It was a matter of a balance of energy that wasn't right. As a result, I couldn't fall asleep and that caused a lot of unrest.' At summer training camp in Austria, Kökçü went to Slot. 'I had to save myself from that trauma. The trainer immediately said, "Go ahead." I didn't wait for a plane and went on an eight-hour bus ride home.' Kökçü sought help from a behavioural coach and used EMDR therapy to overcome his insomnia. 'It was difficult. There was a lot on my mind. The trainer was one of the few who knew about it. He is more than a trainer; he understands exactly how to deal with people. That's why I had to cry when I hugged him after the championship match.'

Slot would also talk about that particular hug later. 'Football-wise, physically and mentally Kökçü was the leader. He always repaid my trust. On the field and in the dressing room, he was an example. That's why I said during that hug: "You deserve this so much."'

Team development is the magic word for Slot. 'For me, the most important quality of a coach is the ability to make [the players] believe in what we are doing. I think about that a lot more than about how we should play against the next opponent.' That does not mean that he does not pay attention who his team are playing against. Before every match, Slot and his staff carefully analyse the opponent. Where can gains be made? 'What are our own vulnerabilities and what are theirs? To a large extent, that is where the strength of your coaching staff shows. If you ensure that the analysis is completely correct, it will become easier to persuade the guys in subsequent team talks. If I then say to them, "We should just drive off such-and-such a player, because he is not strong in possession," and I also show a few fragments to back it up, they believe it. And if he then loses possession three or four times in a match as a result of us chasing him, it helps to gain confidence.'

He adds, 'One of the most important aspects, apart from football tactics, is that I put myself in the position of the opponent. If they have already lost a few games in a row, and we have just won a few games, then I know that they will train very hard that week to turn the tide in the match against us. Meanwhile, we are prone to underestimate them. At the beginning of the week, I say to my players, "Don't give away the advantage now that you are feeling good by training less hard than the upcoming opponent." I try to show my players through examples like this why hard work is so important. There are two rules for a good result. 1: Work harder than the opponent. Simply put: just fight more physically and block balls and crosses as much as you can. And point 2: Play good football. Then I show some images of great actions of my players in previous matches. That's enormously motivating.'

Slot often refers to his so-called 20 per cent rule. 'If you are not 20 per cent better than your opponent in matches, you may lose points. I want as many good football players as possible in the team and I want to make them work as hard as possible. I believe that when we work to perfect our habits every day, we have a better chance to cut out [our reliance on] luck. Our habits will decide what our future will look like. You can have good luck or bad, but this will decide what place in the table we reach. I believe that all the hours we invest will enable us to perform beyond our capacity. Michael Jordan said: the harder I worked, the more luck I had. That is why I was so happy that Messi still won the World Cup at 35 – because he deserved it so incredibly. [Dutch fitness coach] Raymond Verheijen has a nice theory that I also subscribe to. When he talks about assessing players, he talks about four stages: unconsciously incompetent, consciously incompetent, consciously competent and unconsciously competent. If you, as a team, can get through those first two stages quickly enough and you manage to make your players consciously competent, then things will get really interesting. At some point they don't need to think anymore.'

As a manager, Slot draws inspiration from other sports. 'Of course, not on a tactical level. But the way in which people deal with the mental aspect in some sports can help. I sometimes use it during team meetings. At Roland Garros we saw Novak Djokovic win a very difficult match. I think it is one of his qualities that, despite it not really being his day, he still finds a way to win. I think those are examples that you can use with players. But to be clear: we are mostly talking about football. I only use it when I think it is necessary.' Slot generously supplies players with stats and clips. However, he says that he only uses statistics when it suits him. 'If there are statistical data that do not support something I want, then I ask you to hide them for the time being.' The emphasis is always on how the information is communicated to the person. He will pull a player by the arm to give him some instructions and move him into a better position, which usually is closer to the opponents' goal because 'attacking' and 'exerting pressure' are essential to the Slot way.

Arne Slot is an educated man who is accustomed to conducting team meetings in English. He developed the habit at Feyenoord because of the collection of international players present. Even then there were language hurdles to be overcome because of the presence of 'Portuguese players who did not speak a word of English'. Slot explained a little of what it took to get Feyenoord to new levels. 'You build a team at your training complex, not by going karting or padel.

I think we only did that once this season. A football player wants two things. The first is working in a nice environment. You get that by putting together a good staff that gets along well with each other and has a nice interaction with a group of players. You get it by looking at what kind of characters you bring in, the type of person. And the second thing that players find important is that they can develop while enjoying the game. This is hidden in your practice forms. I know that Feyenoord players always feel like training.' Players love his subtle tactical tweaks, his attention to detail and the clarity of his instructions. They know exactly where they stand with him. He is a man who explains things – repeatedly if necessary – until the lesson is fully absorbed.

His teaching style extends to his communication with the media. The assembled Scottish football writers were surprised by the length and quality of Slot's press-conference answers when Feyenoord played Celtic in the Champions League. 'Nobody else does it like that,' was their verdict. Slot explained his rationale: 'It's the only time of the week I can tell my side of the story.' The Dutch Sports Press (NSP) selected Arne Slot as Sports Personality of 2023. He was praised in the NSP jury report for the time he takes to interact with the media, the clear way in which he communicates and his constructive attitude. According to the jury, he is a pleasant person to work with, willing to answer every question, and someone endowed with exceptional communication skills – qualities that contributed to his positive relationship with the media. He received the award during the annual NSP awards ceremony in The Hague. 'A great honour. I think it is important to get your message across well, and I am happy to hear that people appreciate that in me. Football is often very simple, but sometimes also complex. As a coach, knowing how to add the right nuance to the story is, in my opinion, an essential part of the job.'

Slot received further endorsement from unexpected quarters. Former Ajax manager and Dutch national team boss Louis van Gaal is no stranger to tense encounters with the press. 'I could have dealt with the media in a different way. I am generally very emotional and raise my voice. It would have been better if I had just responded calmly. Actually, just like Arne Slot does. Arne has all of it. I have a lot of admiration for that.'

In England, there is a certain appreciation for the 'gaffer', the manager 'who shows them who's boss'. Slot does not fit that image well. On the contrary, he is cheerful, friendly and modest. It is difficult to consider him a tough manager. He thinks that is not necessary. 'What you see is who I am. You can be calm, analyse well and, at the same time, be very clear. I certainly am and that is also reflected on the field. When people see a coach who shouts loudly and is angry, they think of him as hard. It's mainly about giving clarity to players. Every coach knows that players want that, but you have to do it.' He is not always quite as composed on the inside as he appears on the outside, however. 'The constant pursuit of perfection means that as a coach I can hardly enjoy games. I'm always concerned with the momentum of a match. How can we keep that to our advantage? Should I make a substitution? Is some small direction enough or a small adjustment? I always pay attention to the things we have agreed on. Are they still sharp? Will they continue to do the things that, for example, helped us to get the game off to a good start?'

Slot does not deviate from his vision but is constantly looking for ways to draw the maximum potential from players within that framework. He likes to play as much as possible with a fixed eleven. By creating consistency in his line-ups, he creates the conditions during the season to fine-tune the tactical details of his game plan. It mainly comes down to the coordination between the different lines and the execution of the team agreements for the duration of an entire match. As Slot says, 'Whoever maintains discipline the longest often has the best chance of winning. For me, mature football consists of doing your job as well as possible for the full 90 minutes. That often is the difference between achieving something or not.' Yet, flexibility is important. If the situation calls for it, Slot is prepared to make concessions. 'There are several teams playing with many systems. We have a team where you can see the changing system in the game. We play 4–3–3 and if the opponent is trying to pressure us in a certain way, then we need to have an answer to that. These differences can be quite small.'

One of Slot's targets is to confuse opposition analysts so they are unable to recognise a set formation or structure. 'I don't prefer a system. But when we don't have the ball, we have to be aggressive.' Lutsharel Geertruida serves as a good example of Slot's managerial versatility. Geertruida can play at right-back, in central defence or as a holding midfielder, and Slot used this flexibility to his team's advantage. He discovered how to best exploit Geertruida's skills by placing him in important positions all over the pitch. On several occasions, the 24-year-old performed different roles in the Feyenoord back line or defensive midfield within one game. Slot helped him progress from an academy graduate to a first-team player.

To quantify Feyenoord's improvement under Slot, it is worthwhile to consider FiveThirtyEight's Soccer Power Index, which calculates a team's attacking and defensive strength. Slot's arrival at the club coincided with a steady rise up the rankings. By the end of the 2022–23 season, they were on a score of 76.6, the 21st-highest in world football, a very good standing for an Eredivisie club. Perhaps more than these numbers, players' experiences tell the story. Gernot Trauner, Feyenoord's captain after Orkun Kökçü's departure, said, 'I came to Feyenoord as a 28-year-old, but learned more in a few months under Arne Slot than in all those years before. I sometimes think: where would I be now if I had met him earlier?'

12

SYMPHONY FOR THE COMMON MAN

'If Klopp is heavy metal football, then
Slot is classical music.'
CARTERET ANALYTICS

On 12 July 1974, Bill Shankly, the father of the modern Liverpool FC, announced his retirement and fans responded with stunned disbelief. Similar emotions washed over everyone allied with Liverpool when Jürgen Klopp announced, nearly half a century later, that he was leaving Anfield at the end of the season. When he signed his last contract extension in 2022 – a deal supposedly running until 2026 – he said he fully intended to see it out. On the field, 'Liverpool 2.0', as the manager had coined it, were flying after the summer rebuild. But in an announcement via the club's media channel on 26 January 2024, he revealed he would step down two years early. Just like with Shankly in 1974 and Kenny Dalglish in 1991, there had not been any hint of an impending retirement, but it became clear that the toils had taken their toll.

Shankly's replacement came from the inside: Bob Paisley, his assistant for 15 years, took charge and built on the Scottish manager's groundwork to turn Liverpool into England's most successful club during the 1970s and the early 1980s. The difficulty in moving on from a figure like Shankly or Klopp is finding a successor who brings in important innovations that propel the club further forward, without dismantling the valuable foundations their predecessor laid.

The Freedom of the City of Liverpool is an honorary title granted to people in recognition of their exceptional services to the Merseyside city. Only months apart in the mid-80s, Bob Paisley and all four members of The Beatles received the honour (posthumously in the case of John Lennon). In 1994, Nelson Mandela became the first foreign recipient. It is a measure of what Jürgen Klopp meant to the region that in 2022 he became the second. Under Klopp, Liverpool won the Premier League, Champions League, FA Cup, two EFL Cups, the FIFA Club World Cup and UEFA Super Cup in nine enthralling years. In a 25-minute interview with the club's media department, an emotional Klopp explained his reasons for leaving. 'I love absolutely everything about this club, I love everything about the city, I love everything about our supporters, I love the team, I love the staff. I love everything. But that I still take this decision shows you that I am convinced it is the one I have to take. It is that I am – how can I say it – running out of energy. I have no problem now, obviously, I knew already longer that I will have to announce it at one point, but I am absolutely fine now. But I know that I cannot do the job again and again and again and again. After the years we had together and after all the time we spent together and after all the things we went through together, the respect grew for you, the love grew for you, and the least I owe you is the truth – and that is the truth. It is not what I want to do. It is just what I think is 100 per cent right. That's it.'

A month before the season ended, Liverpool were the Premier League favourites. In the last eight Premier League games, losses against Crystal Palace and Everton, and draws with Manchester

United, West Ham and Aston Villa, undid Liverpool's title hopes. The defeat in the Merseyside derby was most notable. Klopp had lost just one of his 18 meetings with Everton before this one. The home fans relished putting their rivals to the sword on a memorable night. The chant of 'You lost the League at Goodison Park' resounded in the old stadium in the closing minutes as Everton held on to their two-goal advantage and Liverpool simply could not break through. The fairytale ending was not meant to be and the script had to be rewritten to a third-place finish and Carabao Cup victory.

This was not what was hoped for. Liverpool had last won their major trophies – the Premier League and Champions League – four years earlier. Most expressed the conviction that Klopp would leave a legacy to be proud of, rather than a new building project for his successor. Others were not quite as certain and were worried that all the backroom staff were going – assistants Pep Lijnders and Peter Krawietz, first-team development coach Vitor Matos, head of fitness and conditioning Andreas Kornmayer, and goalkeeping coach John Achterberg – at the same time. As one supporter commented, 'This has the echoes of Manchester United when Alex Ferguson went. Careful forward planning is essential if Liverpool are to maintain their high standards.'

While searching for Klopp's successor, Fenway Sports Group (FSG) preferred deliberation to speed. For a while, it seemed like former Liverpool midfielder Xabi Alonso might appear at Anfield in a glorious homecoming. He was a wanted man after transforming the fortunes of Bundesliga club Bayer Leverkusen and achieving their first league title in their 119-year history. But the Spaniard turned down both the Reds and Bayern Munich, deciding to stay and continue his successful work in northwest Germany. Ruben Amorim was also considered, but the Sporting CP boss's fondness of the 3–4–3 formation appeared to be an obstacle. The group of players Klopp left behind wasn't exactly overrun with centre-backs, especially ones who have played in a back-three before. There was also concern about Amorim's playing style, which was regarded as slower and less front-foot, both in and out of possession, than what Liverpool are accustomed to. Ironically, after the dismissal of Erik ten Hag a few months later, the Portuguese landed at Manchester United, Liverpool's old rivals.

Other names suggested in the English press included Julian Nagelsmann, Roberto De Zerbi and Franck Haise, an indication of the managerial profile Liverpool had in mind. They all are coaches who have played successful pressing football without having huge budgets at their disposal. Arne Slot emerged at the top of the club's data model in all three major areas: playing style, improving players and injury prevention. The outcome was something of a surprise, given that the model is weighted against the Dutch Eredivisie, where standards aren't as high as in some of the major European leagues. By April, negotiations over a compensation package were underway. Slot, who earned approximately €4.6 million during his last year at Feyenoord, saw his salary jump to around €7.3 million (£6.2 million) at Liverpool, enough to pry him away from the Rotterdam club. Slot's departure to Liverpool was welcomed by Ajax fans as the best news of the year. The troubled capital-city club had been blown away during Slot's last season, losing by embarrassing margins both in Amsterdam and Rotterdam.

The circumstances in which Slot arrived in the immediate shadow of an Anfield icon were compared to the appointment of Bob Paisley, Liverpool's most unassuming manager and one of the greatest. Reluctantly taking on the job in 1974, Paisley needed a little time to prove himself a worthy successor to the great Bill Shankly. He was trophyless in his first season, suffering 11 league losses and a European exit in October. He went on to manage the club during a decade of triumphs, outdoing his mentor in number of trophies won. Liverpool fans hope that Slot will emulate the stellar successes of Paisley's reign while avoiding his first-season experience. Familiarity breeds contempt, the saying goes, but sometimes the opposite is true. Unlike Paisley, Slot did not come with a Liverpool pedigree, which was cause for concern for certain people in the close-knit Anfield community. Some opened fire on Slot's modest CV, which they thought fell short of meeting superclub standards. Former Liverpool defender Jamie Carragher wrote in the *Telegraph*, 'For the last nine years, Liverpool have possessed one of the top two managers in the world. They are now gambling on the next big thing rather than appointing a proven, real deal.'

Marco van Basten, Dutch attacking legend and former Netherlands and Ajax manager, saw no reason to fear a Slot failure. 'I've spoken to him a few times and what he does and how he sees the game is very impressive. He gets along very well with the group of players, has excellent tactical skills, can explain things well and is calm and intelligent. I think he can go to any club, even the very difficult clubs, because he is so intelligent. If you get AZ and Feyenoord to play good football, you will also get the big clubs to play good football. I think it would only become easier for him because you have better players who understand what you want sooner. They are often also more stubborn players, but I think Slot is smart enough to manage that.' Feyenoord were unhappy to see their star coach go, but there was little they could do to extinguish Slot's Premier League dream. The compensation deal worth up to £9.4 million (just over €11 million) Liverpool agreed to would go some way to assuage Rotterdam grief. Never before had a club paid so much for a Dutch manager. Only

Julian Nagelsmann, Graham Potter and André Villas-Boas, went to other clubs for more.

On the whole, there was enthusiastic endorsement of Slot as the new Liverpool boss. Liverpool's stadium was soon nicknamed 'Arnefield' and the red carpet was rolled out. Some went as far as asserting that, at Feyenoord, Slot 'did a Leicester on a shoestring' – a mild exaggeration because the Rotterdam club usually features in the Eredivisie's top three. But by any measure, Slot's accomplishments in Rotterdam were outstanding. After three years, a Conference League final, a national title and a KNVB Cup, the 45-year-old left for Liverpool with his head held high. He had resisted the advances of Leeds United, Crystal Palace and Tottenham the previous year, but the opportunity that beckoned at Anfield was impossible to reject.

At the same time, the prospect of taking over at one of the Premier League's top teams seemed daunting. Liverpool have over 37 times more followers on X than Feyenoord's 649,000; the media demands, global interest and revenues all dwarf those of the Rotterdam club. Slot was not intimidated and reported soon after his arrival on Merseyside, 'Wherever you look, there are images and murals of Klopp. You can't help noticing his legacy and overall impact. But, so far, I haven't seen or heard anyone talking about the days of old.' Before leaving, Klopp had prophesied, 'When I said Liverpool 2.0, that didn't include me for the next 10 years, but the team is there, the basis is there. Whoever comes in cannot give anybody a guarantee to win trophies but can give a good chance to play really good football. They will get a top manager here. Changing from doubters to believers and staying believing in difficult moments . . . if we keep all of that, then it is a wonderful future ahead.'

Liverpool weren't looking for a copy of Jürgen Klopp. The American owners and British executives understood that a replica of the charismatic German would not be found. Yet, in some respects, Arne Slot resembles Klopp. His former Zwolle coach Jan Everse points out that 'Arne shares some details with Klopp, particularly where they come from: rural men turned city boys. Klopp did it in Dortmund and Arne did it in Rotterdam: working-class cities, similar to Liverpool.' While Slot in 2024 was not at a comparable level of prestige, his CV was similar to Klopp's in 2015, having taken two outsiders to big league highs and shown brilliant man-management and communication skills. Like Klopp, Slot is resolute and relies on attacking football. The way of pressing is similar. Slot wants his team to tempt opponents into a short build-up and force them into making risky passes, which often results in his team winning the ball in attractive positions. Like Klopp, he is didactically strong, surrounds himself with skilled assistants, brings wit into his media dealings and is searingly ambitious.

With his love for attacking football and a high line, Slot seemed a natural fit. Liverpool's tactical identity under Klopp was built upon the much-acclaimed *gegenpressing*, harrying opponents immediately after Liverpool lost possession and sabotaging attempts at building up from the back. After Slot was appointed in 2021, Feyenoord won possession in the final third more than any team in the Eredivisie and in Europe's top five leagues – 722 times. Klopp's Liverpool followed close behind with 706 times over the same period. Slot's Feyenoord ranked first across Europe with 201 high turnovers – open-play sequences that start 40 metres or less from the opponent's goal – resulting in shots. Liverpool were fourth in this metric with 182. Feyenoord scored the most goals from high turnovers with 29, exceeding Liverpool's 17. Slot's team did not always attempt to immediately strangle their opposition out of possession, but high pressing had been a constant theme at Feyenoord. Since the start of the 2021–22 season, Klopp's

Liverpool had scored the third most goals in Europe with 244. Slot's Feyenoord were fourth with 234.

The English media will be well served by Klopp's successor. Arne Slot is an excellent speaker who, unlike Unai Emery, Mikel Arteta or Erik ten Hag, does not hesitate to go on at some length about his visionary football tactics, while colouring his explanations with illustrative and sometimes humorous digressions. Like Klopp, he is socially aware and approachable. Few foreign managers are able to convey the same depth and subtlety in a second language as in their native tongue. Slot has a good grasp of English, and his syntax and accent are easier on the ear than that of his compatriot Ten Hag, who sometimes struggled to communicate the necessary clarity and charisma during his time as Manchester United manager. Slot gives intelligent, well-considered answers, without getting rattled and becoming defensive or condescending. When a reporter makes a quasi-funny comment or dresses up criticism as a question, he easily deflects without coming across as an annoying know-it-all. Slot press conferences are informative, even educational. Out of concern for protecting club image in the tabloids, reporters often have to make do with template answers. 'Ten Hag says nothing, Van Gaal was often angry. This man strikes the right tone. What a talker,' was the judgement about Slot of one reporter. Journalist Chris Bascombe was delighted: 'Liverpool's coach has not just answered every question put to him since replacing Klopp, he has delivered impressive responses worthy of a PhD graduate.'

Arne Slot is among the growing cast of top-level people in football hooked on padel, the high-paced racket sport that lands somewhere between tennis and squash. He stood out on the court when he played with his brother at a tournament at Peakz Padel in Zwolle, an event organised by Jakko Slot. The love for tennis was instilled at home in Bergentheim. In their youth, the brothers combined two sports until a choice had to be made; they both kept playing football. 'Of course there is little time, but playing a game of padel once a month is often possible. And an evening without thinking or talking about Feyenoord is also nice, yes,' said Arne Slot. He asked Feyenoord chief executive Dennis te Kloese for a padel court to be built at the club's training ground. It was agreed that he would get his wish if he won the Eredivisie title. Shortly after doing so in the 2022–23 season, the court was constructed. This means Slot and his Anfield predecessor have at least one thing in common: Jürgen Klopp had his own court at Liverpool's training centre, competing against members of his backroom staff and calling padel 'the best game I've ever played'.

Taking over from the successful, charismatic and very popular Klopp was never going to be easy. But the entry point for Slot was favourable. Klopp is a legend in Liverpool, but his last season was not quite legendary. The impossible job no longer looked quite as daunting. Talk of winning the quadruple had evaporated and Slot instead would inherit a squad that had added the consolation prize of Champions League qualification to their Carabao Cup success. Former Liverpool midfielder and manager Graeme Souness said, 'It's been a disappointing end to the season for Liverpool. I thought they would win the Premier League. They were playing a brand of football where they didn't have to play well to win games because there was so much firepower in the team. That's gone in the last couple of months and they've gone from a team that could score for fun to a team that can't score. They've got to look at themselves. At the time it really mattered, they couldn't deal with the pressure for whatever reason.'

One of the things on Slot's to-do list was motivating some

veterans to stay at Anfield. Mo Salah, Virgil van Dijk and Trent Alexander-Arnold's contracts were to expire in 2025. As Slot's tenure at the club unfolded, no press conference went by without questions asked about the contract situations of the awesome threesome, with the answer invariably being: there is no news. Liverpool's academy had proven fertile ground, and Klopp had promoted such talents as Conor Bradley, Jarell Quansah, Bobby Clark and Jayden Danns. That would be sure to continue under his successor. Slot awarded 12,334 minutes to academy talent in the season Feyenoord won the league. 'Youth players in your first team give energy. And if people feel they can grow inside the club, that drives the culture. I don't believe that much in experience; I believe more in game intelligence, and young players can have that much more than an older player.'

Dirk Kuyt is in a good position to assess Arne Slot's qualifications to be Liverpool manager. Kuyt spent the decade from 2003 to 2012 at Feyenoord and Liverpool in equal measures before returning in 2015 for a second helping of Feyenoord. The forward scored 102 goals for the Rotterdam club and precisely half that number for Liverpool.

Arne effectively had to build a new side at Feyenoord. People doubted the new players who arrived and said he would need time to get things right, but he proved them wrong. Slot has his own style. He knows exactly what he wants and he believes in it. It's attractive, attacking football. He likes to play an aggressive defence, high intensity, with the game played in the opponent's half. It's different from Klopp but a lot of the principles are the same. The news that Liverpool had decided to go for Slot came out of the blue, but they have made a very good choice. Arne wouldn't go anywhere unless he really believed in the project. If he says 'yes' then it's because he's convinced he can do great things in the job he's taking on. It's interesting to me as a Dutchman who is both a Feyenoord and Liverpool supporter. I'm a bit excited, to be honest. Slot is loved by the Feyenoord fans. They don't want to lose him and will be sad to see him leave – but from my perspective, if he has to go anywhere, I'm happy that it's to Liverpool. He's not only a very good manager, but also a very good human being.

In an in-depth interview with LFCTV, Slot zeroed in on improving on the previous season's showing. 'I've seen many games already, I've seen many training sessions as well. Of course, the fans can see the games, so they know we have some very good players. A real good team, real good players, managed to be on top for a very long time, but in the end we would all love to see Liverpool a bit higher than third place. This is the challenge we are facing now – to build on what we have. We are going to try to work on what Jürgen left behind and we will see a lot of similar things. He gave me more than a few good tips, but what stood out for me was that he was so happy for me and would be my biggest fan from now on. He supports Liverpool in the best possible way, and you don't see this very often. It says a lot about his character, the way he handled this situation as well. There is a change, but the change hopefully isn't that big, because we still have the same players, we still have the same fans – and if both of them are going to do the same job, that will make my life a lot easier. I'm expecting the fans to show up again in the upcoming season, and the same for the players. I will do everything within my power to lead the team in the best possible way.'

He continued, 'Of course, I bring my own things to the table as well and I think that's also what is expected of me. I think that the similarities in playing style was also one of the reasons why I came in, because of the way Liverpool "scouted" me – I'm not sure if that is the right word to use. They were looking for not the exact same type, but when a certain way of playing has been successful you would like to extend it or to go on with it. This is probably one of the reasons they came to me as well. It is my style but I think it is the style of many modern coaches at the moment: we were all inspired because of the rivalry between City and Liverpool. We were all inspired by Guardiola and Klopp, and at a big club, which I worked in at Feyenoord as well, it is probably the only style you can play: to have the ball a lot, to have a lot of energy. We have to find a way that people get used to me and the new staff that's coming in, and get the same energy in this building and eventually into the stadium as well, because that's what it's all about – we have to perform during the games.'

In October 2015, Jürgen Klopp had been introduced to a packed executive lounge in Anfield's Sir Kenny Dalglish Stand, with global media representatives in attendance. Arne Slot's first encounter with the Liverpool press corps in the congested surroundings of the AXA Training Centre press conference room was on a more modest scale. A positive relationship with the fans is important, Slot explained, referring to a match he attended at Anfield in 2017 on the invitation of Pepijn Lijnders, when he saw Liverpool beat Tottenham Hotspur 2–0. Slot watched from the stands with Liverpool's sporting director Michael Edwards. 'It was before they won the league and Champions League. You know better than anyone that people liked what Jürgen did here. He changed the style of play and the number of times the team won. Everyone was positive, even back then without the team winning trophies at that stage. Our fans are so important. Of course the players are important, but the fans can create this atmosphere between the players and the fans so we can score. We need them. We like the fans to come into the stadium and see a team that plays with a lot of energy, that plays good football. That is the thing I am focused on most. If we do that in the best possible way, it will probably give me some time as well, and if I have time then I can get to know the city a bit better. But it all starts with improving the team and winning as many games as we can.'

After winning his first Premier League match, Slot would add, 'My way of doing things is to let the team play in the best possible way. That way the fans will hopefully admire it and I will get a bond with them. But don't expect me to go out after the game and make fist pumps. That is not going to be my style. It is more: let the team play in a certain way, then they like the team and, because of that, they will like the manager as well. You never know – things can change. I am young. But normally you wouldn't see that from me. I might run down the touchline, but that would be to help the team, not to create something with the fans. I don't think it is necessary because the fans are always behind the team. I don't think they need me to do something different or special. The only thing I can do is help the team before and during the game and then afterwards the lads have done so much work that they will be there to thank the fans. I might be there but I will never be in front of them, always behind them.'

It had been a busy and lucrative June for Liverpool FC, albeit not with the usual cast of characters. Pop diva Taylor Swift played three sell-out concerts at Anfield, followed by fellow artist Pink putting on two. By July, the excitement had subsided and there was a notable lack of big-name presence, including of Liverpool's own. With many of the club's stars on a break after playing with their countries at the European Championships or Copa America, the early weeks of pre-season presented an excellent opportunity for the club's youngsters to show the new manager what they were worth. The team's departure to Pittsburgh for the start of the pre-season tour of the United States was scheduled for 23 July, and open positions in the squad were beckoning. Alexis Mac Allister, Luis Díaz, Darwin Núñez, Alisson Becker, Virgil van Dijk, Cody Gakpo, Ryan Gravenberch, Trent Alexander-Arnold, Joe Gomez, Diogo Jota and Ibrahima Konaté would not be part of the tour. Youngsters like Stefan Bajcetic, Luke Chambers, Kaide Gordon, Ben Doak, James McConnell, Owen Beck, Amara Nallo, Lewis Koumas, Harvey Blair, Luca Stephenson and Trey Nyoni had a chance to impress.

It was to be a much quieter summer than a year earlier. Back then, there was an urgent need for reinforcements after the exits of James Milner, Naby Keita, Alex Oxlade-Chamberlain, Jordan Henderson and Fabinho. This time around, Liverpool didn't have major gaps to fill. Slot also wanted to carefully assess the merits of the players he inherited before making final decisions about the team composition for the upcoming campaign. Darwin Núñez, Dominik Szoboszlai and Ibrahima Konaté had underperformed in the previous season and their confidence dipped. As a coach known for his ability to dramatically improve players' performance levels, Slot was keen to help them exploit their very considerable potential. As is his custom, he pored over footage of countless matches and training sessions. Obviously, relying on data does not replace personal encounters with players. 'To see the maximum level of a player, you have to be together for a long time. It's a disadvantage that many of them aren't here yet. The positive is that it's an ideal way to see the younger players and give them playing time. The standards are really high when it comes to bringing in new players because we have such a good squad. Of course Richard [Hughes, the sporting director] and I are trying to improve the squad where possible, but that's not that easy.'

Arne Slot's arrival as manager gave Liverpool a fresh feel for the season, but the team was notable for its lack of change. Eventually, the sole new arrival in the summer was Italian forward Federico Chiesa, who would only feature as a substitute. Liverpool were alone among the 20 Premier League clubs in not having introduced a new face into their league starting eleven – and they would become the first champions not to have fielded a newcomer since Arsenal in 1970–71.

Slot had brought his first pre-season training sessions forward by a week. The squad was to reconvene in the first week of July so that he could begin acclimatising to his new environment and assessing his charges. Andy Robertson noticed that Slot not only gives instructions but also asks a lot of questions. 'When he arrived, Mohamed and I were the only players with a leading role who were there. He wanted to know everything, from our phone use to the times we eat. And tactically he is incredibly good. Together with his staff, he also puts in a lot of work. Mo and I are often the first players at training, but we still don't beat the manager: he is always there first. And he also goes home last.'

While Klopp would typically observe and leave the training drills to Pep Lijnders, Slot was at the heart of everything during the sessions. He said, 'In pre-season, it's all about getting players fit and getting your game idea, your game model, into the players. We have quite a lot of training time with a few of them. It depends how far players will go in the tournaments they are playing, how much time we have to work with these other players.'

• • •

Journalist Nico Dijkshoorn, who has gained some notoriety in the Netherlands with his weekly columns in *Voetbal International*, thought that Liverpudlians might need some incentive to embrace their new manager.

> Arne Slot in Liverpool is going to be heartbreakingly beautiful. Slot, one of the baldest men I know, right in front of the Cavern Club, where The Beatles once grew their hair long. We, as Slot connoisseurs, have an advantage over the English. You have to learn to love Arne a little. A crushingly ordinary man. Technically, there is no one better than Slot, image-wise he needs a little nudge in England. What could work very well is if Arne bicycles to the stadium for every away game. That will be a thing. Thousands of people along the side of the road, and then the arrival. Arne has to do something strange right away, otherwise he's lost.

All of Liverpool's pre-season games in the United States began with the opening bars of Aaron Copeland's 'Fanfare for the Common Man'. It was written in response to the US entry into the Second World War as a tribute to the soldiers' heroic effort. The New York Philharmonic's version of the work was traditionally played when the ball was raised at Times Square for the New Year's countdown. It was also played at Independence Hall in Philadelphia as Pope Francis came outside to make a speech on religious freedom from the lectern used by Abraham Lincoln when he delivered the Gettysburg Address.

Liverpool's pre-season tour may not have been an event of similar magnitude, but the music seemed well chosen to herald the arrival of Arne Slot. In response to José Mourinho's boisterous claim of being 'The Special One', Jürgen Klopp once suggested he was 'The Normal One'. Slot may well be called 'The Common One'. For all his managerial ingenuity, he is a refreshingly unpretentious man, on the pitch and off. His personality is reflected in his football strategy. Klopp, in a now famous metaphor, once compared his Liverpool, known for direct balls forward, with Arsène Wenger's Arsenal, the team that was particularly deliberate with the ball. 'He likes having the ball, playing football, passing. It's like an orchestra. But it's a silent song. But I like heavy metal more. I always want it loud.' The kamikaze football that Liverpool saw at times the previous season changed to controlled attack under Slot. 'Under Klopp, every opportunity was used to play the ball as far forward as possible. As a result, it was sometimes very open. I say: make a better assessment of the risk and the reward.'

Like almost all managers in the top leagues, Slot has moments when he gets animated, but overall he is surprisingly restrained and composed, even when he is under pressure. If anything typifies Slot, it is a lack of fanfare. You do not see Mourinho theatrics, Conte antics or Van Gaal gymnastics. He takes some justifiable pride in his self-management. Once he was compared to José Mourinho following a spirited touchline display after Feyenoord's cup triumph over PSV Eindhoven. Slot responded, 'That's really embarrassing that you say that. Then I would like to ask you to look back at the images, because I just stood very quietly on the sidelines. Not more than that. At the end, I just asked if it was a throw-in or a free kick, in peace. Because that makes a big difference in how my players have to position themselves.' His focus is unchangingly on the football and on the team harmony that he believes will bring results. Not fanfare, but symphony.

The pre-season 'Rivals in Red' tour in the United States would feature three matches with Arsenal, Liverpool and Manchester United facing each other. Liverpool would kick off on 26 July against Spanish club Real Betis at the 68,400-capacity Acrisure Stadium, home to the NFL's Pittsburgh Steelers. Then they would fly to Philadelphia to take on Arsenal at the 67,590-seat Lincoln Financial Field on 31 July. The final match was against Manchester United at the 77,560-capacity Williams-Brice Stadium in Columbia, South Carolina, on 3 August. A double-header at Anfield against Spanish clubs Sevilla and Las Palmas on 11 August (the latter match behind closed doors) would conclude the string of pre-season games.

The modest size of the crowd – 42,679 – for the game against Real Betis could be explained by the fact it was a relatively late addition to the schedule. The games against Arsenal and United were sold out, with tickets selling for $101 to $500 against Arsenal and $145 to $616 against United – but considerably more on the resale market. Liverpool have 67 official supporters' clubs spread across 35 US states. They sell more kits in the US than in any other international market. Liverpool icon and club ambassador Ian Rush said, 'I travel all over the world with Liverpool and in America, the size of our fanbase gets bigger every year. It will be something different for Arne, something he has never experienced before. He will realise the size of the club he has joined. For lots of these supporters, coming to Anfield isn't possible, so we have a duty to take Liverpool to them.'

Curtis Jones was in excellent spirits at the UPMC (University of Pittsburgh Medical Center) Rooney Sports Complex in Pittsburgh, the elite training facility of the Pittsburgh Steelers, as he shared his first impressions of working with Arne Slot. 'He's amazing. It's probably the happiest I've been. As a style of play, it suits me. It is a clear plan. Arne is fully involved in the training, he coaches us a lot, he's big on the finer details. He knows it's going to take a bit of time because it's a big change. I felt like, under Klopp, the centre-mids were more disciplined runners. Of course, the principles are the same, but now the midfielders are going to be the heart of the team. I say that in a way that, of course, Mo is always going to get his goals. But in terms of our build-up and being comfortable on the ball, we have to be more calm and play more as a team. We're not in a rush to attack. We want to have the ball and break teams down. I feel more in the past it was like a rush. We got the ball back. It was a bit too direct I'd say. Arne wants us to get the ball down and completely kill teams. This now is more me. I can get on the ball more. I can "do me" more. Arne always has a smile on his face. You can approach him at any time and ask for help. He's brought in a new thing that we've all got – a guy we work with showing us our clips from training of what we're doing well and what we can improve on. I find that a huge help. We were told we had six weeks off, but I wanted to come back after four. I knew other lads would be away and I wanted to be under the new manager from the first day.'

Arne Slot secured his first victory as Liverpool coach when Real Betis were defeated 1–0. Mohamed Salah was one of the few stars present and immediately provided the assist for the first Liverpool goal under Slot. Salah found Dominik Szoboszlai and the Hungarian fired the ball into the far corner. For most of the first half it looked like a 4–2–4 formation, with Harvey Elliott and Szoboszlai both operating as false number 9s. Later they moved between 4–4–2 and a more attacking 4–2–2–2 to cause Betis problems. After the match, Slot said, 'During the season you will see us play with a real striker, but at this moment we don't have one available. With Dom and Harvey we have two number 10s, so we put them in that position and played with double 10s. It was maybe out of necessity.' Preseason was an education for Elliott. 'The football is very elegant, the Dutch School. It is very beautiful. The style of play is very different. We're three weeks into pre-season and the details we've learned and the depth we're going into is really interesting. It is more about possession now. The gaffer's style is about keeping the ball, one-touch and two-touch. The players are enthusiastic, we play through certain patterns. It's been really enjoyable. We have full belief in what he is saying and what he wants us to do.'

Harvey Elliott was the star of the show against Arsenal. He set up goals for Mohamed Salah and Fábio Carvalho in Liverpool's 2–1 win. His performance was of such quality that it earned him special recognition from Philadelphia Eagles cornerback Avonte Maddox; Elliott was gifted a signed shirt by the NFL star. The manager was more parsimonious in his praise of his young midfielder. When asked about Elliott, Slot said, 'Two great assists, but what I believe is that the team created this for him as well – playing out from the back, getting him or another number 10 in the right positions, and then it is up to him to bring the most out of those situations and he did that today with two assists. If I am a bit hard on him, I think there are maybe two other situations where he could have done better.'

While Slot is vocal and assertive on the touchline and in the dugout, away from the pitch he keeps a low profile. He accepted requests for fan selfies but avoided extra publicity, as he is keen for the focus to be on his team and not him. However, as the head coach of Liverpool, it is hard to go under the radar in the US, where Liverpool support is sizeable. Fans waited patiently outside the Four Seasons Hotel in Philadelphia to get a glimpse of their heroes.

The city proved to be an excellent place for team-building experiences. The players enjoyed their visit to the iconic Rocky Steps, the site of Sylvester Stallone's character Rocky Balboa's training routine, running up the 72 stone steps leading up to the entrance of the Philadelphia Museum of Art in preparation to defeat his nemesis Apollo Creed. They also visited the Front Street boxing gym where other scenes of the movie were filmed, and Curtis Jones tried on an Apollo Creed gown for size over his Liverpool training kit. The team also watched some baseball at Citizens Bank Park.

Columbia, with a population of less than 140,000, hosted one of the sport's most famous rivalries when Liverpool faced Manchester United. It would also be the first encounter between Arne Slot and Erik ten Hag as coaches of the English clubs, although the two were well acquainted with each other from their time as the respective Feyenoord and Ajax bosses. Two years earlier, in the friendly between the clubs in Bangkok, Ten Hag's United defeated Klopp's Liverpool 4–0. This time, the result was almost the reverse, a 3–0 win for Liverpool. Afterwards, Slot said that there was still plenty of room for improvement. 'I was satisfied, but not completely. We didn't have enough control over the game, because Manchester United were dangerous more than a few times. We gave away too many chances. United deserved more than a 3–0 loss. The score could have been different.' Slot was impressed by the fans. 'I knew it when I arrived, but what you experience here is enormous. I really can't wait to play at Anfield.'

The three-city tour was, at times, a challenge for the players. Double sessions in the intense East Coast humidity, as they tried to get to grips with the style of the new head coach, were supplemented by gym and stretching sessions. Three games, three wins, six goals scored, just one conceded and no injuries. New head coach Arne Slot declared himself satisfied with Liverpool's preseason trip to the United States. 'The results are what everybody is looking at, but players stayed fit and performed in the way we want. We saw some great goals during this tour, some great build-up situations, and I see them working really hard not to concede.'

Liverpool produced a 4–1 win over Sevilla at Anfield in their penultimate pre-season game. A Diogo Jota volley and Luis Díaz double had the home side lead 3–0 at half-time. Striker Gerard Fernández, better known as Peque, pulled one back for the visitors in the second half, but the exciting 17-year-old Trey Nyoni added a fourth a minute later to complete the scoring. It was only a friendly, but was watched by a crowd of more than 59,000. 'You can see that we focus a lot on the build-up, a lot more responsibility for our centre-backs with and without the ball,' said captain Virgil van Dijk, who was making his first appearance under his fellow Dutchman following a three-week break after Euro 2024.

Fist pumps to the Kop were consigned to the past; Klopp's successor was a model of composure. At the end of his first Anfield win, Slot gave a polite little wave to supporters behind his dugout and whistled along as 'A Town Called Malice' boomed from the PA.

13

ARNE AT ANFIELD

'You don't play around with ideas that have proved to work. You just feed and water them.'

BOB PAISLEY

The nineteenth-century 'great man theory' is the idea that landmark events can be explained by the influence of great men: unique and gifted individuals who, through their superior intellect, charisma, heroic courage or extraordinary leadership abilities had an outsized impact on the course of history. The theory is attributed to the Scottish essayist, historian and philosopher Thomas Carlyle, who gave a series of lectures on heroism in 1840. As the influence of modern sociology grew, the causes of tidal shifts in human development have come to be regarded as more complex: social, political, cultural, economic and environmental factors all have an effect. So, which is primary: the man/woman or the moment?

Sports theory has not been immune to this chicken-or-egg-first debate. In *Soccernomics*, the economist Stefan Szymanski and the journalist Simon Kuper argue that money determines somewhere between 80 and 90 per cent of the performance of professional football clubs. That leaves 10 or 20 per cent for other factors, one of which is the manager.

The impact of excellent coaching is impossible to ignore. Outstanding team bosses are placed on a pedestal, sometimes literally. Some of the greatest managerial geniuses in England's football history are commemorated with statues outside their clubs' stadiums: Herbert Chapman and Arsène Wenger at Arsenal, Bill Shankly and Bob Paisley at Liverpool, Sir Matt Busby and Sir Alex Ferguson at Manchester United. At top English clubs, the long-serving manager – Ferguson, Wenger, Guardiola – has often been influential in football policy. Liverpool went through such a phase under Jürgen Klopp. His record in charge of Liverpool was extraordinary, but he also had been a very demanding presence to the players, staff and executives. When the energetic, driven and very effective German left, the Liverpool boardroom authorities realised it was time for a reset. They understood that relying heavily on the charismatic presence of one individual makes a club vulnerable at a time of leadership transition. At Arsenal, Mikel Arteta spent years winning the public's trust and proving he was the right man for the job. Unai Emery, who came in immediately after Wenger, succumbed to the towering expectations and overwhelming legacy. Despite being an excellent coach, as he has demonstrated at Aston Villa, managing a top club takes more than skill. It requires the ability to change deep-rooted dynamics. The decade-long turmoil that Manchester United have been going through since Ferguson's departure serves as a compelling example.

As Klopp grew more successful and powerful at Liverpool, his grip on recruitment became stronger. While the club will continue to welcome input from its team boss, they would like to simplify the role and allow the person to concentrate on the demanding occupation of developing players, preparing the team and selecting the line-up for the next match. Rather than manager, Slot would be 'head coach' at Liverpool, a notable shift in England perhaps, but nothing out of the ordinary to the current bearer of the title. 'For me, it's not a change as in Europe we work like this. At my former clubs, it was always like this. There are not many clubs in the world where one person decides everything. It will be a collaboration between people. I don't think many sporting directors bring in players that the head coach doesn't like or the other way around. At a club like this, there are many more people than the two of us who can bring their opinion. That's how I've worked in recent years and how I like to work. I'm not interested in what you call me: you can call me Arne, head coach or manager. I don't care as long as I can do what I like and that is being with the players on the pitch, working with them and being at the games, as that is the most special.'

Where Klopp argued for Leverkusen's Julian Brandt to be added to the squad in 2017, sporting director Michael Edwards preferred Mohamed Salah, based on data and scouting reports. The former Portsmouth and Tottenham Hotspur analyst has proved time and again that he has a good eye for new players. Edwards left Liverpool in the summer of 2022. His successor Julian Ward departed the club at the end of the 2022–23 season. The following two transfer windows were handled by Jörg Schmadtke, a Klopp confidant. 'Klopp determines the policy at Liverpool. I purely am a support worker. I am the assistant, the right-hand man,' he insisted. Together with the rest of Klopp's entourage, he left when the manager resigned. Meanwhile, the enterprising Edwards had set up a data company together with Ian Graham, Liverpool's former head of research. He was persuaded to return to the FSG fold as its chief executive of football. He appointed Richard Hughes as the new man taking care of the daily implementation of sporting policy at Liverpool, which includes overseeing the coaching, recruitment, negotiations, medical and sports science operations. Feyenoord stars Marco Senesi and Luis Sinis-terra (on loan from Leeds United) were signed for Bournemouth by Hughes while he was the club's technical director, so he'd already had some exposure to the impact of Slot's work.

The wish to set boundaries to the influence of the top dog is also the result of a cultural shift. Millennials and Gen Z-ers are not quite as tolerant of authoritarianism as members of earlier generations were. This coincides with the risk-assessment of club leadership: giving one person too much control is not good business. Thus, these days the ability and willingness to work within a management team and to accept restraints is becoming increasingly important. Many of the game's most accomplished managers have been colour-ful and forceful characters, but nowadays neither the players on the pitch below nor the hierarchy in the boardroom above accept the dominance of one man. Even apart from issues involving style of football, Liverpool wisely did not consider individualistic and vola-tile characters in the mould of José Mourinho or Antonio Conte. Their choice of Arne Slot was based on his outstanding quality as a coach, but also on his willingness to work within a structure, as he demonstrated at Feyenoord. Slot is eminently well-equipped to work with a team. In fact, he rarely fails to share the credit with the mem-bers of his staff.

There was no personnel continuity from the Klopp era, with the entire backroom staff changing as part of a complete revamp of the club's football operations structure. In his first Liverpool interview, Slot highlighted what motivated the backroom-staff composition of the new-look Liverpool. 'You want to take some people with you as well [from your previous job] because they know who you are, they know your playing style and they can translate this to the other people in the staff. But if you go to a club like Liverpool, there are a lot of good people working here as well. We are going to use, hopefully, the best of both worlds to implement a few things from us and to use the knowledge that is inside this club already.'

The move of assistant coach Sipke Hulshoff would help to reinforce Slot's preferred style at Liverpool. The two had worked well together on a management team at Cambuur, a decade earlier. Hulshoff had been Slot's assistant at Feyenoord since mid–2022 and, simultaneously, Ronald Koeman's assistant at the Dutch national team. He stepped down from the role in May 2024, just before the European Championships in Germany started, because he was eager to join Slot on Merseyside. Hulshoff is an unassuming presence in the dugout, watching closely from his seat with a clipboard in hand, but his role as Slot's assistant should not be underestimated. They have a strong bond based on mutual trust and a shared football philosophy. Known as a 'field trainer', Hulshoff is a vocal leader of Liverpool's training sessions and plays a vital role in player development.

Besides winning silverware, Slot's management has proven its effectiveness when it comes to preventing injuries. For three seasons, player availability levels in Rotterdam were above 90 per cent; Slot played a key role in that by listening carefully to the experts. He was committed to replicating that tradition at Liverpool. Their players missed a combined 362 games through injury in Klopp's last season. At Feyenoord, Slot was aided by the same exercise physiologist who now oversees fitness at Anfield. Ruben Peeters is a 32-year-old with a master's degree in sports sciences from KU Leuven. He was head of performance in Rotterdam, and Slot indicated his Liverpool role would be focused on working on the physical dimension of team management. His main responsibility is the 'periodisation' of training planning, mapping out individual timetables for each player, gauging the required workload and deciding when to push them or rest them, so they peak at the right time.

German Fabian Otte, who was previously a goalkeeper coach at Burnley, had not worked with Slot before. For a time, he combined his activities at the US men's national team with his role as first-team goalkeeping coach at Borussia Monchengladbach. He joined up with Liverpool after the US team's Copa America campaign ended. Otte has a PhD in skill acquisition training in modern football goalkeeping from the German Sport University Cologne and has published numerous research papers on the topic. There was an instance during pre-season training when the German's creative methods were on open display. He asked 21-year-old Brazilian Marcelo Pitaluga to wear a pair of American-designed Swivel Vision training goggles, which limit peripheral vision and force the goalkeeper into closer visual tracking and use of audio cues. Former Manchester City analyst and coach Aaron Briggs was appointed as the club's new development coach. He would be the key link between the academy and the first-team set-up.

The addition of John Heitinga made the staff puzzle complete. Slot–Heitinga at Liverpool may seem like an unconventional pairing. Heitinga was a key player with Ajax in two stints over eight years. Rarely have men on either side of the Amsterdam–Rotterdam football divide joined forces to take on a new project elsewhere. And never before has someone who spent so much time with Everton as a player taken a high-profile role on Liverpool's managerial team. Heitinga made 140 appearances on the blue side of Liverpool, from 2009 to 2014. When he retired at the age of 32, the former central defender set his sights on a coaching career. He spent four years with Ajax's under-19s and then two years with the club's reserve team. When Slot's former NAC teammate Alfred Schreuder was relieved from his duties as Ajax first-team coach, Heitinga was appointed as the Amsterdam club's caretaker manager. Ajax were sitting fifth in the Eredivisie, seven points behind Slot's title-bound Feyenoord. During his short time in temporary charge, he promoted a style designed to keep possession, press high and win the ball back quickly – all essentials of Slot's football vision. After winning 14 and losing 5 of his 24 matches, Heitinga was disappointed when he was not appointed on a permanent basis. Instead, he joined forces with his former Everton coach David Moyes at West Ham, where he worked as first-team assistant coach for eight months. On 17 July 2024, Heitinga was appointed as new assistant at Liverpool.

The number of team meetings at the AXA Training Centre increased dramatically. Slot likes show-and-tell, which means he works closely with the club's video analysts. Training sessions as well as matches are thoroughly reviewed in video presentations. There are team meetings on tactics and technical aspects, and individual meetings, where the players receive feedback on how they can improve. Slot enters the presentation room well supplied with information, sometimes using a whiteboard to illustrate the strengths and weaknesses of an opponent. Assistants Hulshoff and Heitinga tend to be more involved in individual or small group meetings. Defender Conor Bradley explained, 'We have meetings almost every day, but that's only right. He wants to get his tactics embedded into us so he needs to keep having meetings to show us what we are doing well and not doing well. Some are short and sharp, some are longer. They are really good. I learn a lot from them which is the main bit. It helps me understand the way he wants us to play. We didn't really have meetings last year – only the day before the game. There's differences from what Jürgen did and what the gaffer does now. I'm enjoying learning new things, so it's all been really good.'

Training days are longer but often less intense than they were under Klopp, reducing the risk of injury. Under Slot, an average day begins at 9:45am with a wellness check where the players enter information into an app that records the quality of their sleep. Before the start of training two hours later, there may be yoga or hydrotherapy sessions. The backroom team introduced breathing exercises ahead of matches and training sessions, while ice baths have been encouraged post-exercise. More time is spent in the gym on individual programmes determined by the performance and medical team. Rather than warm-up exercises, rondos are now an integral part of Slot's training programme. He likes one-vs-one drills because he thinks they add a layer of competition between the players. Training usually lasts for an hour and a half and most players are on their way home by 3pm. Some may stick around a little longer. Liverpool had a coffee bar built just inside the players' entrance in the summer of Slot's arrival to encourage them to socialise. Salah is one of the regulars, spending time with Kostas Tsimikas, Dominik Szoboszlai, Trent Alexander-Arnold and others. Players sleep in their own beds ahead of home games – a departure from the Klopp custom of having the squad stay at the Titanic Hotel on the Liverpool waterfront. Slot believes they are more likely to get a good night's rest in a familiar bed.

Club watchers held their breath, wondering how the Klopp-to-Slot shift would unfold. Some suggested that the presence of a number of Dutch players in the squad – Virgil van Dijk, Cody Gakpo and Ryan Gravenberch, people familiar with the 'Dutch way' of playing and managing football – may have helped to cushion the transfer of power. In particular, the opinion of Liverpool team captain Virgil van Dijk, an admired player and respected authority at Anfield, would matter. Alyson Rudd wrote in the *Sunday Times*:

We do not know exactly how those first meetings and coaching sessions developed, but it is a safe bet to assume the team looked across at Virgil van Dijk to see his response and if the Netherlands international was nodding along, then all was well with the world. Van Dijk possesses an aura like no other player. He is intelligent, calming, authoritative and intimidating. When you ask him a question, as is occasionally allowed after matches, he looks you straight in the eye as if weighing up your IQ, your sincerity, your decency.

After a sluggish start at Ipswich Town, Liverpool eased to an opening-day Premier League victory. Portman Road was bouncing in celebration of Ipswich's return to the top flight, but Slot was unperturbed by the din. No gesticulating, no confrontations with the fourth official when decisions went against his side. There was a clear and well-organised managerial team effort. As Slot headed straight to the dressing room at half-time, it was his assistant Sipke Hulshoff who approached referee Tim Robinson to voice Liverpool's complaints about the officiating.

Slot's in-game intelligence enabled him to quickly spot problems and find solutions. He replaced Jarell Quansah with Ibrahima Konaté at half-time, concerned about how the 21-year-old was struggling against Liam Delap. Slot realised that he needed a defender who could win duels against the physical force of the Tractor Boys. Quansah won only 50 per cent of his aerial duels; Konaté won 80 per cent. In the second half, there was increased tempo, better movement, precision with passing and more confident defending. Alexander-Arnold masterfully passed to Salah, who sent the ball wide to Diogo Jota: 1–0. Individual class also helped Liverpool to make the score 2–0. Van Dijk launched his classic cross pass to Salah, as he had done many times before. Salah then combined with Szoboszlai to score, marking his 350th appearance for Liverpool in style. Slot enjoyed the closing stages as the away end chanted his name. He became the first Liverpool boss to win his opening league game since Roy Evans and Gerard Houllier oversaw a 2–1 victory as joint-managers in August 1998.

'The first taste in the first half was not as expected,' Slot told TNT Sports. 'I have to give credit to Ipswich, because they were aggressive, they were not afraid, they were playing one-vs-one all over the pitch to defend against us. Then it is about winning your duels and winning your second balls. I think they won more than us and that's why it was absolutely an equal game in the first half. We couldn't find a rhythm or any balls in behind. That's what I said to them at half-time, "If you want to win here, then you need to go a step up in terms of winning your duels first and make a fight out of it, instead of accepting that every time we play a ball long that the ball ends up in our 16-metres [penalty area] again." The second half was a joy to watch.'

Spectators and commentators were coming to grips with the change in flavour. At AZ and Feyenoord, Slot usually let his players absorb supporters' end-of-match applause. He did likewise after his debut game at Ipswich. He walked off the pitch immediately after the victory, with fans left wondering where their new manager had gone. The faux pas did not lead to overt criticism, but did cause some misunderstanding among supporters. Used to exuberant Klopp post-match fist pumps, they wanted to express their appreciation to the new arrival, but the down-to-earth Dutchman had already disappeared into the tunnel. Slot learned, and from then on also waved to the crowd after matches, politely returning applause to his admirers, while skipping dramatic arm gestures.

In post-game analyses, some were quick to point out that Slot may be more 'ruthless' than his amiable exterior suggests. Unnerving for some was his substitution of Quansah at half-time and his calling the defender's performance symptomatic of the team's lack of aggression. Gary Lineker expressed concern. 'Speaking out publicly about a player's performance is not something that I think you'd have ever heard from Jürgen Klopp, so there's already a slight difference there. It always makes me slightly nervous when managers are critical of their players.' Slot addressed his substitution in his next press conference, saying that he took time to fully explain his decision to Quansah. 'I spoke to him immediately after the game and again on the day after. At the end of that conversation, he asked if he could train on Sunday. He reacted in the way every player should. I don't think that much should be read into it. I did not say that he lost every duel. But he lost one or two important ones. It was not about Jarell. We as a team did not do well. I was trying to get that strength by bringing in Ibou [Konaté]. I think you earn your respect by what you tell them in video meetings and what you tell them on the training ground. I'm not losing it in terms of throwing things through a dressing room, but I can be hard and tough on them if I think it's necessary. You always look at your team and think, "What do they need?" And if you feel they need a bit of this [punches his palm], you are a bit harder on them, sometimes really hard on them, but never in a way that you are losing your mind.'

Dutch journalist Richard Dubbeld gave some insight into Slot's time at De Kuip and how his operations at Liverpool might compare. 'If you are a coach at that level, you have to be like this – you can't win by just being nice. Arne does not beat around the bush. There is no player at Feyenoord who, over the three years he was there, ever said anything negative about him, even when they left. What they like about him is that he is not playing around. He is clear with his opinions. There is no fussing about. His door is always open. When he makes a substitution, as he did last weekend, he will offer an explanation. I'm not sure I would describe it as ruthless. What some say is ruthless, others call honesty, and I am sure he would have had a good chat with Quansah the day after last weekend's game. He would tell him what he did right and wrong. And it would never be [a] one way [conversation].'

Fans behind the dugout held up a banner that welcomed Slot to Anfield: 'From Bergentheim to Anfield. We got your back Arne.' Slot spent three-quarters of the match against Brentford in his signature posture, with his hands in his pockets. He did something the four Liverpool managers before him could not do: win his first Premier League game at Liverpool's home base. Brendan Rodgers: 2–2 with Manchester City. Roy Hodgson: 1–1 against Arsenal. Kenny Dalglish's second time in the dugout: 2–2 with Everton. Klopp: 1–1 against Southampton. Two games, two wins, two clean sheets. No Liverpool manager had done that since Graeme Souness in 1991 and that was before the Premier League existed.

Possessing a scintillating front three was a gift to Slot. He offered them freedom in the final third, making them a more dangerous prospect by improvising rather than choreographing. That freedom, in an otherwise structured set-up, was productive. Speed, touch and directness led to Luis Díaz's opening goal, originating from a Brentford corner and a breakaway that started in the home team's penalty area. It was, in many ways, a classic 'Jürgen Klopp goal'.

The post-goal play was different: settle, regroup and safeguard the lead. The crowd warmed to Slot's controlled but also fast-paced style.

The head coach suggested this would be part of leading Liverpool to the next level. 'I inherited a team and we try to keep a lot almost the same and adjust maybe one or two things where we think we can gain. If Jürgen would have stayed, he also would have tried to find these one or two things where he could improve the team. It's not a surprise the team plays like this. And it shouldn't be a surprise to you if you saw them playing like this many times this season.' Football is about keeping possession for Slot and he has plenty of passers that can maintain control. They successfully completed 92 per cent of their passes against Brentford. There were important changes in midfield, where Klopp had often deployed ball-winner Wataru Endō. Slot turned instead to his compatriot Ryan Gravenberch to be the deepest of three central midfielders, not because he is the most likely to win the ball back but instead is unlikely to lose it. Gravenberch was afforded an injury-time standing ovation when he was substituted after a shrewd piece of man-management from Slot, who had pushed him into an unfamiliar role.

Trent Alexander-Arnold was taken off 18 minutes before time, after Mohamed Salah had scored Liverpool's second goal. It was the second game in succession that the full-back had been taken off early. His body language spelled disagreement to such an extent that the boss decided to share some words of guidance during match time, seated next to the player. 'He didn't look that happy. I understand. Every player wants to play 90 minutes, but I also don't think the players who were on the bench at the start were really happy with the choice I made. Trent came back from the national team. He had a few weeks off and this was only his third game. We have to take care of him because we need him for the whole season, not just the first few games. The good thing for me is I have a very good backup in Conor [Bradley].'

The crowd were serenading the new head coach at the game's end. Slot commented on the reception. 'Two good wins against difficult opponents. Both teams deserve respect for the way they have played against us, but there's still a lot to prove for us. Always good to start out with two wins and clean sheets. Every manager who comes here feels the warmth of this club and the appreciation of the fans. The most important thing I have to do is make sure we play in the style the fans want to see. That's what we are trying.'

· · ·

Liverpool vs Manchester United is the major clash in English football and one of the biggest football matches in world. Few people understand the roots of the intense antipathy between the two teams and their supporters. It has been fuelled by the proximity of the two cities, their historic economic and industrial standing, and the shifting fortunes of domestic footballing dominance and European success. Liverpool and Manchester are located 50km apart in northwest England. In the heyday of the first Industrial Revolution, Manchester was the far more populous city and was considered the hub of the north. By the late eighteenth century, Liverpool had grown into a major seaport – critical to the expansion and success of the northern cotton mills. Liverpool outgrew Manchester and throughout the late nineteenth and early twentieth centuries was often referred to as the British Empire's second city. The construction of the Manchester Ship Canal, funded by Manchester merchants, was opposed by Liverpool politicians and bred resentment between the two cities. Tensions between Liverpool dockers and labourers in Manchester peaked after its completion in 1894, just three months before the first encounter between Liverpool and Newton Heath – as United were called at the time – in a play-off match that would see Newton Heath relegated to the Second Division.

Liverpool and Manchester United are the two most outstanding clubs in the history of English football. Between them they have won 39 league titles, 21 FA Cups, 16 League Cups and 9 European Cups/UEFA Champions Leagues. By May 2024, they had won the same total number of trophies – 68. Though the contest may have lost some of its lustre since Manchester hegemony was seized by Manchester City, players, fans and the media consider the fixture the fiercest rivalry, more so than the respective local derbies with Everton and City. Arne Slot was well aware of the rivalry. 'A lot of people try to tell me about it, but that's really not necessary. Every player and every coach at Liverpool knows how important a match against United is. It's just like at Feyenoord, how much the matches against Ajax weigh there. If you follow football, and I have been doing that for a long time, you know the importance of United–Liverpool, and vice versa.' Of course, the northwest derby is *not* quite like De Klassieker. Feyenoord–Ajax games are watched by between 500,000 and 600,000 people. Broadcast in approximately 170 countries, Liverpool–Manchester United matches are followed by between 600 and 700 million viewers, more than any other game in world sports besides World Cup finals.

The 'Battle of the Baldies', the *Daily Star* called it. Across the Netherlands there was considerable interest in the double Dutch clash at Old Trafford, with Erik ten Hag in one dugout and Arne Slot in the other, Ten Hag in a suit, Slot in a sweater. The two men know each other well from their Feyenoord–Ajax encounters. A reporter wanted to know whether they are friends. Slot replied, 'No, not friends. Friendship is something different. We have a good relationship, but a friend is someone you go out with, out to dinner. But we've never done that. We don't know each other well enough for that.' Slot consulted with his players: 'I haven't experienced this game yet but the players have experienced it many, many times. Of course, we have to not only prepare them for the tactical part. I want to know what you can expect and how you should play in the best possible way so that it doesn't happen that the crowd is going completely crazy.'

Red balloons with the numbers '7' and '0' floated in the away section in happy memory of the result at Anfield a year and a half earlier, when Liverpool demolished United 7–0. Cody Gakpo, Darwin Núñez and Mohamed Salah had each scored a brace, with Roberto Firmino adding a seventh. But it can be intimidating to play at Old Trafford, a venue where even Klopp won only twice in 11 visits. On the two previous trips to Manchester, the celebrated 'organised chaos' of the German did not produce good results. In March 2024, Liverpool led 3–2 in the FA Cup tie but lost 4–3. In April, they only managed a 2–2 draw in the league, which was a blow to their title hopes. Liverpool's more measured approach under Slot served them well. Centre-backs Virgil van Dijk and Ibrahima Konaté calmly threaded pin-point passes between the lines. In midfield, Ryan Gravenberch, Alexis Mac Allister and Dominik Szoboszlai outclassed and outworked their opponents. All of Liverpool's goals came from United midfielders losing possession and leaving the home defence outnumbered. Luis Díaz scored twice before half-time after being teed up by Mohamed Salah. In the second half, Szoboszlai set up the third for Salah, who made it 15 goals in 16 appearances for Liverpool against United. Liverpool's comprehensive 3–0 win left the so-called Theatre of Dreams a gallery of empty seats well before the final whistle. At the end, Slot waved, raised a clenched fist and then briefly returned applause before walking towards the tunnel in business-like fashion.

Slot became the first Liverpool manager to win his first game against United since Bob Paisley in November 1975, and the second to do so away from home after George Kay in November 1936. 'I normally don't use the word "proud", but what we did very well in all three games is our work rate without the ball,' he said after the match. 'We try to press the opponent as high as we can, but if they play through or over our press, I see everybody working really hard to make sure we don't need Alisson. Sometimes we do and it's a really good thing that we have a really good goalkeeper.'

Liverpool had scored seven goals and not conceded in their opening three matches under Slot, but were found wanting in their home match against Nottingham Forest. Liverpool had almost 70 per cent of possession and 34 touches inside Forest's box, but were unable to beat Matz Sels. Callum Hudson-Odoi came off the bench to secure Forest's first win at Anfield since 1969. Ibrahima Konaté was slow to react and Alisson didn't cover himself in glory as he was beaten from outside the box. The goalkeeper said later, 'Hudson-Odoi had too much freedom to do whatever he wanted with the ball, dribbling inside and shooting. It was poor defending from us and we have to improve for the next game.' The Liverpool performance was far from the fluency and control they had shown in the victory against Manchester United a fortnight earlier. The introduction of Darwin Núñez, Cody Gakpo and Conor Bradley just before the hour mark actually made things worse. Trent Alexander-Arnold was moved into midfield. It brought little benefit in attack, while at the back Bradley struggled to contain Hudson-Odoi. The switch to a back three late on did nothing to improve things. Liverpool pushed and probed but there was no end product.

Slot said, 'If you lose a home game, that's always a setback and especially if you face a team – we never know, maybe they will go all the way to fight for Champions League places – but normally this team is not ending up in the top 10. If you lose a game against them, that's a big disappointment, although they were organised and structured really well. We had a lot of ball possession, but only managed to create three, four, five good chances – that's by far not enough. If you play so much in their half, we need to do much better. We lost the ball so many times in simple situations. It wasn't good enough because too many individual performances in ball possession were not up to the standards that I'm used to from these players. I want to see the same attitude every single day, after a big win, after a small win, after a draw, after a loss. There were enough things we could improve from in the United game. But this is a different game than the ones we've played till now because we faced a low block.'

Former Liverpool manager Gérard Houllier once said, 'You may miss out this weekend and be the hero next time. I don't have 11 players. I have a squad of players.' Slot's history with Feyenoord shows that he is reluctant to tinker with his line-up. But with more depth at Anfield came greater selection dilemmas and a challenge to some of the ideals that got him the Liverpool job. Other than Ibrahima Konaté, all starters had made two appearances for their countries in between Premier League games. Mohamed Salah had played in Botswana, while Alexis Luis Díaz, Mac Allister and Alisson had commitments in South America. Dominik Szoboszlai and Ryan Gravenberch had played in Nations League matches for Hungary and the Netherlands. 'What would Klopp do?' had been a moot question reiterated by commentators in the English media in the early days of Slot's Anfield rule. This time, it seemed apropos. Klopp never played the same starting line-up in games directly before and after an international break.

Slot had demonstrated his fondness for unchanged teams and, for the third successive game, named the same starting eleven. Maybe he could have rotated more, beginning with some players who hadn't been away on international duty. Curtis Jones might have given the midfield the edge that was lacking. When asked about his squad returning from their national teams, Slot insisted the hiatus was not the problem. 'I don't think it had anything to do with it. The players came back strong and I saw a team that wanted to fight until the end. So it had nothing to do with energy in my opinion. Everyone can have their own opinion but it is too simple to put it down to rotation, with too many players not at their best level. If you drop home points in a game against Nottingham Forest, then something is wrong. Forest made it difficult for us and when you don't win, you look at as many arguments as you can. I prefer to look again at the game and find what we didn't do well.'

Physical stamina did seem to be an issue. Szoboszlai lost possession 18 times and Gravenberch 12 times. Salah won two out of eight duels, Díaz two out of seven and Jota two out of six. 'We lost too many second balls,' Virgil van Dijk admitted. 'We know how direct they are, so playing against a big striker you can sometimes lose a challenge, but you have to be ready for the second ball. Every time there was a second ball they were on the right side of it. They got momentum in terms of winning the right challenges and they did their job very well. We weren't good enough. Everyone is coming back from different places and playing a different way, but we expect a lot better from ourselves. Losing at home is something that can't happen.' He added, 'If you want to dwell on things, it is only going to backfire on yourself. We're already thinking about recovery and being ready for [the Champions League match against AC Milan]. That's how we live our lives but the disappointment is still there.'

A new coach usually learns more from defeats than wins. Slot later said, 'My former teams were able to actually play almost every game with the same players, but it is a different league so I might have to adjust to that. I get some feedback from the medical staff and performance staff about where they are and what is the best thing to do, and then we make the decision before every game.'

In the mind of a Liverpool fan old enough to remember, playing against AC Milan conjures up images of the great 2005 Champions League final in the Atatürk Olympic Stadium in Istanbul. Liverpool, who had won the competition four times, were appearing in their sixth final, and their first since 1985. Milan, who had won the competition six times, were appearing in their second final in three years and tenth overall. They were regarded as favourites and took the lead within the first minute through captain Paolo Maldini. Striker Hernán Crespo added two more goals before half-time to make it 3–0. In the second half, Liverpool scored three goals in a dramatic six-minute spell to level the scores at 3–3, with goals from Steven Gerrard, Vladimír Šmicer and Xabi Alonso. The score remained unchanged during extra time, and a penalty shootout was required to decide the winner. The score was 3–2 to Liverpool when Andriy Shevchenko's penalty was saved by Liverpool goalkeeper Jerzy Dudek. It was Liverpool's fifth European Cup, which meant they were awarded the trophy permanently and the right to wear a multiple-winner badge. Liverpool's comeback is known as the Miracle of Istanbul and is regarded as one of the greatest finals in the history of the tournament.

Not all memories associated with Milan are happy. In 2007, the Rossoneri's seventh and so far final Champions League victory was secured against Liverpool at the Olympic Stadium in Athens, Greece. Milan won the match 2–1.

Alisson Becker insisted that being out of the competition during the 2023–24 season would only make them hungrier to win this time. 'Playing in the Champions League was one of the reasons that I came to Europe from Brazil. Not being able to play last season was really hard. But here we are again after a really good season qualifying in a really difficult league. We are looking forward to it. It is a big chance to go back to the good start we had in the season.' Slot agreed. 'I think it is the first time my birthday is not important tomorrow. It's a big game for me and because of the history these two teams have, the venue, it's one to look forward to. I don't think any manager is scared to play the other team, but we have a lot of respect for AC Milan. They have quality. We're not scared but we respect all their players.'

Milan's most glorious decade revolved around their Dutch stars Marco van Basten, Ruud Gullit and Frank Rijkaard, who showed stellar form in Serie A at the same time when Johan Cruyff was wreaking havoc elsewhere in Europe while managing Barcelona. Virgil van Dijk, Ryan Gravenberch and Cody Gakpo showed the Italian team that Dutchmen still know how to play the game. Gravenberch gracefully pirouetted through midfield and outclassed his surrounding opponents with mazy dribbles and clever passes. While Slot had made only two changes to his starting eleven, Gakpo used the opportunity to continue the form he had demonstrated for his country at the European Championships.

Within three minutes, though, Christian Pulisic took advantage of some lax defending from Konstantinos Tsimikas to score from a tight angle. It was the worst possible start for Liverpool, but Slot got a pleasingly strong reaction from his side. Ibrahima Konaté and Van Dijk's first-half headers were evidence of Milan's Achilles' heel – defending set-pieces. The two goals had much in common. Liverpool had identified a weakness of Milan in goalkeeper Mike Maignan coming slowly off his line when defending corners. Perfecting set-piece routines on the training pitch is Aaron Briggs' domain and he had evidently done his job. Trent Alexander-Arnold supplied Konaté with a well-delivered cross from the left and Tsimikas redeemed himself by providing the assist for Van Dijk from the right. Szoboszlai added a third goal after the break. Slot commented on the set-piece routine. 'We were disappointed about getting eight corner kicks and not scoring against Nottingham Forest, but we were very close. We felt with all the work we put in on set-pieces that at some moment we should get the reward. It was two very good set-pieces and two very good headers that got us two goals. It was important because I think we were very comfortable on the ball and pressed really well, but in the end, you need goals as well. We hit the crossbar a few times from open play, so we needed set-pieces and it was good to see that we scored them after all the work my assistants and the players put in.'

Liverpool outclassed their opponents to such an extent that the San Siro crowd turned on their own near the game's end. 'Fuori coglioni!' the home fans chanted ('Show some balls!'). Finally, Arne Slot could give some attention to the fact he had turned 46 on the day. 'The fans were singing for my birthday. What a great way to celebrate. That was the positive thing. Losing on Saturday was a blow for us, and then to be 1–0 down, how we reacted. I won't say it's a disgrace, but it is unbelievable to lose to Forest when you can play this well. I would have played Cody on Saturday, but he played two games for the Dutch team for the first time and [Díaz] was more fit. This is a special place for Dutch players to play because of the former players that have played here. To put a performance in like this is always nice as a Liverpool player and, at a venue like this, it's even nicer.'

In Liverpool's fifth Premier League match, Bournemouth appeared to have opened the scoring early in the first half courtesy of

Antoine Semenyo, only for the video assistant referee to rule the goal out. Liverpool then took their opponents apart in an 11-minute spell around the half-hour mark. Luis Díaz struck twice in three minutes. The 27-year-old was flourishing under Slot, adding more end-product to his game. Darwin Núñez then sealed the win with a curled effort in the 37th minute. He looked like a player who had a weight lifted off his shoulders, ending a run of 14 matches without a goal. Slot and his coaching staff had been working with Núñez to help him adjust and adapt to the new system. The Liverpool board were hoping the head coach could apply his magic touch to the misfiring Uruguayan, pointing to Slot's work at Feyenoord where young Santiago Giménez scored 49 goals in 86 appearances.

Slot commented on Núñez's performance. 'If you play for a team like Liverpool, you will always score or assist. For me, it is mainly about the work you do without the ball. Darwin is fitter now and understands better what we expect of him, but he is in competition with Diogo [Jota] who has done really well. First and foremost, you have to work really hard for the team. In the beginning of the season, it was Mo who made a difference, then Lucho [Díaz], then Cody and Diogo were involved in goals. Today it was Lucho and Darwin. That's what we want to see. You get consistency with two things: work rate and team performance. If the team performance is not consistent, it's so difficult for an individual to be consistent. So we just have to create our habits day by day, on the training ground and in the games, to get this consistency. He showed a good game today and maybe he can show it again. On first instinct when he shot, I said, "Why did he shoot?" I could have said, "Why don't you keep on building?" because he freed up the ball and I think the defender was on the ground. A fraction of a second later, I saw that the ball went in off the post. I was like, "Okay, maybe you are a better football player than I was".'

14

LIVERPOOL 3.0

'Before I worked with Arne Slot, I didn't expect he was this good. He's great with details, he's great on tactics, and doesn't have ego when he makes a mistake. He says things straight to your face. It is important for players to know what a coach wants.'

MOHAMED SALAH

'Beginner's luck' is the label for the odd phenomenon of novices disproportionately often outperforming experts. It can apply to winning a new board game or knocking over all the bowling pins with a first throw. One would expect veterans to beat newbies, and when the opposite happens, it is counterintuitive. Twelve of the 25 winning albums at the British Album of the Year awards this century have been an artist's debut. Harper Lee's first novel, *To Kill a Mockingbird*, became an instant classic, winning her the Pulitzer Prize. J.K. Rowling's first try, *Harry Potter and the Philosopher's Stone*, catapulted her to literary stardom. The world of sport is rife with stories of new arrivals scoring a goal or hitting a home run in their first match. Eleven different managers have won the Premier League title since the division's formation in 1992. Five of them – Arsène Wenger, José Mourinho, Carlo Ancelotti, Manuel Pellegrini and Antonio Conte – won it in their first season, or first full season, in Wenger's case. Claudio Ranieri won it in his first season with Leicester City, having been away from the league for a decade. Before there was a Premier League, Joe Fagan and Kenny Dalglish won the Football League First Division title in their first season as Liverpool managers.

In a way, it makes sense. A manager's best chance to succeed may come when they are newly appointed at a club, when they bring in fresh ideas that rally the players and before their systems have been decoded by opponents. Arne Slot repeatedly referenced the rather light early-season schedule when assessing his team's excellent start. 'If you judge your team after only a week, that would not be fair. We have to judge ourselves as a team after this [upcoming] spell of games – not three of them but six, seven or eight. The best way to judge us is in four weeks.' When the BBC surveyed 30 of its pundits at the beginning of the 2024–25 season, each one predicted that either Manchester City or Arsenal would win the league. Most made the safe bet by assuming City would prevail because that is what City most often do under Guardiola. About one-third of the way into the season, there was some indication that the script needed to be rewritten.

New Opta records kept rolling in, with Liverpool historians filling in the details. Slot became the first Liverpool manager since Tom Watson in 1896 to register six wins from his opening seven matches in all competitions. Diogo Jota and Cody Gakpo each scored two goals as Liverpool began their defence of the Carabao Cup against West Ham United, who were eliminated in a 5–1 mauling. The lone West Ham goal was scored by Liverpool when Wataru Endō's attempted clearance struck teammate Jarell Quansah and rolled over the line to give the Hammers an early lead. Federico Chiesa marked his first start with an assist when his acrobatic volley into the ground bounced up for Jota to head in the equaliser. With an eye on the list of upcoming fixtures, Arne Slot refused to get caught up in fan euphoria and contrasted his experience in England with the Netherlands. 'One thing I noticed in the Premier League compared to the league I have come from is that every team has a few players who cost £40 million to £50 million and have a lot of quality, so there are no easy games in the Premier League. I know every manager says it, but it is true. If you work in the Eredivisie and you play a lower league team – take my final game with Feyenoord against Excelsior, a newly promoted club, and they didn't have one chance. They didn't get close to the goal once and Feyenoord were not even playing that well in that game. With the Premier League, every team is able to buy players for a lot of money, every team has a lot of quality and you can never feel that the game is yours.'

The vulnerability of a Premier League top team was brought home by the ugly 2–1 win over struggling Wolverhampton Wanderers, which took Liverpool past Manchester City to the top of the table. Slot puffed out his cheeks and breathed a sigh of relief at the final whistle and was far from impressed. In his press conference after the match, he cautioned, 'It's more at 19 games when you start to feel where you are. We still have to prove it when we come across teams like Arsenal, Newcastle, Chelsea and Aston Villa to see if we can stay up there. If you have so much quality as a team, you cannot accept mediocrity. You have to demand of yourself every second of the day, every second of the game, the highest standards that this shirt brings. I, and we as a staff, have to set those standards very clearly. I think Wolves only had two shots in the second half, but in promising situations we lost the ball before it led to a chance. I don't think it is a good idea to lose your temper every single day because then players feel at a certain moment, "There he is again, screaming at us". I think it is better to show them the actual things they do. The positive thing about this group is: maybe I don't accept mediocrity, but these players don't accept it either.'

The midfield is still composed of players who were already there under Klopp, but it operates in an entirely different way under Slot. He wants his midfielders to control the game by building attacks and preventing counter-attacks. This tactical tweak should be welcomed by Liverpool fans, as the style of play of the past left the back door open. In the previous season, Liverpool's number of attacks conceded per 90 minutes was the sixth-highest in the Premier League, just ahead of relegated Luton Town. Now, when Liverpool won the ball in midfield, Slot would urge calm with arm gestures on the touch-line. He wants the ball to be kept in possession a bit longer instead of his players forcing a risky solution. A telling statistic for midfielders showed that they were giving 18 per cent fewer 'progressive' passes – forward shots and shifts – than the previous season.

Ryan Gravenberch went through a metamorphosis under the new coach. He was named man of the match after the 2–0 Champions League win against Bologna. The day after his fine performance at Anfield, he was voted player of the month by Liverpool fans. Slot said, 'I was very happy with him, because Ryan played excellently again. I don't say that to players at half-time, because there are still 45 minutes to go, but after the game I called him over and said: "This was another great performance".' Had Liverpool had their way and signed their midfield target Martín Zubimendi from Real Sociedad, Gravenberch would have been left wondering where he fitted in at Anfield. Instead of looking for an alternative, Slot recognised that the Dutchman's qualities had been underused. Gravenberch had been given his senior debut by Erik ten Hag – eclipsing Clarence Seedorf as Ajax's youngest player – aged 16 years and 130 days. Gravenberch looks at home in the deep-lying midfield role in Slot's system. Liverpool's head coach believes that his number 6 should focus on leading a possession-based approach through controlled but fast build-up play, the phase where Gravenberch is now so influential. Few anticipated it would prove so spectacularly effective. He plays freely with both feet. He is calm but doesn't take too many touches. The nice little flicks and quick releases have a great impact.

Slot said, 'There is no point talking about Zubimendi anymore because he stayed with Real Sociedad. We've moved on and we are really happy with Ryan. You see a Ryan who is full of confidence and that comes normally with good performances, trusting your team-mates and knowing that you can do what you have to at that level. I wouldn't say I am surprised, because he's Dutch. I'm Dutch, so I saw him playing at Ajax when he came up into the first team. Everybody saw back then what a special talent he was and probably for that reason he went to two amazing clubs, Bayern Munich and Liverpool. You can only go to these clubs if they see you have a lot of quality. Then it is up to us to make sure we get the best out of him. But it is not only down to what we, as a training staff, do. He is the most important for that. He can be a really important player for our build-up game. What impressed me most when I started working with him was how much he can run and then still be good when he arrives in the duel.'

The 22-year-old spent extra time working with John Heitinga, who knew his skill set from their time together in Amsterdam. Gravenberch said, 'John Heitinga – I had him at Ajax so he knows me really well – and I had chats about good positioning, where the ball can come and also about where I have to stand attacking-wise.' No Premier League midfielder made more passes than Gravenberch in the first two months of the season. His ability to receive the ball from the defenders on the half-turn and turn defence into attack was a major reason why Slot's Liverpool were performing as well as they were. In the first half of the season, he averaged 66 passes per match, significantly more than his predecessors in the role – Alexis Mac Allister last season and Fabinho during the previous four years – and was high-ranking in his recoveries and interceptions. Slot commented, 'It's up to him to keep setting the bar as high as it is now. He, like everyone else, has to play every three days. That's a challenge for all of us, but especially for him because he didn't play many games last season. I think he's played more 90-minute games now than he has in the last two seasons. So far, he's doing very well.' In the previous season, Gravenberch got only 35 per cent of all playing time, while halfway through the new season it was 90 per cent – with captain Virgil van Dijk the highest percentage of all players.

Gravenberch's repurposing at the base of Liverpool's midfield by the head coach transformed his individual performance and the operations of the team. Slot said, 'There are a few ways to overload or outplay [the opposition], and one of them is a player who can drive with the ball, dribble with the ball, and that is what happened. Ryan was outstanding again with his dribbling ability and that was important against this team [Bologna]. But if we only focus on the dribbles he had then we forget how important he is without the ball, where he does a lot of work and wins a lot of second balls as well.'

By superbly setting up Mac Allister for Liverpool's early opener and scoring the second with a stunning finish, Mohamed Salah became the quickest player to reach five goals and five assists in a season for Liverpool in 35 years. Slot thanked his players and staff for helping him to an eighth win in nine games. 'It says a lot about how much the players want it, how much effort they have put in and how the staff have helped me to create this start.'

Slot said he hoped that Liverpool fans would remember him in 10 years' time for more than the greatest start to a manager's career at their club in its 132 years of eventful history. After defeating Crystal Palace 1–0, his record stood at nine wins in ten games in three competitions. Not even Bob Paisley managed that. 'It's quite special, if you look at the managers Liverpool have had,' Slot said afterwards.

'Defence wins championships,' Trent Alexander-Arnold said. Remarkable words from a right-back who until recently seemed to regard defending as a side issue. Former Slot critic Jamie Carragher had been won round. 'Defensively, Liverpool are the best team in the Premier League. That's the biggest difference from last season.' Slot's team conceded only two league goals in their opening seven games – four fewer than the joint-second lowest, Arsenal and Nottingham Forest. In their ten matches in all competitions, they let in just four goals and kept six clean sheets. That was a considerable improvement on the previous season when they kept the same number of clean sheets in their final 27 games. Liverpool had the division's lowest expected goals (xG) against. Crystal Palace had managed just one shot by the 64th minute.

Chelsea had won all their previous away league games of the season, but Slot's Liverpool passed their first big test. Slot had learned from the loss against Nottingham Forest and left out Alexis Mac Allister and Luis Díaz following their long journeys back after playing in South America. Mohamed Salah scored a first-half penalty after Curtis Jones was brought down by Chelsea centre-back Levi Colwill. Nicolas Jackson capitalised on a defence-splitting pass from Moisés Caicedo and poked the ball past Caoimhin Kelleher, but Liverpool restored their lead within three minutes. As he darted towards the penalty area, Curtis Jones pointed exactly where he wanted it and Mo

Salah didn't let him down. Jones prodded a close-range finish past Robert Sánchez. The academy graduate had just become the proud father of a girl. Buoyed by the bliss of new parenthood, the energised midfielder lit up Anfield with arguably the most complete perform-ance of his Liverpool career. He simultaneously celebrated the birth of his first child and his goal as he vindicated Slot's decision to hand him a second league start of the season. 'It's the best thing ever,' he told Sky Sports. 'I'm playing with a smile on my face. It's a different type of joy. She's a little dream.'

It was not an easy win, and the usually composed manager dis-played more emotion during this match than at any of his earlier games. Commentators gleefully discovered that Arne Slot found occasion to 'channel his inner Klopp' when a refereeing deci-sion in injury-time went the wrong way. Enraged by John Brooks's bizarre decision to award the visitors a foul after Darwin Núñez was shoulder-barged by Portuguese back Renato Veiga, Slot turned on his heels and screamed at the ground in front of him. His passionate reaction to the injustice warmed the hearts of those watching from the stands, but Brooks booked him for remonstrating once too often. It was the first time Slot had been shown a yellow card. The positives outweighed the negatives: Liverpool's performance against the other teams composing the so-called big six had been mediocre in the pre-vious season, with just 12 points taken from a possible 30. This time around it was six out of six so far, with first Manchester United and now Chelsea defeated.

When praise was showered on Slot in the early stages of his Anfield reign, the caveat was routinely added that the fixture list had been kind to Liverpool. After the bar had been raised impres-sively with victories over Chelsea and RB Leipzig in the Champions League, that reservation no longer applied. The only goal of the

Leipzig game was not typical of the Núñez repertoire. The spectacular is more likely than a tap-in, but the striker was alert and tucked away Mohamed Salah's nod down from Kostas Tsimikas's cross. Virgil van Dijk completed 70 of his 74 passes and won possession on six occasions. Caoimhin Kelleher made a couple of big saves. This was Liverpool's seventh clean sheet thus far in the season, with just five goals conceded. Only once in club history had they let in fewer in 12 matches and that was in 1977–78.

'You were not inside the stadium? You thought we didn't dominate?' Slot reacted to a journalist questioning his team's performance. 'If you play good teams and if you play a Pot 1 team in an away game, there will always be moments in the game for the other team. The way I looked at this game was that we had, for large parts, total dominance. This is how I like to see our team play: many more chances than the other team, much more ball possession, much more time freeing up the midfield from build-up. We are really happy with the win. We knew it was a difficult away game but what pleased me most was that we controlled large parts of it, except for the last 15 to 20 minutes when we definitely needed our two centre-backs to keep a clean sheet, and also our goalkeeper in two big moments. That was, in my opinion, unnecessary.' Tsimikas, making his fourth start of the season, was handed UEFA's man of the match award. The recipient said, 'One of the goals of the new manager is he asks us to defend as a unit. So I think that is the important thing. We don't want to concede. Every game we all defend together. I enjoy playing for this manager very much. He and his staff work on every kind of detail and they want you to improve and are always there for you to help you do the right stuff for the team.'

In his analysis of matches against top teams, Slot frequently dwelled on the importance of set-pieces. Throughout his career he experienced how decisive corners and free kicks can be in determining whether a game ends in success or failure. In Feyenoord's championship year, a match had been won by Ajax by scoring from a corner kick. A season later, Slot's team lost at home to PSV, when the visitors scored from a corner kick. Slot also experienced the small margins in top matches at Liverpool. His team had turned a deficit into a lead at AC Milan with two set-pieces. Before the encounter with Arsenal at the Emirates Stadium, Slot took up the theme of set-pieces once again. Both in defensive and attacking respects, that proved to be an appropriate message. Just before half-time, Arsenal converted a good spell in the game by means of a set-piece. Declan Rice produced a well-taken free kick from the right, which Mikel Merino expertly headed in. A long VAR check showed that Van Dijk had tried to put the Arsenal midfielder offside a fraction too late. In attack, Liverpool's focus on set-pieces had already paid off in the 18th minute. Trent Alexander-Arnold's corner kick from the left landed at the near post, where Luis Díaz headed it onwards to the goalmouth and Virgil van Dijk finished the sequence by nodding the ball into the net. Bukayo Saka had opened the scoring for the home side. Mohamed Salah's second-half finish restored parity after Merino's goal. Liverpool had twice come from behind.

Slot said he was unfairly penalised by referee Anthony Taylor when he vociferously complained about the home team slowing the game with apparent time-wasting during the thrilling 2–2 draw. He was shown the second yellow card of his Liverpool career because of his outburst. 'Last time I said I completely deserved a yellow card. This time, I don't think I did. They always fell down once they had ball possession and that took the energy out of the game in my opinion. I said to Ibou Konaté, "This is [a] fucking joke." The fourth official [Sam Barrott] thought I had said it to him. That's definitely not what

I did. I got a yellow for that so now I am on two. I have to be careful now.' Sky Sports pundit Roy Keane seemed to agree with Slot's assessment. 'If I were to look at the mentality of this Arsenal team today, when you're watching them live and they're 2–1 up, can you go on and take the initiative? Every time a player is tackled they're going down, they're rolling around, they're time-wasting. They're trying to kill the game, I get that. But you're the home team, you're 2–1 up. Use the initiative, use the fans behind you.'

Despite his altercation with the fourth official, Slot was happy with the match. 'Going two times behind against a very strong Arsenal team, to get a point is pleasing to see, especially as we played away in Europe this week and had one day less to recover and prepare. We came back so strong in the second half after deserving to be one goal down at half-time. You face Arsenal, with a manager who has been working here four or five years and has done an incredible job; his team can play in so many different set-ups. They always play 4–3–3, but the way they position themselves, I think he said himself once, they can do it in 40 different set-ups. You prepare a game plan, but you can't tell your players about 40 different options. We could prepare them a bit better for the second half with what we had seen in the first half. We took more risk but the main thing was we put more energy into it. We pressed them more aggressively. You saw also we could keep going, where they had to take a few of their quality players off. To see we can compete with such a strong Arsenal team, in their stadium, that is very pleasing.'

Liverpool headed to the quarter-finals of the Carabao Cup after a 3–2 win over Brighton & Hove Albion. The match at the Amex Stadium allowed Arne Slot to try out a couple of tactical ideas. With Diogo Jota and Federico Chiesa missing, and wary of overloading Darwin Núñez, he started with not one but two false number 9s. 'I prefer to play with a number 9, but if there are none available, then this was what we came up with. Yes, Núñez was on the bench. We have to be careful with him not to start three games in a row.' Managers of both sides recognised that the Carabao Cup's principal purpose is to give opportunity to fringe players. Slot used the occasion to give young players a chance to prove themselves. Tyler Morton, Conor Bradley, Jarell Quansah and Vítězslav Jaroš were in the starting line-up. 'I'm very happy with what I've seen. I haven't seen them play much yet. They were able to play in a similar style to what we normally do. And they brought quality football into the game. That makes it even more difficult for me to decide the line-ups in the coming weeks.' Cody Gakpo's two goals early in the second half were evidence of a player thoroughly enjoying himself. 'Cody has been a good player for Liverpool for a long time – that is a good thing for me. For me, he is a regular, even if he does not start every game.'

Brighton were then beaten for the second time in four days, this time in a hard-fought league match at Anfield. They were caught in what Mikel Arteta once described as the Anfield 'washing machine', with new manager Fabian Hürzeler attributing his team's collapse to the raucous environment. He said he would ask his retired countryman for some pointers on how to better cope with the venue next time. 'I will have to call Jürgen and ask him. I only experienced the atmosphere on television so far, and now in person. A wild environment is the time to stay calm . . . With Jürgen, Liverpool were really good in transition. They played with a lot of intensity. What I see now is like that. They sprint backward, everyone. So when they're overplayed, you think you're out, you break their lines. But in two seconds the situation changes completely because they all have the attitude to defend. And that's something special.' It was, as they call it, a game of two halves. After a listless and disjointed first half, there was a transformation after half-time. Trailing 1–0, Cody Gakpo came to the rescue with yet another goal against Brighton. Two minutes later, Mohamed Salah unleashed a thunderbolt beyond Bart Verbruggen, his 48th match-winning goal in the Premier League.

Slot's post-match assessment indicated lessons would need to be heeded. 'We didn't show up at all in the first half. If you face a team like this, you have to keep running. They all could have been taken off at half-time. We changed a bit tactically but that had nothing to do with us coming out stronger. It was all to do with our players showing a different attitude and a different intensity. When things go against you, you have to show up. Winners always do. Fortunately, we have a lot of winners in our team. The crowd were incredible in the second half. That's the loudest since I've been here. This is the kind of win you need in a season.' Slot's changes made a huge difference. He brought on Curtis Jones and Luis Díaz for Alexis Mac Allister and Dominik Szoboszlai. It was now a four-pronged attack and, within six minutes of that double substitution, Liverpool had gone from trailing to leading. Once they were in front, Slot responded by replacing Darwin Núñez with Wataru Endō – a move designed to ensure Liverpool secured their advantage. The victory was made sweeter as news of Manchester City's defeat in Bournemouth filtered through by full-time.

In Europe, Liverpool were sitting atop the Champions League's new 36-team table, guided by someone whose every tweak and adjustment seemed to produce good results. They were the only club to have won all four of their Champions League matches. The 14th victory of the season was secured against Bayer Leverkusen. No new Premier League manager had ever won 14 of his first 16 games across all competitions, as Slot did. The victory took him clear of

José Mourinho, Carlo Ancelotti and Ole Gunnar Solskjaer, who all managed 13. Leverkusen had won the 2023–24 Bundesliga title without losing a game and were Europa League runners-up – the final against Atalanta was their only defeat in 53 matches. If Jürgen Klopp was celebrated for his heavy metal football, Slot is all about the fine tuning. He replaced Dominik Szoboszlai with Curtis Jones, while Luís Díaz came on for striker Darwin Núñez. Liverpool vanquished the German champions with a magnificent second-half display. Díaz scored the first hat-trick of his professional career, while Salah's cross for Gakpo's goal was flagged offside by Dutch assistant Jan de Vries only to be restored by the VAR.

It was a night to celebrate. After he was serenaded by the Anfield crowd, Slot said that the Dutch rarely sing a manager's name. He quipped, 'Some players get used to having their name sung. I was only sung about a few times in my playing career.' Díaz left Anfield holding the player of the match trophy, with the match ball – signed by his teammates, as is the tradition in football when somebody scores three goals – tucked under his arm. The manager had unearthed some untapped potential in the shortish Columbian. Slot and his coaching staff made sure Díaz got on the ball more centrally and in more advanced areas. He had never played the central role for Liverpool before, but he was having the time of his life, taking his tally for the season to 9 goals in 15 appearances. 'I really enjoyed playing in that position. The manager makes it very clear exactly what he wants from us. It wasn't easy for him to come in and fill Jürgen Klopp's shoes, but things have gone so well with him. He's been spectacular from the first day he's been here. He's very focused on the things you need to improve, but he'll also praise you for the things you're already doing well. His game plan is spot on every time.' Curtis Jones put in another great performance and more than repaid Slot's faith in him, which earned him the manager's praise. 'So comfortable on the ball, you can trust Curtis closer to your defence. Like we saw against Chelsea and again tonight, he is also able to penetrate inside the 16-metre [penalty] box and give the last pass. He's really made a step up after pre-season and that's why he gets his chances now. If players do well – and I have quite a lot of them at the moment – they will get their chances.'

Between 2004 and 2009, Xabi Alonso served Liverpool FC with distinction. The former Spain midfielder had enjoyed being back in Liverpool, taking a mid-morning run through the city, past his old apartment at Albert Dock. He said, 'It's always special. You notice the development of the club. The new Anfield Road Stand looks pretty amazing. I know the city very well. I loved it and I have friends here. Liverpool are in a great moment. I followed Arne Slot when he was at Feyenoord. I know his approach. That, combined with the intensity here at Liverpool, is a nice mixture. That's why they are top of the Premier League and the Champions League. In all areas they are strong. The manager has done a fantastic job in the past three months. For us it's a big challenge to come here. At the moment Liverpool are one of the best, if not the best, team in Europe. We have our plan so let's see what happens.'

When he walked through the tunnel, he paused for a moment to touch the 'This is Anfield' sign. By the time the Liverpool fans began serenading him with a couple of minutes of the match remaining, his team were 3–0 down and heading for just their third loss in 69 matches in all competitions. 'I think they are a complete team,' Alonso said in his post-match news conference. 'They are able to defend, to score, they have power in both boxes, they can keep clean sheets and they are able to score with not many chances. That is a great strength in the Champions League, especially in the next round.'

In an interview with the *Athletic*, Alan Shearer was asked whether he thought the praise for Arne Slot was over the top. After all, he had taken over 'a team of leaders and winners that pretty much runs itself'. Shearer disagreed.

On the contrary, I think Slot has done brilliantly. Yes, Liverpool are a well-oiled machine with some very good players, but he's added to it, he's made them tougher defensively and they've only lost one game. That doesn't feel like a case of too much hype. Sometimes, new managers give their teams a bounce, but there have been enough occasions when influential long-term figures have gone and things have fallen apart. Intensity or identity can dip. That's certainly something Liverpool would have been desperate to avoid when Jürgen Klopp left. I was lucky enough to be at Anfield doing co-commentary for the Champions League game against Bayer Leverkusen, and the German team were blown away in the second half. Slot has implemented a few interesting tweaks. You're not seeing Trent Alexander-Arnold going into midfield as much as he used to and he's defending better as a consequence. In midfield, Liverpool have Curtis Jones, Dominik Szoboszlai, Alexis Mac Allister and Ryan Gravenberch – in other words, they have really good options. They have depth upfront, so they're really strong.

Slot's substitutions helped to finish matches and ensure that Liverpool did not lose points in the closing stages. His incisive second-half decision-making has made the difference between narrow defeats and crucial draws, or frustrating draws and pivotal wins. Liverpool had yet to concede a goal after the 72nd minute of a game in the

Premier League or Champions League, proof of their stamina but also excellence in organisation.

Slot puts a lot of trust in the reports his staff produce on the state of each player's physical condition. The information helps to plan substitutions in advance, instead of them just being reactions to changing match conditions. Rotation is also taken into consideration. This careful management of personnel helped to keep injuries to a minimum, a hallmark of Slot's leadership that had drawn the attention of the Liverpool board. At other times, his replacements are targeted to deal with a specific problem. Switching full-backs, often for the last ten minutes of the game, is one of Slot's most commonly used interventions. Joe Gomez, at the back, and Wataru Endō, in midfield, are brought on to secure a good outcome. No one is guaranteed playing a full 90 minutes. Even Mo Salah was substituted four times in his fourteen starts, an indication that every player, no matter how brilliant, is subservient to team interest. Slot plays down his influence, saying that substitutions are only hailed as strokes of genius when they work.

Before players understood Slot's management strategy, his interventions had caused some displeasure, as was shown by Trent Alexander-Arnold's brooding countenance when he was taken off against Brentford. Gradually, he and other members of the team came to understand and appreciate Slot's modus operandi, helped by the manager's patient explanations and the relentless flow of good results. The full-back said, 'We agreed that he will be strict with me. I told him that I want to become the most feared defender in Europe. We analyse every game together and then he shows me what I need to improve. It is really refreshing to have a manager who helps, directs and teaches me how to become a better player.'

The 2–0 victory over Aston Villa gave Liverpool a five-point lead at the top of the table going into the November international break. In August, Liverpool had been given only a 5 per cent chance of winning the Premier League by Opta's supercomputer. That figure had surged to 59 per cent by the time the match against Aston Villa was concluded. Champions Manchester City had lost 2–1 to Brighton & Hove Albion earlier and their chances of winning the league had slipped from 82.2 per cent to 36.2 per cent. City had lost four games in a row while Liverpool had won four in a row. Núñez put Liverpool ahead against Villa from a tight angle in the 20th minute and, from another counter-attack, Salah scored his eighth goal in his last ten matches against Villa. Caoimhin Kelleher superbly saved twice in quick succession and had kept four clean sheets in eight games. He drew level with Alisson on appearances for Liverpool in the season. The Premier League's best centre-back pairing was Van Dijk–Konaté. The defensive togetherness was on display when the back line formed a huddle at full-time and celebrated another clean sheet.

Everyone expected a cakewalk against Southampton, but the Saints held their own before folding in some unfortunate game moments. They continued to play out from the back, a risky tactic when playing against a team like Liverpool, who wield a potent high press. Liverpool entered this fixture with the best defensive record in the league but looked wobbly at the back and trailed 2–1 with 25 minutes to go. A clever finish by Salah got the team level before he fired home an 83rd-minute penalty to secure the win. Liverpool ended the afternoon eight points clear of Manchester City at the top. After the final whistle, Slot walked towards the travelling supporters, took in his song, returned their applause, did some low-key chest-tapping and turned on his heels to head to the tunnel.

Almost routinely, Slot downplayed the significance of another win. 'We are really happy, especially because we were 2–1 down. Maybe that wasn't a reflection of how the first hour went because I think we dominated the whole game. We always know we can trust Mo if things are difficult for us because after we went 2–1 down, I didn't really feel that was the moment we could score. It was a fantastic pass from Ryan Gravenberch and the timing of the run and how Mo finished it was special. That helps you back in the game. The first goal we scored was from them playing out from the back. That didn't happen a lot for them today. It has happened a lot for them in other games, and I showed the players yesterday how many times Southampton can play through the press. We know what we have to put into it to get these leads and these wins. These players have been longer in the Premier League than I have, but even later on last season, Arsenal led by eight points and Manchester City still came back. You know if you face Arsenal, City, Chelsea and all these other teams that they are all able to win so many games in a row. It's nice to have this position but we are not getting carried away.'

Liverpool hadn't beaten Real Madrid in eight attempts since Rafael Benitez's side beat them 4–0 on Merseyside in March 2009. That miserable run includes losing Champions League finals in Kyiv and Paris, in 2018 and 2022. With Arne Slot at the helm, Liverpool took European game management to new heights, dominating the Galácticos in almost every department. Midfield star Jude Bellingham's impact was reduced to near insignificance. Conor Bradley excelled in both attack and defence, the 21-year-old filling in for injured Trent Alexander-Arnold and coming up against Kylian Mbappé. He launched himself at the French superstar in a classic crunching tackle, took the ball, upended his opponent and was met with the kind of roaring response from Anfield usually reserved for goal-scorers. He not only contained Mbappé but found time to get forward in the second half, teeing up Alexis Mac Allister for the opening goal after 52 minutes.

Mohamed Salah and Mbappé both failed from the penalty spot; Salah hit the outside of the post and Caoimhin Kelleher saved the Frenchman's attempt. Mbappé's slip was in keeping with his evening. Salah's miss was more shocking, but Liverpool had the capacity to absorb it. Substitute Cody Gakpo headed past Courtois from Robertson's cross 14 minutes from time, putting Liverpool on top of the Champions League table with five wins from five. Slot's decision to play Curtis Jones ahead of Dominik Szoboszlai was rewarded. The 23-year-old was involved in both goals and completed 55 of his 59 passes, comfortably outclassing Jude Bellingham in midfield. After the match, Bellingham said, 'From the first minute, they took control of the game. We tried to force the counter-attack a few too many times. They were more up for it than us, which is really disappointing to say. But it's no disgrace, against probably the best performing team in Europe.'

Slot said that what he found most challenging at Liverpool was not picking apart the opposition or devising the best game plan, but delivering the right words, at the right time, to motivate and inspire each team member on a daily basis. Yet, he appears to have no difficulty getting his message across in 15 minutes. His half-time team talks have effected dramatic second-half improvements. They are short and sharp, and backed up with video analysis. Since the start of the season, Liverpool had noticeably raised their level after the break – with the 2–0 victory against Madrid just one more addition to the list of impressive second halves. In the first half, they were patient in possession as they worked to decode Madrid's set-up and settle into game rhythm. By introducing tweaks in their attacking phase after half-time, Slot provided the key to break down

Carlo Ancelotti's defence, producing Liverpool's first victory against Madrid in 15 years.

'Before they go out, we always prepare them for what to expect from what we have seen from the opponent till now. But what we saw from them until now was with Vinicius Junior,' said Slot after the game. 'Now they lined up without Vinicius, so after the first half we knew better what to expect than we knew before the game. Sometimes these small adjustments help as well, but it has mainly to do with the effort we put in in the first half already.' He gave credit to the Liverpool academy. 'Did Conor play the ball to Macca [Mac Allister]? – he was in a strange position then. It is nice for him, his family and us, but also for the academy. Not only him, Caoimhín and Curtis were outstanding. To have three academy players doing so well is a big compliment for the academy. For Caoimhín, the penalty was a big moment. You see Mbappé behind the ball and I thought what everyone thought – this will probably go in.'

Liverpool, at the top of the revamped Champions League as the only team with maximum points from five matches, looked well positioned to continue their advance to European glory in Slot's first season. They swept aside AC Milan, Bologna, RB Leipzig, Bayer Leverkusen and Real Madrid while only conceding one goal. Slot managed to maintain his team's ability to score, including in classic Liverpool-style counter-attacks, but with a new versatility in midfield and steeliness in defence that makes them far less likely to concede. 'The market doesn't lie' is the adage, and Liverpool dislodged Manchester City as favourites in Champions League betting on the strength of their convincing victory over Los Blancos. Hours after Real Madrid were sent packing at Anfield, the updated odds to win the Champions League were: Liverpool at 9/2, Manchester City at 5/1, Barcelona at 6/1, Real Madrid at 13/2, Arsenal at 13/2. The *Daily*

Telegraph opined, 'It is only late November, no trophies are handed out at this time of year, but there is little doubt that Liverpool are the best team in Europe right now. The hope will be that they maintain that status come the final in Munich on May 31.'

At one time or another, almost every Dutch coach has cited Pep Guardiola as an inspiration. Arne Slot never made a secret of his admiration for the Catalan manager and finally found himself at a level where he had to look Guardiola straight in the eye. He was no longer a fan and an apprentice, but a direct competitor tasked with defeating him. And he did, comprehensively, on 1 December 2024 when Liverpool beat Manchester City 2–0. For 20 minutes Liverpool played Jürgen Klopp football as they tore into City, with Cody Gakpo scoring in the 12th minute. In the remaining three-quarters of the match, they demonstrated Arne Slot football. Slot preserved the best of what he inherited and added his own ingenuity to the mix. With more control but still plenty of threat, they wrapped the match up in the 78th minute through a Mo Salah penalty. It was a score that flattered City; Liverpool could have scored four times. The difference in expected goals (xG) between the teams was 3.43–0.83 in Liverpool's favour. Virgil van Dijk might have scored a hat-trick of headers, hitting the post with one effort. At game end, Slot applauded the Kop and blew two kisses to his family in the Main Stand before heading down the tunnel. The jubilant Anfield supporters assured his parents, Arend and Fennie, brothers Edwin and Jakko, wife Mirjam and children Isa and Joep that Liverpool loves Arne Slot. The family flew back to the Netherlands having seen the fruit of his investment in England and a great game of football.

'You're getting sacked in the morning,' sang the Liverpool fans, taunting the City manager. Pep Guardiola responded by holding up six fingers, referring to his club's six titles in seven years. It was hard to see them making it seven; the result pointed towards Liverpool winning the title. Post-match, Guardiola expressed frustration with the chant. 'I did not expect it from the people of Liverpool.' But in the light of Liverpool's experience of the last years, the reaction should not have come as a surprise. City have prevailed at the expense of Liverpool, particularly in the title races of 2019 and 2022 when the Reds were painfully edged out by a solitary point. Arne Slot said, 'I've already experienced a few nice moments here as a manager. But today stood out with the energy we delivered on the pitch and the energy the fans delivered for us. Only being 1–0 up at half-time, we would have loved to see a bigger margin. In an ideal world we would have scored the second earlier. You have to put a lot of effort in and force them into mistakes to give us energy. The crowd was fantastic today. We are a competitive team and it's difficult to beat us, but we need to put in the effort and we have injuries at the back. I would have liked to see the second half be as good as the first half, but to win against City you have to be perfect in every part of the game – high press, low press, build-up, every part – because they bring so many problems to you. We weren't perfect, but we came close to perfection today.'

Arne Slot knows that it's not a good idea to incentivise the opposition by making bold claims. He downplayed the impact the results would have on the course of the season. 'When playing against Real Madrid and Man City, teams that have been and are so good, with managers that have won so many trophies, it's always nice to come out in both situations as a winner. But the reason these teams won so many things is not that they won once or twice, they were able to win every three days. Winning once or twice, even against these big teams, is not enough to win anything at the end of the season. Let's not get carried away. It's all about consistency until the end of the season, keeping the players fit and playing with this much energy. There's a long way to go and so many challenges.' Be that as it may, by the final whistle at Anfield, Opta Sports' model gave City a 4.4 per cent chance of winning the Premier League, Arsenal 9.8 per cent and Liverpool 85.1 per cent.

English football over the last 50 years has featured several dominant and long-lasting managers: Bob Paisley's Liverpool, Alex Ferguson's Manchester United and Pep Guardiola's Manchester City. There is something in human nature that dislikes marked superiority and appreciates a fall from grace. Journalist Nico Dijkshoorn praised Slot while indulging in a bit of schadenfreude.

A new king is coming, and the current king knows it all too well. Pep Guardiola resignedly has to watch how Arne Slot winds all the football journalists around his little finger. I can watch him for hours: Arne Slot entertaining himself twice a week with TV interviewers in flawless English. They love this new bald Dutchman. The ease with which he speaks and the time he takes to talk to interviewers about tactics in great detail – I find it impressive. It suspiciously looks like fun. That is probably why I enjoy the downfall of Pep Guardiola so much. Because of Arne Slot, Guardiola suddenly belongs to an old-fashioned group of managers. Slot shows that there is a different way of doing things. He never breaks off an interview. That is why I enjoy Pep Guardiola's losing streak. He has opted for bored arrogance for years.

After the glory of defeating heavyweights Real Madrid and Manchester City, momentum slightly decreased. Against Newcastle United, a thrilling second-half resurgence ultimately failed to yield an eighth successive win in all competitions. Having fought back from 1–0 and 2–1 down, Liverpool were 3–2 up in the closing stages but couldn't hold on to their lead. Salah struck twice, created one for Curtis Jones and saw another effort bounce back off the bar. He had 15 goals and 12 assists in 21 appearances thus far in the season, a goal involvement every 63 minutes. 'Mo had a massive impact on the game,' Slot said. 'It's difficult for me to predict the long-term future, but he is in a very good place at the moment, in a very good team that provides him with good opportunities and he is able to do special things. In the first half we had a lot of problems with their intensity and aggressiveness. They forced us into too many mistakes. It wasn't that difficult to be better in the second half and that's what we were. We dominated the second half. Being 3–2 up one minute before the end, it is a disappointment to drop two points.' It was the first time in Slot's reign that Liverpool had conceded three goals in a game.

Liverpool extended their 100 per cent record in the Champions League group stage to make it 18 points from 18 with a 1–0 win at Girona. The modest victory came courtesy of a Mohamed Salah second-half penalty. The Egyptian master of attack became the first Liverpool player to score 50 goals in European competitions. Liverpool had to work for the win, with the returning Alisson making some important saves. 'We have to thank Alisson that he kept a clean sheet,' Slot said. 'Maybe his teammates wanted to make sure he was really fit, by giving him a lot of work.'

15

HISTORIC TITLE RUN

'I love you. The football you can play is ridiculous, and I can't wait for you to make the next steps. With new ideas and new energy . . . the sky's the limit for you boys.'
JÜRGEN KLOPP, FAREWELL MESSAGE TO THE LIVERPOOL PLAYERS

A Boeing 737 jet was dragged along by airport staff and teams from local businesses in a spectacular charity feat. The challenge took place at Liverpool John Lennon Airport to raise money for Alder Hey Children's Hospital in West Derby. The teams competed to see who could pull the aircraft a set distance in the fastest time. Fortunately, Arne Slot, Virgil van Dijk, Mohamed Salah, Alisson Becker, Kostas Tsimikas, Dominik Szoboszlai and Joe Gomez were not required to over-exert themselves in similar fashion. They simply participated in the annual Liverpool FC Christmas visit to Alder Hey. Slot was donning a Santa hat for the occasion and made a tour of the wards together with some of the most famous members of his squad. They spent time with patients and their families, posed for photographs and handed out LFC gifts and treats. They also met with the doctors and nurses at the hospital. Speaking about the visit, Slot said, 'If you look at how passionate the people that work here are, how much they want to help everyone over here, to give them the best possible time, it's special to see. As a coach, we always think that we are doing very important things, but when you come back from a visit to a children's hospital, you remember who does the really important work in life: it's the doctors and nurses. Our work is not so special then.'

Slot's charity reached across borders. Serious Request is a series of annual multi-day, multimedia fundraising events, hosted by radio stations in the week before Christmas. The project was begun in 2004 by Dutch public pop music radio station 3FM and has since been adopted in Belgium, Switzerland, Sweden, Kenya, South Korea, Austria, Latvia and Portugal. Every year on 18 December, three DJs get locked up in a 'Glass House' that is built somewhere in the centre of a Dutch city. They broadcast for six days, 24 hours a day, raising money for a good cause chosen by the Red Cross, and are not allowed to eat, but can only drink for the entire period. In 2024, the Glass House stood in Slot's beloved Zwolle. Slot was called in during the live broadcast and said he wanted to donate a Liverpool shirt with all his players' signatures to help raise money for the charity Metakids, an organisation conducting research on metabolic diseases in children. 'If more than €5,000 is offered, I will make sure that there will be another signed shirt. I hope that you will collect a great amount and that Zwolle and surroundings will show themselves from their best side.'

Mid-December, Liverpool dropped points in the Premier League, coming from behind twice with only 10 men at home against Fulham. They had played 450 minutes at Anfield without conceding before Andreas Pereira's opener. Many things went against the home team. Fulham's Issa Diop and Andreas Pereira were fortunate not to be awarded red cards. Kenny Tete sent Joe Gomez tumbling in the box, only for penalty calls to be ignored. Slot struggled to keep his emotions in check and received a yellow card for a third time in the season when complaining about a booking handed to Curtis Jones. After going 1–0 behind on 11 minutes, Andy Robertson was sent off after 17 minutes for bringing down Harry Wilson when he was through on goal. Given the situation, salvaging a point with a 2–2 draw was an accomplishment. Liverpool endured a shaky 10 minutes after Robertson's dismissal but then settled into the game. Ryan Gravenberch dropped back into central defence and operated there like he was in his natural domain.

Liverpool had been reduced to 10 players for the first time under Arne Slot. 'It was exactly the opposite of the Girona game where I was pleased with the result but not the performance. Now I am very, very happy about the performance, I couldn't have asked for more. But if you drop points in a home game against Fulham, it's definitely not what you want. So many things went against us, except for one thing: our performance and our fans.' When asked, Slot said his team had not practised playing with 10 men in training sessions. 'You never know which player is going out. It always depends on which players you have available and how you will react. Are you a goal up or down, if you're up, you might consider defending with more players. One goal down, it's different. First you take a look at the tactic board and think this might be a good option. That's what we did for five minutes, but it looked better on the tactic board than on the pitch. At half-time we were able to get our message across better. We told them clearly what we expect from them. Then it helps by scoring straight away. But the game was delayed when they were on the ground, that happened a bit too much when we were trying to keep the momentum going.'

Despite the many changes and young players in action, Liverpool then qualified for the Carabao Cup semi-finals after defeating Southampton 2–1. 'It would be normal if I played with all the regular starters that we would have a better team than we had tonight! Otherwise, I would make the wrong decision every week, which maybe is a possibility,' Slot joked. 'But we also trust these players. I heard the fans singing a song about the Scousers for Trent Alexander-Arnold. I don't know exactly what they sing, but it probably has to do with him coming from the academy as well. We already have a few starters from our academy.'

According to the *Telegraph*, Slot had taken a risk by fielding a B-team against Southampton. 'This is the one where Arne Slot gambled. The Slot machine chanced his arm and won. Again. The Carabao Cup is not high on the priority list for Liverpool, top of the Premier League and the Champions League, but a Wembley final is close and so they just about squeezed past Southampton and into the last four.' After receiving three yellow cards, Slot was serving a touchline ban and watched the game from the press box. He found the positive in it by saying that it was warmer there than in the dugout. It was another sign of his confidence that he did not have an earpiece to stay connected with his staff. The *Daily Mail* wrote, 'He looked calm, with no headphones or direct line of communication with the bench. It was a pretty relaxed evening for Slot. He sat quietly next to analyst Roderick van der Ham, who joined from Feyenoord last month. The two could just as well have tuned their laptops to a Christmas movie on Netflix.' Slot said, 'It was actually a "light" version of a suspension. If you get suspended in the Netherlands, you're not allowed to enter the dressing room and you're not allowed to speak to the media. Here I can still do what I want, because you have the most influence before the game and at half-time. Ideally you're on the sidelines, but it is what it is. This is the first time I've been suspended.'

Prior to their Premier League encounter on 22 December, Slot lavished praise on his Spurs counterpart Ange Postecoglou. 'If I look at Tottenham – and I come from Holland, but I did watch a lot of *Match of the Day* – I think about David Ginola, Paul Gascoigne, Glenn Hoddle, and more recently Luka Modrić, Rafael van der Vaart and Gareth Bale. They've always been a certain brand of football for me and have a certain identity. I think Ange Postecoglou gives them that identity back completely. Ange is doing great work over there. I hope this is seen a bit more. I also hope, hope, hope that he wins a trophy – not the League Cup [Liverpool beat Tottenham 4–1 on aggregate in the two-legged semi-final]. I completely am a fan of his team for the Europa League. [Tottenham won the final against Manchester United.] People always talk about trophies and that it's so important. For his brand of football and his style, if he can combine that with winning something, that would be so good for football in general because people can stop talking about it being too attacking. How on earth can you play too much attacking football? I think it is a privilege to be a season-ticket holder at Tottenham at the moment because they play such a great style. They always won the sympathy of the fans in Europe because of the style of play they had. If I think about Spurs, I think about the shirt, the playing style and their identity and certain players. For me, he brought that back completely. I've said so many positive things about Ange now that if I say another thing it will seem like I'm his agent!'

Perhaps Slot succeeded in lulling Postecoglou asleep with his panegyric. The match found Tottenham wholly unprepared for the Liverpool onslaught. Attacking football is indeed wonderful, as long as you remember to also defend. Both teams did the former, only Liverpool did the latter. Slot had made seven changes from Liverpool's League Cup win over Southampton and reaped the reward of resting players. Midfielder Dominik Szoboszlai drove Liverpool forward and was also among the goals and assists. It turned into a nine-goal thriller, with six scored by Liverpool and three by Totten-ham. Díaz and Salah were the stars, both getting a brace. Salah, who also collected two assists, became the fourth-highest goal-scorer in Liverpool's history. It took his goals total for Liverpool to 229, which lifted him one ahead of Billy Liddell in the club's all-time scorers' list. Every dedicated Liverpool fan knows the significance of Salah's achievement, in just 373 games. It took Liddell 534 appearances. Only Gordon Hodgson (241 in 377), Roger Hunt (285 in 492) and Ian Rush (346 in 660) are still ahead of Salah in that storied list.

By the end of 2024, Salah's record stood at an incredible 37 goal involvements in 26 games of the new season. There was nothing inev-itable about the productivity of the 'Egyptian King', given his poor conclusion to the 2023–24 season. He gave the impression of a star whose time at the top was over and that a departure to Saudi Arabia or the United States seemed inevitable. Under Slot, there were tweaks to his positioning – he started wider, with the right full-back and central midfielder at some distance to give him extra space – and his timing of runs. Slot's focus on deep runs, with midfielders breaking into the penalty area, meant there were more teammates for Salah to assist. In 2025, he was no longer considered an individualist, but an ideal team player. Setting up a teammate in front of the goal was just as easy for him as scoring.

His manager was understandably pleased. 'Apart from him being a good footballer, he is very likable as a person. He is always there to help his teammates, always down-to-earth. He under-stands what it takes to be at this level every three days. That's what impresses me: that, as a top player, he understands how hard he has to work for the quality he shows.' Slot was not happy with the goals conceded. 'Until 60 to 65 minutes, I really, really, really enjoyed what I saw. But then you also saw that no matter how much quality players have, if they think they don't have to run any more in this league, especially against Tottenham, they immediately scored two goals. I was happy when the sixth one went in. Maybe it is human when you are 5–1 up to think, "Okay." But Tottenham always keep on going and they have the ability to create. You have to be on top of your game every second of the game and if you're not 100 per cent, then it hurts you.'

In truth, the scoreline flattered Spurs. Liverpool had 24 shots, 12 on target, and they created nine 'big chances' as defined by Opta. With more clinical finishing and sharper defending, it could have been 7–2 or 8–1. Slot said it probably had been Liverpool's best away performance of the campaign so far.

Reflecting on Manchester City's sudden and spectacular collapse, Slot told reporters, 'I think if you're in this game for a long time – like these players are and I am as well – then 20 games before the end you don't look at [the table]. You know so many challenges are still ahead of you. I think it was two months ago when we were one point behind Manchester City and look what has happened there. You can have injuries and then you have a bit of bad luck, you have a suspension. This can happen to any team, so it's far too early to already be celebrating. You go game by game and you know how many you have to play. Especially in the Premier League, you see results which make you go, "Oh, I didn't expect that." Of course it means something [to be top of the league] because you always prefer to be where we are at the moment rather than another position in the league table. But you know as well as I know – as I've won the league once – just how hard it is to win it. You have to keep on going every three days. You have to be on top of your game every minute of the game. You see last week, in a moment you can get a red card. At Newcastle, we're 3–2 up and you expect to win it but we drop two points. That's the

Premier League. I didn't expect Chelsea to drop points today as well, so it can happen in every game and that's what makes this league so special. That's why people want to watch it, and that's why we play at Christmas time.'

Boxing Day may come to be recognised as the day when Arne Slot's Liverpool were no longer merely early frontrunners and became the team whose trophy it was to lose as rivals Chelsea lost 2–1 to Fulham. Salah scored his 100th home goal in the Premier League, giving Liverpool the last word against Leicester City after Gakpo had cancelled out Jordan Ayew's early opener just before half-time. Liverpool's decision-making before the break was poor. Slot cut an agitated figure on the touchline, but the interval gave him the opportunity to produce the requisite tactical tweaks. The change of approach reaped rewards. 'Patience' is on Slot's keyword list and his players showed a lot more of it in the second half as they waited for openings to emerge.

Cody Gakpo followed his manager in not thinking about the title yet. 'We can't deny that we're in a good position, but we have to keep thinking game by game.' Mohamed Salah agreed but dared to dream out loud about the title. 'The most important thing is that the team keeps winning and hopefully we win the Premier League. It feels different this year, but we have to stay humble and keep going. It would be very special if we win the Premier League. That's what I dream of with this club.' The Kop chanted about being top of the table and serenaded Slot.

On 29 December 2024, Liverpool overpowered West Ham 5–0, putting them nine points clear of Arsenal and ten ahead of Chelsea. Their five goals at the London Stadium came from five different scorers, reflecting the success of a strikerless system that deploys Cody Gakpo and Mohamed Salah as wide forwards, allows nominal centre-forward Luis Díaz to roam freely and score goals, and creates space for midfielders Curtis Jones and Dominik Szoboszlai to make runs beyond the ball.

In 2024, Slot lost only once – the home defeat to Nottingham Forest – in 49 matches (22 at Feyenoord, 27 at Liverpool). 'You could say that it was twice, because we lost to AS Roma on penalties. But compliments to Nottingham Forest for succeeding in that. It was very special. It was a very nice year. It was nice to be able to work at a big club like Feyenoord. I wondered if there was another club where I could do better. It is not just as good here, but even better. To do it in another country is special.'

During 1999–2001, Sander Westerveld played 103 matches for Liverpool. In an interview with the *Algemeen Dagblad*, the former goalkeeper and current analyst with Viaplay paid tribute to Slot.

Admittedly, I didn't expect it to go so well. But I was convinced from day one that Arne was the right person. In all those years, he hasn't changed a bit. He's still that modest man, like most people from the East [in the Netherlands]. He prefers not to be in the spotlight and was like that when I played with him at Sparta, sixteen years ago. I notice it when I have a cup of coffee or a bite to eat with him. He will never act cool because things are going well but keeps both feet on the ground. Always. That's also why Arne is a perfect fit at Liverpool. Look how respectfully he talks about Klopp and keeps saying that he laid the foundation for this team. They like that at Liverpool. How sympathetic he is, how well he speaks English, how calm he is. It's not for nothing that the fans love him and now sing the most beautiful songs about him. He is comfortably ahead in the Premier League and at the top of the Champions League. I have every confidence in it. It's only just starting.

Harvey Elliott spoke about training under Arne Slot with a degree of psychological poise you don't commonly find with players in their early twenties. He explained how he practises mindfulness and painted a picture of a theatre stage where a refined art is being honed.

> I think, for me, the most important part is my drive into training. I give a lot of thought to things then, so that as soon as I come through the gates and I park my car up, everything that I've needed to think about, whether it's good or bad, it's out of my head. As soon as I walk into the building, my mind and my focus is just on football. With the games coming thick and fast, it's now just about practising the new style of play that we've learned with the gaffer and how we're going to keep applying it in games. It's completely different to what we used to play before, so it's like if you're performing, if you've got a show, you keep going over and rehearsing it and rehearsing your lines or your part of the play. That's kind of what we're doing at the moment. We just keep going over and over things and making sure we're getting it to a tee, really.

Brentford manager Thomas Frank's praise of Liverpool as 'probably the best team in the world' was instructive considering that his team recently had also played Manchester City and Arsenal. Darwin Núñez replaced Luis Díaz midway through the second half at the Gtech Community Stadium in mid-January, and his exploits late in the game gave Liverpool a much-needed victory following a sequence of disappointing results. The photograph of the elated Uruguayan removing his jersey and celebrating in front of the travelling supporters will become a treasured club heirloom, a reminder of a possibly campaign-defining moment. He doubled his league tally for the season with two clinical finishes in stoppage time to break the hosts' stubborn resistance and Brentford fans' hearts. Wastefulness in the final third almost cost Liverpool. Their total of 37 shots was their highest since they had the same number in a 4–0 home win over Everton in April 2016. With just eight of them being on target and one hitting the woodwork, the 36th and 37th attempts were vital. The value of Núñez's contribution was magnified when rivals Arsenal threw away a 2–0 lead at home to Aston Villa.

Núñez had been criticised for his unsteady finishing, and he sorely needed a breakthrough moment. When the final whistle sounded, he clenched his fists and looked to the heavens. Arne Slot had been unfailingly supportive of his errant forward, as he had been of Trent Alexander-Arnold and Harvey Elliott when their status in the squad had been questioned. The manager said, 'The first hour is often open but the last 30 minutes dominant. Then to have someone like Darwin is nice. He brings energy and power. In most of our games, especially in the last half-hour, we control and completely dominate around their penalty box—that's where he's at his best when we can bring the balls in. I'm very happy with him – not only because he scored two goals today. I'm very happy with the other performances he put in for us as well. He's having a good season, he scores goals, he works very hard for the team, he assists.'

Liverpool's head coach was forced to address suggestions that his team's results had not been convincing since the turn of the year. With league draws against Manchester United and Nottingham Forest and a defeat in the first leg of their Carabao Cup semi-final against Tottenham, there seemed to be room for improvement. There was a hint of irritation in Slot's response at the press conference after the Brentford match. 'You are talking about the result. I focus on my own team. If you look simply at the number of chances created, and I think you are all a bit aware of xG, that is something familiar to you? Do me a favour and look back at the Manchester United, Nottingham Forest and Brentford game, and see what the xG of both teams were – and you will probably see that nothing has changed between now and the first half of the season. What you do see is that at this moment, it's a bit harder for us to convert our chances into goals.' Indeed, Liverpool's performances in the season continued to be strikingly consistent, with their non-penalty xG of 2.2 per 90 minutes the best of the Premier League and their January games barely deviating from their average.

As before at Feyenoord, having Slot in the Liverpool dugout proved to be a good thing for the club bank account. The near-flawless run to the last 16 of the Champions League earned the club £85 million in UEFA prize money. But for the head coach, the positive of being able to rest key players for the game against PSV at the Philips Stadion ahead of the next Premier League match, three days later, mattered more. 'Normally I would only be looking at PSV but I'm looking at Bournemouth as well. Like all the teams in Europe, we are playing many, many games and the [players] we left behind could have played, but we need to think long-term. It took me a while to understand this new format, but I'm now 100 per cent sure it doesn't matter at all if you end up first or second because we will play the team that is 15th, 16th, 17th or 18th, and then it's down to the draw. It has no impact on the league table. But a wise man once said to me, he's never seen anything good come from losing a game, so we will do everything to try and win.'

Slot lined up a second-string squad. Cody Gakpo and Andy Robertson were the only players of Liverpool's starting eleven to make it to the Netherlands, the latter featuring in the position otherwise always occupied by Virgil van Dijk. Gakpo received a hero's welcome at his boyhood club, where he scored 55 times in 159 games prior to a move to Liverpool exactly two years earlier. A PSV supporter held up a sign: 'Cody Gakpo, *Eindtovenaar* – may I have your shirt please?' a play on words suggesting that the Eindhoven native is a wizard.

The Liverpool reserves failed to clear the final hurdle to make it eight wins from eight when they were beaten 3–2. In the process, Amara Nallo established an unwanted new club record when he received a red card four minutes after coming on as a substitute. He became the youngest Liverpool player to be sent off, at 18 years and 72 days, replacing Ballon d'Or winner Michael Owen, 45 days older when he was dismissed in a match against Manchester United in April 1998. Arne Slot said, 'He'd never played first-team football and then to make a debut at Champions League level is probably the hardest way to make a debut. It's a big moment for him to learn from and it's cruel. You think, "I'm going to make my debut in the Champions League," and then a few minutes later you go off with a red card. That's always difficult. He has to fight very hard to make sure he plays a second Champions League game. It is not going to be easy but hopefully he will.' Despite the defeat, Liverpool finished in the top spot of the league phase.

Topping the Champions League's first phase, Slot believed, could present a distorted picture. 'The format of the tournament is different now, which makes it very difficult to judge based on the ranking. It is a strange format, where you are also dependent on the teams you meet. If you are at the top, that does not mean you are the best. In tennis, if you are number-one seeded, you know it is always better to face the number 24 than number 8, but now we are in a new format so we don't know yet. Some teams are high because they had a lucky draw and some teams are low because they had a tough draw. It's too far off to know if it is an advantage finishing first or second. We still don't know yet, might be lucky or unlucky. For me, it doesn't tell me anything. The most important thing is that we now skip a round.'

• • •

Liverpool had returned from the Tottenham Hotspur Stadium aggrieved after their 24-game unbeaten run ended in controversy. Arne Slot was incensed that referee Stuart Attwell did not show Lucas Bergvall a second yellow card for a foul on Kostas Tsimikas shortly before the teenager scored the late winner in the Carabao Cup semi-final first leg. Liverpool emphatically responded by thrashing Tottenham 4–0 at Anfield in the second leg. Cody Gakpo struck in the 34th minute, and Mohamed Salah added his 26th goal of the season from the penalty spot. A dominant midfield display was key to their control. Dominik Szoboszlai, whose £60 million move from RB Leipzig had yielded a mixed first season, had struggled under the weight of early comparisons to Steven Gerrard. He had been relegated to the bench in the closing stages of Jürgen Klopp's tenure but was rejuvenated under Slot. Against Spurs, he had five shots, nine box touches, five chances created, nine possession recoveries, and scored the third goal after a well-worked move. Virgil van Dijk sealed the rout with a powerful header in the 81st minute.

Slot's composed demeanour had clearly rubbed off on his players throughout the season. For much of the campaign, the head coach's calmness was mirrored in Liverpool's measured performances. Their style of play showed a level of composure that had often been missing under Klopp, allowing them to neutralise opponents and close out games with cool efficiency. Yet those familiar with Slot from his time in the Netherlands knew he wasn't immune to emotional surges. Beneath the calm exterior was a fiery competitor, easily riled by questionable officiating. 'There are too many referees [in the Netherlands] who have no idea about the impact and consequences of their decisions on a team,' he once said while managing Feyenoord. That combative edge inevitably spilled over into his spell at Liverpool.

Everton first played at Goodison Park in 1892, but with ambitions for a bigger future, the club will move to the new Everton Stadium for the 2025–26 season. The 120th and final Merseyside derby at Goodison descended into chaos during added time. These encounters are famously incandescent, and Arne Slot may have wondered what hit him. Fireworks, blue smoke bombs and deafening cheers greeted Liverpool's team bus upon arrival – a mere prelude to the evening's pandemonium. Everton struck first in the 11th minute, with Jarrad Branthwaite smartly working a free-kick that striker Beto shot past Alisson. That lead lasted just seven minutes until Alexis Mac Allister headed home after a pinpoint Mohamed Salah cross. Salah seemed to have sealed the win with his 27th goal of the season in the 73rd minute, quieting the raucous home crowd. Liverpool fans broke into chants of 'We won the league at Goodison Park' a little prematurely. James Tarkowski smashed in a stunning volley deep into injury time to secure a dramatic 2–2 draw. The balance was maintained: Liverpool and Everton each finished with 41 wins at Goodison, with the other 38 meetings ending in draws.

Abdoulaye Doucouré celebrated provocatively at the away end, prompting Curtis Jones to react by shoving the Everton midfielder away from the Liverpool supporters. The confrontation quickly escalated into a melee between both teams, with bottles thrown from the stands as police and stewards struggled to regain control amid the din. At full time, referee Michael Oliver produced four red cards. Jones and Doucouré were both sent off after receiving second yellows, while Arne Slot and his assistant Sipke Hulshoff were shown straight reds for their post-match dissent. Slot, riled by heavy tackles, pitch invaders, and bullying from Everton players, had grown increasingly frustrated with the officiating, repeatedly protesting to the fourth official during the match.

The Premier League website featured the announcement that 'Liverpool head coach Arne Slot was dismissed at the end of the Merseyside derby for using offensive, insulting or abusive language. He is handed a two-match touchline ban as a result.' It was an unwarranted judgement, given the Football Association (FA) deals with disciplinary matters, and the statement was removed soon after it appeared. The FA had to decide whether to issue a charge, a warning, a reminder of responsibilities, or take no further action. Speaking on the episode a few days after the match, Slot admitted his emotions had gotten out of control. 'The extra time, the additional five minutes ended up being eight minutes. A lot happened. The emotions got the better of me. I should have handled it differently after the game. There is an ongoing process. I have to respect that, so I can't go into the details. It's an emotional sport. Sometimes individuals make the wrong decision in their emotions. That's clearly what I did.'

Reflecting on the bedlam, Chris Bascombe wrote an article in *The Telegraph*, titled, 'Arne Slot – How Liverpool's king of Zen lost his cool in Goodison cauldron':

Arne Slot had called for his players to keep cool heads in the derby cauldron. Suffice to say, the Dutchman's guide to Buddhism will not be a bestseller any time soon. So much for the calmer, more controlled and less emotional

Liverpool . . . Slot's takeaway from his first Merseyside derby is that there are no reports, testimonies or videos of the previous 244 meetings between the neighbours that prepare you for the turbulent reality. Only when living and breathing every snarling tackle, venomously debated decision and raging passion released by every goal – multiplied after injury-time equalisers – can you truly understand what this fixture means . . . Slot cannot allow these late lapses to become frequent in his task of keeping his nearest rivals at bay. On home turf, Liverpool are usually perfectly equipped to cope with the most tempestuous encounters with professionalism and poise.

Veteran Everton manager David Moyes was more magnanimous toward his younger colleague. During a press conference ahead of his team's next Premier League match he said, 'It was an emotional night. It was a game where everyone was involved. We were playing against a really good Liverpool team, probably the best in Europe and certainly in our country. We had to do a job on Liverpool to make sure we got a result and we just about did on the night. I feel a bit for Arne Slot. This was the sort of thing that I was always getting involved in when I was a younger manager. It tells me that he cares a lot for his club and is fighting for his players. Everybody has to do what they can and he did it for his team. When you get a bit older, you sit back and say, "What was I doing?" I have had a lot of moments and a lot that I am not proud of.'

It took two weeks for the FA to deliver its verdict, allowing Slot to remain on the touchline for Liverpool's league fixtures against Wolves, Aston Villa and Manchester City. The strain of the Premier League title race was beginning to surface. Against Wolves, Luis Díaz bundled in an early goal, and when Mohamed Salah added a second from the penalty spot before half-time, it seemed Liverpool were set for a comfortable win. However, a second penalty award was overturned by VAR, and Matheus Cunha's superb finish halved the deficit, setting up a tense and nervy conclusion. Slot said, 'It was mentally difficult the second half because we thought we scored the third, then thought we got a penalty, both situations were correctly handled by the referee. They got better and better, we got worse and worse. We had to show a different mentality which we did and got it over the line.'

A frenetic 2–2 draw between Aston Villa and Liverpool saw Mohamed Salah and Trent Alexander-Arnold score either side of goals from Youri Tielemans and Ollie Watkins. Taking three points from a team unbeaten in 12 home league matches was always going to be difficult, but Liverpool should have defeated Villa. They outshot their opponents 17 to nine and posted an xG of 2.51 to 0.67, only to be let down by missed chances and defensive lapses. Slot commented, 'It was a great game but I am not happy with the result. We scored two good goals and created enough chances to get the winner. We desired more and that is the only thing we can blame ourselves for a few times now we did not get what we deserved. We must not make a habit of that.'

Manchester City were well below their best, but Liverpool still had a job to do at the Etihad, where they hadn't won a league match since 2015. Slot's team delivered a controlled, clinical performance. The head coach's tactical tweak had four midfielders – Curtis Jones, Ryan Gravenberch, Alexis Mac Allister, and Dominik Szoboszlai – deployed, with no recognised striker. Jones and Szoboszlai operated as dual number 10s tasked with disrupting City's rhythm. The opener came from a a cleverly worked corner routine: Szoboszlai pulled the ball back for Salah, whose shot deflected into the net off Nathan Aké.

Szoboszlai later credited set-piece coach Aaron Briggs, a former City analyst, for spotting the weakness. Liverpool's second was equally well-constructed. Trent Alexander-Arnold released Salah down the right, who cut inside and teed up Szoboszlai to slot home through Abdukodir Khusanov's legs, leaving Ederson unsighted. Liverpool scored twice from their only two shots on target. As the home fans streamed out, the away end erupted in chants of 'Hand it over, hand it over,' followed by a defiant 'We're gonna win the league.'

Slot spoke about how the match demanded different qualities from his team, as they had far less possession than usual, but praised their outstanding ability to adapt quickly in every transition. 'No one saw us as a title contender when we started. No one in the world of football would expect City to not be close to the one who leads the league. Three days ago we had a draw at Villa and people told me we were not in a good place and then three days later we win and it is the complete opposite again. We work every single day to achieve this and it is three months of very hard work to keep this going. There is no secret. You always have to adapt to the challenge you get. A week ago we experienced how difficult Wolves at home was. This result was more about defence than attack. It is normal for fanbases of teams leading the league to be positive, but it is important to understand why we are where we are.'

The FA issued Arne Slot a two-match touchline ban, ruling him and Sipke Hulshoff out of the matches against Newcastle United and Southampton. Slot was fined £70,000 and Hulshoff £7,000. After a disciplinary hearing, Everton and Liverpool were also fined £65,000 and £50,000 respectively. In its statement, the FA said, 'An independent regulatory commission has sanctioned Everton, Liverpool, Arne Slot and Sipke Hulshoff in relation to the Premier League fixture between the clubs on Wednesday 12 February. It was alleged that both clubs failed to ensure their players and/or technical area occupants did not behave in an improper and/or provocative way following the final whistle.'

Slot and Hulshoff watched the contest against Newcastle from the Anfield Main Stand, but their absence from the touchline made little difference. Under assistant coach John Heitinga's guidance, Liverpool eased to a 2–0 win, with goals from Dominik Szoboszlai and Alexis Mac Allister. In September Slot had said of Szoboszlai, 'For an attacking midfielder at Liverpool, his numbers need to go up, but I am really happy with the way he has done until now. I am 100 per cent sure that if he plays in a team with so much quality around him and with the quality he has, he will, in the end, score more goals as well.' The Hungarian delivered in the second half of the season, with his sharp finishing complementing his overall game. After the match, Slot praised his team's professionalism in seeing out a comfortable victory. 'This was more like the way we've won the previous games. It was more like how we have been winning games all season. After Everton, Wolves and Villa, people started to doubt us. Then you have to react to that.'

Liverpool beat Southampton 3–1, with Arne Slot making it clear that his absence from the bench didn't mean he wasn't involved. 'The fans always sing great songs. We'll be hearing them again during the match. I'll be listening from the stands – maybe I'll even start one,' he joked beforehand. Southampton struck just before half-time after a mix-up between Van Dijk and Alisson, prompting a furious Arne Slot to storm down from the directors' box to the dressing room. Known for measured half-time talks, he instead delivered a blistering critique of Liverpool's flat first-half showing, slamming their lack of energy and intensity. His triple substitution – Elliott, Mac Allister, and Robertson – sparked an instant response, as Liverpool came back with three goals in nine second-half minutes to seal a commanding 3–1 win. Slot said, 'It's a sign of a good team that you can win in different ways. It was a poor performance first half – not only because of the way we played but also because of the energy we brought. I know these players are capable of doing much, much better. They were not the energy levels I am used to with these players.' Following the victory, statisticians placed Liverpool's chances of claiming the title at 98.9 per cent.

Excitement was mounting as Liverpool sat atop the Premier League and had the best record in the league phase of the Champions League. With the physical demands on players intensifying, managing workloads and rotating the squad became just as crucial as executing tactics. Liverpool cruised to a 4–0 FA Cup third-round win over Accrington Stanley at Anfield, highlighted by the senior debut of Rio Ngumoha. At just 16 years and 135 days old, he became the youngest player to start for the club, dazzling the crowd and opponents alike with his sharp dribbling, quick feet, and body feints. First-half goals from Diogo Jota and Trent Alexander-Arnold put Liverpool in control, Jayden Danns added another in front of the Kop, and Federico Chiesa sealed the win with his first goal for the club in the final minute.

Liverpool's fourth-round FA Cup tie at Plymouth Argyle, the Championship's bottom club, did not go as well. Plymouth's players were up for the fight, with Bosnian defender Nikola Katić even losing a tooth for the cause in a collision with teammate Adam Randell. With bigger priorities looming, Slot fielded a weakened side, expecting that his line-up would be able to do the job. Pundits later criticised him for lacking a plan B and naming an inexperienced bench. Key players like Alisson, Salah, Van Dijk, Gravenberch, Konaté, Mac Allister, Szoboszlai, and Robertson had been left at home. When the match didn't go to script, Slot had few alternatives, and it proved costly. Liverpool created little and were knocked out by a Ryan Hardie penalty early in the second half. Asked afterwards if he regretted his line-up. Slot said, 'No, because you never know what would have happened if we played with our starters. We've seen so many times this season that it is a playing style that is very difficult – constantly long ball, second ball, long balls, second balls. It's hard for any team to play against.'

Liverpool had secured automatic qualification for the Champions League last 16, avoiding the two-legged playoffs reserved for teams finishing from ninth to 24th. Before conceding in the 62nd minute against Lille in the penultimate game of the group stage, Liverpool had gone 599 minutes in Europe without getting a goal against – surpassing the previous club record of 572 minutes set under Rafa Benitez in 2005–06. 'Very pleased,' Slot said. 'I put everything down to, first, the quality of the players and, second, they have an incredible work rate. We keep clean sheets not by defending a lot, we keep clean sheets by attacking a lot. The fans prefer it like this as well. It's definitely a good achievement to end up top of this league. But I said many times it's hard to judge a table after eight games, let alone with the teams playing different opponents. Some have faced easier opponents than others. It doesn't give us any assurances for the next round. I see the four teams we can face and especially one of them is definitely one you are hoping not to face.' He knew the danger ahead: among the potential opponents was Paris Saint-Germain.

If Slot was annoyed by Liverpool's draw, he didn't show it. PSG's quality was undeniable. They demolished Brest 10–0 on aggregate in the play-offs and in Ligue 1 thrashed Lille 4–1 – leading 4–0 inside 37 minutes to notch their tenth straight win under Luis Enrique. Ahead of facing Liverpool, PSG were unbeaten in 22 matches across all competitions, with 66 goals scored and just four draws. Their previous four games alone had produced 21 goals. 'Their form tells us all that we need to know about the challenge that we will face,' Slot said.

The last time Liverpool visited Paris, for the 2022 Champions League final, they left feeling battered, not by the match itself, but by the chaos caused by UEFA, French police, and a few hundred troublemakers. This time, the PSG ultras in the Virage Auteuil sent a clear message with a giant banner: 'Victoire!' Wave after wave of PSG attacks had Liverpool hanging on, but as the match wore on, the home crowd's energy shifted to frustration. In the 87th minute, against all odds, Liverpool stunned the dominant French champions. Mohamed Salah, contained all night by Nuno Mendes and largely ineffective, had been replaced by 21-year-old Harvey Elliott. His first touch, 47 seconds later, came when he latched onto a pass from another substitute, Darwin Núñez, and coolly side-footed Liverpool into a shock lead. The stats were staggering: PSG had 70 per cent possession, 27 shots to Liverpool's two, 10 shots on target to one, and completed 630 passes to Liverpool's 220. Yet Liverpool somehow escaped the Parc des Princes with a 1–0 win to take back to Anfield. France's leading sports newspaper, *L'Équipe*, dubbed it an 'English heist'. It was the ultimate smash and grab.

Liverpool have had no shortage of iconic European nights, and this one ranked among the finest. Once again, Slot's substitutions proved decisive. He admitted it was 'almost a miracle' they hadn't conceded before half-time, with Alisson producing several crucial saves. 'It was probably the performance of my life,' said the Liverpool goalkeeper. 'The manager was telling us how hard it would be to play against PSG, how good they are with the ball and that we would have to be ready to suffer. We knew what was coming. All the efforts the team put in makes my job easier. Then, at the end, Harvey coming in and scoring the goal. It is a great story for us. A great night.' Slot added, 'I have had some very good players as a manager but never the best goalkeeper in the world until now. To go away with a win here was probably a bit more than we deserved. We were not under par. It purely had to do with the quality of PSG. We felt their quality. It was an unbelievable challenge for us to get away with a result and we know it is going to be a hard one in a week.'

Slot knew Liverpool would need a level of performance beyond anything they had shown domestically to keep their European hopes alive. 'They are the most complete team we have faced so far. We have faced Arsenal and City, but the intensity PSG play at is difficult. They have so much quality and a great manager because he has the team playing in a way that is not easy to play against. I was very impressed by the intensity, the team cohesion and the rotations in the midfield. They are such a complete team, such a well-managed team and we experienced that last Wednesday. Some people said we played poorly. I don't agree. I think they played tremendously well. I don't think we have played a team this season who combined that much quality with intensity. But I do think we can play better.'

The volume inside Anfield reached its highest levels. It was the mirror image of the Parc des Princes: this time, Gianluigi Donnarumma was the hero, just as Alisson had been in Paris. PSG struck early, with Ousmane Dembélé leveling the tie on aggregate in the 13th minute. After a tense battle, the match was decided by a nerve-racking penalty shootout. PSG won the crucial coin toss and chose to take their penalties in front of their fans at the Anfield Road end. A PSG supporter with a megaphone unleashed a deafening barrage behind the goal, disturbing Liverpool's takers. It worked – Donnarumma saved penalties from Darwin Núñez and Curtis Jones, while PSG converted all four of theirs to advance to the Champions

League quarter-finals. Luis Enrique had predicted the winner of the tie would reach the final. For Liverpool the European campaign ended in sudden, painful fashion. Slot remained gracious. 'It was the best game of football I was ever involved in. Incredible performance compared with last week. In the first 25 minutes we created chance after chance but maybe we ran out of luck after last week. It feels a bit unfair to go out in this round already – to win the group and then play a team as strong as PSG.'

Arne Slot admitted Liverpool fully deserved their 2–1 defeat to Newcastle United the following weekend in the Carabao Cup final, criticising his team's below-par showing at Wembley. In an attempt to freshen up the squad, he had given the players a rest day before the final, but they still appeared sluggish and uninspired. Nine of Liverpool's ten outfield starters had also featured in both matches against the French side. Yet Slot dismissed fatigue as an excuse. 'Disappointing result, disappointing performance. Completely different than I felt after the Paris Saint-Germain game. Losing twice in a row is something I think we do for the first time. But that probably also comes with going into the latter stages of a tournament, so facing Paris Saint-Germain and Newcastle in a final are two very good teams, both with their own styles.'

Liverpool supporters were stunned by the midfield and attacking struggles, especially against a side they had comfortably beaten just three weeks earlier. By the time Slot led his dejected players to collect their runners-up medals, much of the Liverpool end at Wembley had already emptied. Over 95 minutes, a team that had scored more than 100 goals during the season barely troubled Nick Pope. While the loss in Paris was more forgivable, Liverpool underperformed badly in a domestic final. Slot understandably tried to emphasise the positives after such a bruising week, saying, 'It was a tough week, but we also extended our league lead to 12 points, so not everything was negative. The further you go in tournaments, the tougher the opponents. Even Liverpool can lose games, that's part of football.'

When Liverpool returned to Premier League action against Everton, Diogo Jota celebrated his first goal since rescuing a draw at Nottingham Forest in January, and it proved the only goal of the game. 'Very pleased,' Slot said. 'Everton were nine games in a row unbeaten, hardly ever concede a goal, hardly ever concede a chance, defend with 10 players, apart from Beto, in and around their penalty box.' Jota repaid the faith Slot had shown in him, especially after disappointing starts against PSG and Newcastle that might easily have seen him dropped to the bench.

Slot dismissed suggestions that complacency was behind Liverpool's 3–2 defeat to Fulham, ending their 26-game unbeaten league run. 'No, there's no reason for us to be complacent. We're not number one in the league because we win every game by a margin of three or four goals. It takes so much effort, so much hard work combined with quality for us to win games. The team that won the league for the past four seasons [Manchester City] was already 3–0 up at half-time in almost every game they played. That's not the way it is for us. We are fully aware of the fact we need to compete for seven more games. When we played Everton, it was a close call. Today was a close call. Many times we've been on the right side, today we were on the wrong side mainly because of the errors we made.'

The Hillsborough Memorial is a lasting tribute to the 97 Liverpool FC supporters who lost their lives in the tragedy of 15 April 1989. What should have been a joyous FA Cup semi-final against Nottingham Forest at Sheffield Wednesday's Hillsborough Stadium turned into horror when overcrowding in the Leppings Lane stand led to a fatal crush. The events of that day left a deep scar not only on Liverpool but on the entire footballing world. Erected outside Anfield, the memorial features *The Band of Life*, a powerful bronze sculpture by Tom Murphy, with eternal flames surrounding a marble plaque inscribed with the names of the 97 victims. It is a place of remembrance, reflection and resilience. In the stillness of the early morning, Liverpool manager Arne Slot and club captain Virgil van Dijk paid their respects by laying a wreath at the memorial. Prior to the match against West Ham, Anfield paid its respects ahead of the 36th anniversary of the disaster with a moment of silence at the centre circle.

When the match began, Mohamed Salah delivered a brilliant outside-of-the-boot pass to set up Luis Díaz for Liverpool's early opener. Frustration erupted as Van Dijk inadvertently turned Wan-Bissaka's cross off Robertson and into Liverpool's net, sparking a furious reaction from the left-back. Fortunately, the Liverpool captain was in a hurry to get his hands on the Premier League trophy, and he made amends when he headed in Alexis Mac Allister's 89th-minute corner to seal the win. Alisson, back in goal after recovering from a concussion, impressed with several key saves before the unfortunate own goal. The victory pushed Liverpool 13 points clear at the top of the table with six games to go.

Slot was animated after the final whistle, celebrating in front of the Kop. He praised how Anfield collectively responded to the blow of conceding the equaliser, with the crowd driving the late push that led to Van Dijk's winner. 'A big relief. West Ham showed their quality, Paquetá and Kudus were outstanding in the second half. Maybe we were too afraid and didn't push hard enough. After West Ham scored it seemed there was no time, but our players and our fans thought differently. We saved a big set piece for a very important moment. As a manager, you are always looking at those who have already achieved a lot of things in their careers to step up in the most important moments of the season. At the end of the season, moments get bigger and bigger and bigger. Today, the three of them showed up. Alisson had probably his best game of the season, Virgil scored the header to get us three points, and Mo was again very important in the first goal and really lively in the first half. I don't care where we win it. We know we still have to win two more games and the first 32 games have shown us how difficult that is, as the competition has never been as strong as it is this season.'

Trent Alexander-Arnold's emotional celebration captured the spirit of Liverpool's Premier League champions run. Brought on in the 71st against Leicester at the King Power Stadium to spark a mis-firing team, he was warmly received by the travelling fans, even as speculation about a free transfer to Real Madrid grew. Within five minutes, he made his mark, blasting his first-ever left-footed goal past Mads Hermansen to put Liverpool ahead. Alexander-Arnold ripped off his shirt and sprinted to the away end, arms outstretched as his teammates mobbed him. It was a huge moment, cementing his impact on Liverpool's historic title run.

Liverpool's charge to the title had a soundtrack – 'Sultans of Swing' echoing through the dressing room after every hard-fought victory, the celebratory anthem of a team in flow. Alisson, ever the rhythm-and-mood setter off the pitch, added 'Walk of Life' to the playlist, turning it into another rallying cry. It spoke to a squad and staff in perfect synchronisation, a group who were able to tune out the outside noise and get on with the task of winning matches with polished efficiency. Over the course of the 2024–25 season, no one in the Premier League could match their steady rhythm.

16

TOT SLOT: A NEW BEGINNING

'The accolade of the most successful club – today the debate is over, it's Liverpool football club. For the [United] fanbase it absolutely hurts like hell. Arne Slot, what a spectacular coaching performance. They deserve it, they've been the best team all season.'

GARY NEVILLE, FORMER MANCHESTER UNITED CAPTAIN

Transfer talk is a staple at elite football clubs. Rumours of incoming deals and behind-the-scenes whispers give fans a sense of connection, a chance to critique, and endless material for speculation. Liverpool regularly feature in the Premier League's rumour mill, with familiar storylines resurfacing each window. The Reds are often cast in imaginary bidding wars with clubs like Arsenal or Man City – not because they're always serious contenders, but because the Liverpool name guarantees attention. Many of these stories are agent-driven or designed to jump-start negotiations, yet they still create plenty of noise, even as the club goes about its actual business with quiet efficiency.

Despite the clamour among a section of the fanbase to bolster the squad, Arne Slot made it clear he was happy with his options and that Liverpool were unlikely to bring in reinforcements during the January window. 'It would be a bit weird if I said during the summer break that we're very happy with the team and then I told you something different now. You always look at the market, this club has always done that. We did that with the goalkeeper [Giorgi Mamardashvili] who we don't even have at the moment. If there's a chance in the market then this club always tries to bring someone in, but the team is in a good place. We have a very good squad and if you look at the league table, the players have shown that the trust we had in them was correct. For now, we're happy with the team we have.'

The strength of Slot's bench at Bournemouth was proof: Diogo Jota, Darwin Núñez, Curtis Jones, Harvey Elliott, Wataru Endo, Conor Bradley, Jarell Quansah, Kostas Tsimikas, and Caoimhin Kelleher. For the first time since 2007, a Liverpool manager had a fully fit squad to choose from in February. Even Federico Chiesa and Joe Gomez were available, but there was no room for them in the 20-man matchday squad – a rare luxury, especially after the demanding Christmas period. It marked a stark contrast to Jürgen Klopp's situation in February 2024, when Liverpool were missing seven key players: Alisson, Alexander-Arnold, Szoboszlai, Jota, Núñez, Salah and Gravenberch. Under Slot, the squad missed just 92 matches' worth between them, compared to 159 at the same stage the previous year and 253 the year before. That fitness and depth gave Slot the freedom to make second-half substitutions without weakening the team.

Despite the presence of so much firepower on the pitch, Liverpool had to be at their best to overcome Andoni Iraola's in-form Bournemouth. They rose to the challenge, with Mohamed Salah scoring both goals in a hard-earned 2–0 win on the south coast. The squad then returned to London for a team bonding evening, celebrating their nine-point lead at the top of the table with dinner at one of the West End's trendiest spots. They chose the Japanese-Peruvian fusion restaurant Piraña, located in upscale Mayfair, known for its inventive and artfully presented dishes. Highlights on the menu include £40 tuna tartare and £50 'Premium Sushi' featuring lobster and Wagyu beef – while high-end options like £440 Beluga Caviar and a £495 Australian Tomahawk cater to those with a serious appetite and deeper pockets.

All season long, one recurring topic at press conferences was the futures of Mohamed Salah, Virgil van Dijk and Trent Alexander-Arnold. Journalists pressed for updates, but Slot's response remained steady, 'There is no news.' Despite the contract uncertainty, the trio's situation never disrupted the team's performances, though things could easily have gone another way. These millionaire superstars had to weigh not just what they might gain by leaving, but also what they stood to lose. The Saudi Pro League would have eagerly welcomed them as poster boys of its gold-plated project. True to form, Liverpool's board took a measured approach. Salah and Van Dijk's standout form made a persuasive case for flexibility, and for Slot, retaining them was vital, provided the finances aligned.

Mohamed Salah is revered not just in Egypt but across the Arab world, with his brilliance at Anfield a source of pride and inspiration. He has encouraged millions to chase their own dreams. His Muslim faith shapes his life, and he has been praised by religious leaders for being such a positive role model, someone who is helping to reshape how the world sees the Islamic community. Within the Liverpool dressing room, teammates had long felt he would stay, not just because of his performances, but also because of the strong bond he formed with Arne Slot. He openly spoke about the coach's role in taking his game to new heights. 'He is very honest. The Dutch are quite tough, but he made our lives easier. The tactics are quite different. Now I don't have to defend much. I said, "As long as you rest me defensively I will provide offensively." I am glad that I did. He listened a lot and you can see the numbers.'

In April, finally, there was good news. Salah signed a new two-year contract, ending a year-long saga and securing the future of a Liverpool legend. In a video released by LFCTV, he spoke about how his daughter, Makkah, was 'the happiest one in the family'. She didn't want to leave her school, her friends, her life in Liverpool, and neither did he. 'It's great,' Salah said. 'I had my best years here. I played eight years, hopefully it's going to be 10. I'm enjoying my life here, enjoying my football. I had the best years in my career. I signed here because I believe we can win a lot of big trophies together.'

Salah's base salary stood at £350,000 a week, but bonuses and performance incentives pushed his earnings far higher. With commercial endorsements included, some of which also had performance-related clauses, he made up to £1 million per week. He is worth it. In the victory over West Ham he broke the record for most goal involvements in a 38-game Premier League season. Post-match, standing beside his captain and reflecting on his new deal, he beamed, 'I am glad that we managed to do it early, before the end of the season, and hopefully Virgil will be next. I just say hopefully! He can do whatever he wants, but I would love to see him again next season.'

Van Dijk never turned up the pressure on Liverpool's hierarchy in public. As captain, his priority was keeping the focus on winning trophies. Like Salah, he made it clear he wanted to stay. His family was settled in the northwest, and his bond with the fans was unmistakable when he kissed the badge after his dramatic winner against West Ham. 'I can tell you I'm very proud today to captain my 100th [league] game for Liverpool. It was an emotional day, because of the Hillsborough anniversary. Everyone knows how much I love this club.' He was the cornerstone of Liverpool's title push, producing one commanding display after another. Under Slot, he embraced a more evolved role, tasked with more responsibility in building play with his passing. Van Dijk fully embodies the captaincy, setting the tone on and off the pitch and elevating those around him. A few days after the West Ham match, he too signed a contract extension.

'The journey I've had so far in my career, to be able to extend it with another two years at this club is amazing and I'm so happy. It was always the plan and it was always Liverpool. There wasn't any doubt in my head that this is the place to be for me and my family. I'm one of Liverpool. Someone called me the other day an adopted Scouser – I'm really proud to hear these things, it gives me a great feeling. It is the place for me to be, to spend my best years, be successful with the club as we have been over the years and hopefully the future as well. I love the city, I love the club, I love the fans. I love my teammates. I love everything that embodies Liverpool, and on to many more.'

Replacing Van Dijk would arguably have been an even tougher task for Liverpool than finding a successor to Salah. He was pivotal and played every minute of the Premier League campaign. His new deal includes no break or release clauses, and he won't be taking a pay cut. His salary remains around £400,000 per week, keeping him among Europe's highest-paid defenders. The terms are largely guaranteed, with incentives tied only to team success rather than individual performance.

In the summer of 2027, Salah will turn 35 and Van Dijk 36. The new deals effectively ensure that Liverpool will keep them until they step away from the big stage. The two will be at the heart of Liverpool's aspirations for coming seasons.

• • •

The anticipation on Merseyside had been building to a fever pitch ever since Arsenal's midweek draw with Crystal Palace left Liverpool on the cusp of glory. Street vendors were doing brisk business selling 'Champions of England' merchandise, while fans faced eye-watering prices: over £2,000 for a pair of tickets to witness what could be a title-clinching clash with Tottenham at Anfield. VIP packages were being touted for as much as £3,500 on resale sites, as the black market seized its moment.

When the team bus finally arrived just after 3pm on Sunday, 27 April, it crept forward through a haze of smoke, flares painting the air red and briefly blotting out the sun. It was a scene that swept people up, a city giving itself over to a celebration 35 years in the making. Where the joy of Jürgen Klopp's lone league title in 2020 had been stifled by the silence of empty stands, Arne Slot's encore reverberated at full volume. A decade mostly spent in Manchester City's shadow gave way to a moment of pure catharsis. While 60,000 filled the ground, twice as many gathered outside, turning the surrounding streets into a carnival. Fans climbed lampposts and clambered onto rooftops just to witness the mayhem, a delirious, unforgettable eruption of pride and joy.

Arne Slot said, 'The only moment I was emotional about today was when we arrived at the stadium, to see what it meant for the fans, what it meant for these people. Everybody who was inside that bus felt, if the fans are with us like they are, then it's impossible for us to lose this game of football. This is so, so, so special. To be part of the history of this football club is something I could have only dreamed of two, three or four years ago. I am very, very happy, of course, but to a certain extent it is quite unreal, because you've worked so hard for this moment to happen, and when it does happen it needs some time for you to truly feel it.'

Liverpool briefly trailed against Tottenham, when former striker Dominic Solanke headed the visitors in front, but any suspense over the title was short-lived. Three goals in 18 blistering first-half minutes – courtesy of Luis Díaz, Alexis Mac Allister, and Cody Gakpo – settled the contest. Salah added a fourth and then forced a fifth via a Destiny Udogie own goal. As he celebrated, a club photographer handed him a phone, and Salah snapped a beaming selfie, much to the delight of the fans. On the touchline, Arne Slot stood hands in pockets, exuding the composure of a man watching a procession, not a football match. Red balloons drifted across the pitch as memories were etched and a record-equalling 20th English league title was sealed.

The commanding 5–1 win secured the Premier League crown with four games to spare, unleashing a wave of celebration. Salah dropped to his knees and pointed skyward. Van Dijk was met mid-pitch by Andy Robertson leaping into his arms. Alisson, overwhelmed, collapsed to the turf. Ball boys danced with Salah and Trent Alexander-Arnold in front of the Kop, while Harvey Elliott spun a corner flag overhead. As 'You'll Never Walk Alone' reverberated over the PA system, the squad formed a line across the pitch. A clip of Darwin Núñez went viral as he tried to drench Mohamed Salah with what looked like champagne, though it turned out to be alcohol-free Nozeco, a thoughtful nod to the club's Muslim players. Later, Núñez shared a dressing room snap of himself puffing on a large cigar.

The victory registered as a seismic event – literally. Researchers from the University of Liverpool's Department of Earth, Ocean and Environmental Sciences used advanced instruments, similar to those deployed in earthquake-prone regions like Chile, Italy and Japan, to capture data. Their findings showed that the 60,415 fans inside the stadium generated measurable seismic activity, especially during the six goals. The most powerful tremor came after Alexis Mac Allister's 24th-minute goal, which put Liverpool ahead 2–1 and measured 1.74 on the Richter scale. Dr Farnaz Kamranzad remarked, 'Who knew that football fans could generate seismic energy? This experiment shows us that science is everywhere, even hidden beneath the roar of a goal at Anfield. ... Incredibly, we recorded six seismic events with equivalent Richter magnitudes from 0.7 to 1.75. These were small tremors, not strong enough to be felt in the stands, but powerful enough to leave a clear and lasting mark at Anfield. Every cheer, every celebration, leaves a trace beneath our feet, a seismic fingerprint of collective joy, written into the Earth's memory long after the final whistle.'

In the Eredivisie, champions are typically presented with the trophy as soon as the title is secured, even if matches remain. But Premier League rules dictate that the trophy is only awarded after the final home game of the season. Meanwhile, Liverpool players had to make do with a cardboard cutout version. Liverpool shirts reading 'Champions 25' were passed around the squad and staff, with Arne Slot happily pulling one on himself. He had vowed that he would enjoy 'a glass of beer or two or three' and he was true to his word. Having become the first Dutch manager to win England's top flight, he danced in a circle with his backroom staff at the final whistle. Just before stoppage time, he had turned to the directors' box and blew a kiss to his family – a quiet, personal gesture that gently marked a momentous day.

'Arne Slot! Na-na, na, na-na!' the fans sang, just as Jürgen Klopp had done as he had welcomed and endorsed Slot as his successor at the final home game of last campaign. 'All I can do is show my appreciation for Jürgen Klopp,' Slot said as held the mic and he, this time, stood in the centre of the Anfield pitch before leading a chorus to honour the man he followed with such spectacular, unexpected, immediate success, and who had been so gracious in welcoming him. 'Jürgen Klopp, Na-na,na, na-na.' An imitation of Klopp's signature move then followed. He ran over to the stands to deliver the three fist pumps that the fans had craved all season.

But Arne Slot is all about keeping perspective. The day after the Tottenham match, there was more cause for celebration, albeit on a more modest scale. 'Monday was my wife's birthday. She was here, together with the children and some friends, so we had lunch together. It's not like the whole world has changed by winning this league title. Sometimes you think before you win, "Probably everything is going to change." But when I woke up Monday morning, I still felt the same person, although I felt really happy.'

During the championship celebrations after the final match of the season, Arne Slot was asked at what point he would begin thinking about preparations for the next season. He said, 'From about four weeks ago.' That was no joke. May felt like a soft launch to Liverpool's 2025–26 pre-season. Slot used the month to experiment with his squad, testing combinations and assessing which players might step up next season, and where reinforcements would be needed. Even the ever-present Virgil van Dijk got a break for the first time in the season. The team took their collective foot off the accelerator and matches were played in a lower gear. Results took a back seat. A 3–1 loss to Chelsea, a draw with second-placed Arsenal, and a 3–2 defeat to Brighton – Liverpool's first loss in nine years after leading at half-time – barely dented the mood. With the title already sealed in April, the fans celebrated at full-time regardless.

The final match, against Crystal Palace, yielded another draw, 1–1, with Liverpool's only goal scored by none other than Mohammed

Salah. He concluded the 2024–25 Premier League season with 47 goal involvements – 29 goals and 18 assists over 38 matches – equalling the all-time Premier League record for combined goals and assists in a single season previously set by Andrew Cole (1993–94) and Alan Shearer (1994–95). He won the Premier League Golden Boot (as the top scorer) and Playmaker of the Season (for the most assists). At Anfield, moments of class were on full display. Liverpool players appeared on the pitch with their children, reminding everyone that these superstars are human after all. Liverpool staged an impromptu guard of honour for Crystal Palace to mark their historic FA Cup win. Trent Alexander-Arnold received a rapturous welcome while collecting his final medal with the club. He was in tears after his last match as a Liverpool man. In a defining moment, Alan Hansen passed the Premier League trophy to Virgil van Dijk, symbolically transferring the mantle of title-winning leadership between two of Liverpool's great captains.

Liverpool concluded the Premier League season with more points than Manchester United and Tottenham combined. In an article in the *Telegraph* entitled 'Move over Sir Alex: There's no denying Liverpool are England's greatest club,' former Liverpool great Jamie Carragher wrote:

In winning the Premier League at his first attempt, Arne Slot has scored one of the most celebrated equalisers in Anfield history; Liverpool can proudly call themselves record title-winners again. True, it is an honour they must temporarily share with Manchester United, the giants of English football tied at 20–20. But there is massive symbolic importance in Slot wiping out the advantage, which owed everything to the genius of Sir Alex Ferguson . . . If you had asked me on the day of my retirement how long it would take for Liverpool to catch up to United's total, my honest answer would have been that it might not happen in my lifetime . . . Nobody believed FSG could replace Jürgen Klopp and win the league straight away. Let's be honest and admit that when everyone welcomed Slot last summer saying he could be 'the new Bob Paisley', there was as much hope and romance as absolute faith in that being the case. But Slot has justified those comparisons with Shankly's legendary successor.

Arne Slot overachieved in a transition year. As a result, expectations will mount for 2025–26. ESPN and TNT Sports commentator Ian Darke offered some perspective on what lies ahead for Slot. 'Expectations are always sky-high. This time around, people probably thought this would be a year of transition. On the whole, Slot has barely put a foot wrong, and it's all gone very well . . . Next year, the expectations will be far, far higher. Some will want the Premier League retained and then the Champions League as well, and there is that danger that he becomes a victim of his own success, as it happens with managers. But Slot knew when he signed on the dotted line at Anfield, he was expected to deliver big things.'

The head coach conceded that his main regret from an otherwise triumphant season was not making more changes to his line-up during the most demanding stretches. He suggested that with a deeper squad, Liverpool might have advanced further in the Champions League. 'I'm 100 per cent sure I haven't made all the decisions right. We were in the wrong place at the wrong time facing Paris Saint-Germain. I made six substitutions against Paris Saint-Germain, where the extra time wasn't our best period of the game. The time to reflect even more is when I'm going on holiday again. If I look at the way we think about next season and our squad, these are things that are on my mind. I think we can find one or two extra weapons that this team doesn't have. Maybe by using the transfer market. That is what we are trying to achieve. Apart from the transfer window, we can also improve certain aspects ourselves.'

Slot was confident that Conor Bradley could fill the Alexander-Arnold-shaped hole, following the right back's high-profile move to Spain. 'Let's not compare him with Trent. They are two different types. Conor is in his own league when it comes to running a lot. He is everywhere during the game.' Bradley signed a new four-year contract at Liverpool to underline his status as the club's first-choice right back despite the impending arrival of Jeremie Frimpong from Bayer Leverkusen. Frimpong drives his team forward through his pace and ability to carry the ball up the pitch. While primarily a right back, his versatility allows him to operate as a wing back or winger, offering Arne Slot tactical flexibility. The addition of Frimpong will give Liverpool FC even more of a Netherlands feel: in addition to the manager and several staff members, the squad will feature four Dutchmen. His Leverkusen colleague, attacking midfielder Florian Wirtz, was next in line to make the move to Liverpool.

Virgil van Dijk was convinced that Slot's team are capable of reaching much greater heights beyond this season. 'I think 100 per cent we can improve. If you take it all the way back to last summer, l didn't have a proper pre-season. This year there is a training camp and there is time for the team to work on what the manager wants and I think that will then improve the team. We shouldn't forget the quality that the Premier League possesses. A proper pre-season would definitely help the club in order to be even more consistent than we already have been.'

One of Anfield's most iconic banners is six metres wide and three metres tall, and features the faces of six legendary Liverpool managers: Bill Shankly, Bob Paisley, Joe Fagan, Kenny Dalglish, Rafa Benitez and Jürgen Klopp. The banner is owned by the Irish Kop, an online community established in 2003 by Paul Larkin, a Liverpool fan from Dublin. Positioned prominently at the front of the Kop before every home game, it was inspired by a painting from local artist David Neve (who drew on the imagery of the Five Heads of Communism, depicting Karl Marx, Friedrich Engels, Vladimir Lenin, Joseph Stalin and Mao Zedong). The rule has always been that only managers who've won the league or the top European Cup earn a place. This summer, the banner will be updated to include Arne Slot, in recognition of his extraordinary debut season.

At Anfield, it was playfully called 'the immaculate handover'. Replacing Jürgen Klopp was as much about managing legacy as tactics, but Arne Slot handled it with confident authority. Unlike Klopp, Guardiola or Arteta, he stayed out of the spotlight, uninterested in soundbites, and focused instead on detail and steady progress. He didn't force a new identity on the team but built on what worked. Slot fast-tracked himself into Anfield folklore by masterminding one of the most memorable title wins in the club's history. He became just the tenth manager in over a century of English football to win the league in his first season and only the fifth to do so in the Premier League era. English football is idiosyncratic and unforgiving, yet Slot navigated it with calm precision. Liverpool hit the top on 2 November and stayed there for 177 days, a run that sealed his place in club history as the architect of a truly remarkable campaign.

ARNE SLOT CURRICULUM VITAE

Born on 17 September 1978 in Bergentheim, the Netherlands

Career as player:

VV Bergentheim youth, 1984–92

FC Zwolle youth, 1992–95

FC Zwolle, 1995–2002

NAC Breda, 2002–07

Sparta Rotterdam, 2007–10

FC Zwolle (loan), 2009–10

FC/PEC Zwolle, 2010–13

Career as manager:

PEC Zwolle youth coach, 2013–14

SC Cambuur assistant coach, 2014–16

SC Cambuur head coach, 2016–17

AZ Alkmaar assistant coach, 2017–19

AZ Alkmaar head coach, 2019–20

Feyenoord head coach, 2021–24

Liverpool head coach, 2024–present

Achievements as player:

FC Zwolle, Eerste Divisie title, 2001–02, 2011–12

Achievements as manager:

Feyenoord, Conference League final, 2021–22

Feyenoord, Eredivisie title 2022–23; KNVB Cup 2023–24

Liverpool, Premier League title 2024–25

Special honours:

Rinus Michels Award, Eredivisie Coach of the Year, 2021–22, 2022–23

Premier League Manager of the Season, 2024–25

Manager of the Year, League Managers Association (LMA), 2024–25

ABOUT THE AUTHOR

Maarten Meijer spent his childhood and youth in the rural Netherlands. He hitch-hiked across southern Europe, from Spain to Italy to Greece, and sailed across the north, from Ireland to Denmark to Finland. When Europe became too small, he sailed a two-masted yacht with friends across the Atlantic Ocean to Central America. After touring Martinique, Guadeloupe and a handful of other Caribbean islands, he ended up in the USA. He enrolled at the State University of New York, receiving a bachelor's degree in science and a master's degree in philosophy. In 1982, he met his beautiful Latina wife Myra, a Manhattan native.

In 1991, thirst for new adventure led the family, which by then included two children, to Russia. Maarten taught philosophy in post-Communist Moscow, and again travelled widely, from Riga and Crimea in the west to Lake Baikal and Vladivostok in the east. He received his PhD in Russian literature from Moscow State University, writing a dissertation on 'The Family in the Works of Leo Tolstoy'. He is fluent in English, German, Russian and Dutch, and gets by in French and Korean. Living in a Moscow student dormitory with many friendly Korean families inspired a move to South Korea in 2000.

Maarten taught writing at Seoul Women's University for several years and began to publish. He is the author of *What's So Good about Korea, Maarten?* (South Korea, 2005), *Guus Hiddink – Going Dutch*

(Australia, 2006), *The Korean Education Code* (South Korea, 2011), *Dick Advocaat – Biografie* (Netherlands, 2013), *Louis van Gaal – the Biography* (UK, 2014), *How to Create Top Education – Finland and Korea* (South Korea, 2015, co-authored with daughter Renée), *The Marriage Blessing* (US, 2020), *Smarter than Covid – How South Koreans Beat the Virus* (US, 2021), *Ten Hag: The Biography* (UK, 2022) and *Virgil van Dijk – De biografie* (Netherlands, 2024). Since March 2006, he has been teaching writing and philosophy at an international school in the Korean mountains, while doubling as social critic and football commentator. Maarten and Myra have a daughter, who was born in Montana, and three sons, born in New York, Moscow and Seoul, respectively.

SOURCES

Articles:

Bascombe, Chris. 'Behind his friendly exterior, Arne Slot is as ruthless as they come'. The *Telegraph*, 23 August 2024.

Bascombe, Chris. 'Arne Slot: How Liverpool's king of Zen lost his cool in Goodison cauldron'. The *Telegraph*, 13 February 2025.

Brown, Oliver. 'Arne Slot feels like a new Bob Paisley – the man who built on a Liverpool legend'. The *Telegraph*, 28 November 2024.

Brown, Oliver. 'The making of Arne Slot – "he is more intelligent than Erik ten Hag"'. The *Telegraph*, 20 May 2024.

Burt, Jason. 'The manager every Premier League club should be looking at'. The *Telegraph*, 13 April 2023.

Carragher, Jamie. 'Move over Sir Alex: There's no denying Liverpool are England's greatest club'. The *Telegraph*, 27 April 2025.

Cox, Michael. 'Arne Slot has first-season advantage at Liverpool and their Premier League rivals are in disarray'. The *Athletic*, 13 November 2024.

Crafton, Adam. 'Arne Slot's Feyenoord, access all areas: Kickboxing, Beckham clips and why he stayed'. The *Athletic*, 1 June 2023.

Crafton, Adam. 'What I learnt from meeting Arne Slot – charismatic and innovative, but a big bet by Liverpool'. The *Athletic*, 29 April 2024.

Duncker, Charlotte. 'Arne Slot: I'm happy to wait – it's hard to find stars good enough to sign'. *The Times*, 26 July 2024.

Edwards, Luke. 'Why Dutch managers struggle in Premier League – but Arne Slot can buck trend at Liverpool'. The *Telegraph*, 2 May 2024.

Evans, Gregg. 'Arne Slot: What it's really like to play for Liverpool's new head coach'. The *Athletic*, 12 August 2024.

Hughes, Simon. 'Arne Slot: The borderland "priest" who was born to coach'. The *Athletic*, 21 May 2024.

Hughes, Simon. 'The rise and rise of the Premier League's frontier coaches'. The *Athletic*, 19 September 2024.

Hughes, Simon, James Pearce and Gregg Evans. 'How Arne Slot prepares Liverpool: "Body wake-up", ice baths and wellness checks'. The *Athletic*, 4 October 2024.

Idrissi, Oussama. 'I have played under Arne Slot so here is why he is a great fit for Liverpool'. The *Guardian*, 21 May 2024.

Jones, Andy. 'Arne Slot's first Liverpool interview: "Game model", training videos and transfer chats'. The *Athletic*, 20 June 2024.

Joyce, Paul. 'Harvey Elliott: Training with Arne Slot is like actors learning lines'. The *Times*, 7 January 2025.

Kay, Oliver. 'Is the cult of the manager over? How English football's power structure changed'. The *Athletic*, 9 August 2024.

Khalique-Loonat, Hamzah. 'How Arne Slot's style of play compares to Jürgen Klopp's Liverpool'. *The Times*, 21 May 2024.

Kuyt, Dirk. 'Dirk Kuyt: Arne Slot's style is exactly what Liverpool supporters love to see at Anfield'. The *Athletic*, 26 April 2024.

LFCTV, 'Arne Slot: Following Jürgen Klopp is tough but he'll be my biggest fan'. 19 June 2024.

Northcroft, Jonathan. 'Dutch managers have never cracked England – can Arne Slot be the first?'. The *Sunday Times*, 1 September 2024.

Northcroft, Jonathan. 'How Liverpool knew Arne Slot was the right man for them'. The *Sunday Times*, 4 January 2025.

Pearce, James. 'Why Liverpool are back in the U.S. after five years away – and who stands to benefit'. The *Athletic*, 23 July 2024.

Pearce, James and Oliver Kay. 'How Liverpool hired Arne Slot: The data, surprise contenders and why talks grew tense'. The *Athletic*, 21 May 2024.

Renard, Arthur. 'Slot wants his teams to entertain the crowd'. Premier League.com, 20 May 2024.

Rudd, Alyson, 'Losing Van Dijk, Alexander-Arnold and Salah would rip out Liverpool's soul'. The *Sunday Times*, 23 November 2024.

Shearer, Alan. 'Alan Shearer on Arne Slot, Eddie Howe, Kai Havertz, Premier League hard men and more'. The *Athletic*, 8 November 2024.

Slot, Owen. 'My Dutch road trip to uncover the real Arne Slot'. *The Times*, 3 May 2024.

Vlietstra, Bart. 'Arne Slot: the overachiever and "good guy" who can spark a revolution'. The *Guardian*, 26 Apr 2024.

Zeqiri, Daniel. 'Arne Slot may be the perfect fit for Liverpool – here are the statistics that show why'. The *Telegraph*, 23 April 2024.

Books:

Giphart, Ronald, *Het beste van jezelf*, Uitgeverij Brandt, 2023.

Gouka, Mikos, *Kameraden – Het ongelooflijke kempioensjaar van het Feyenoord van Arne Slot*, ADR Nieuwsmedia, 2023.

Gouka, Mikos, *Slot-bal – Hoe Arne Slot via Feyenoord de top bestormt*, ADR Nieuwsmedia, 2024.

Van Egmond, Michel and Martijn Krabbendam, *Lourdes aan de Maas*, Overamstel uitgevers, 2022.

Vlietstra, Bart and Willem Vissers, *Wij gáán winnen – De fascinerende weg van Feyenoord naar het kampioenschap van 2023*, Overamstel uitgevers, 2023.

Periodicals, websites and broadcast news (write-ups):

Algemeen Dagblad, *AS*, AZ (az.nl), BBC Sport, Bekende Buren, *BN DeStem*, Carteret Analytics, Coaches Betaald Voetbal, *Corriere dello Sport*, *Daily Star*, *De Stentor*, *De Telegraaf*, *De Toren*, *De VoetbalTrainer*, *de Volkskrant*, ESPN, *Feyenoord Magazine*, Fr12.nl, *Helden Magazine*, Indebuurt, KNVB, *La Gazzetta dello Sport*, *Le Figaro*, *L'Équipe*, *Liverpool Echo*, MoederscheimMoonen Architects, Nederlandse Sportpers, *Nieuwe Revu*, NOS Voetbal, *NRC*, Omroep Friesland, *Panorama*, PEC Zwolle (peczwolle.nl), RTV Oost, RTV Rijnmond, Sporf (sporf.com), Sky Sports, Sportclub Cambuur (cambuur.nl), the *Daily Mail*, the *Independent*, the *Mirror*, TNT Sports, UEFA, *Voetbal International*, Voetbalzone.

IMAGE CREDITS